Praise for *The Naked Pint*

"*The Naked Pint* is a great read for anyone interested in all things beer—from beer style descriptions to cooking with beer to brewing your own beer at home. Like a Beer 101 textbook to amp up your brew IQ, if only textbooks occasionally made you laugh out loud. The authors know their stuff; they understand and convey the notion that beer can be complex without being overly complicated, and they take beer seriously but don't take themselves too seriously. *The Naked Pint* is very, um, revealing."

—Sam Calagione, president and founder of Dogfish Head Craft Brewery and author of *Brewing Up a Business*, *Extreme Brewing*, and *He Said Beer, She Said Wine*

"No one turns people on to beer the way that Christina and Hallie do. Along with their passion and expertise, they bring a wit and levity that exemplify the renegade spirit of craft beer. They possess the skills of a sommelier . . . yet take you on the even more inspired journey into craft beer. Share a pint with these ladies; they will rock your world. They did mine!"

—Greg Koch, CEO and cofounder of Stone Brewing Company

"I have always loved beer without knowing much about it. I learned a lot in this factual, enlightening, and funny guide to one of the oldest and most cherished beverages known to man."

—Jacques Pépin, cookbook author, cooking teacher, and PBS television cooking series host

continued . . .

"Whether you want to brew at home, belly up to the bar with confidence, or make magical pairings at the dinner table, *The Naked Pint* makes learning about craft beers as fun as drinking them. You'll be a savvy sipper after reading this educational and engaging book."

—Leslie Sbrocco, PBS television host and author of *Wine for Women*

"An incredibly satisfying read! This book gets better-looking on every page. From Pale Ale to Weizen, *The Naked Pint* covers all of beer's finer points in a fun, witty, and approachable manner. Hallie and Christina's great taste and cool, refreshing style is the perfect introduction to the often intimidating world of craft beer."

—Rachael Leigh Cook

THE
NAKED PINT

AN UNADULTERATED
GUIDE TO CRAFT BEER

Christina Perozzi & Hallie Beaune

A PERIGEE BOOK

A PERIGEE BOOK
Published by the Penguin Group
Penguin Group (USA) Inc.
375 Hudson Street, New York, New York 10014, USA
Penguin Group (Canada), 90 Eglinton Avenue East, Suite 700, Toronto, Ontario M4P 2Y3, Canada
(a division of Pearson Penguin Canada Inc.) • Penguin Books Ltd., 80 Strand, London WC2R 0RL,
England • Penguin Group Ireland, 25 St. Stephen's Green, Dublin 2, Ireland (a division of Penguin
Books Ltd.) • Penguin Group (Australia), 250 Camberwell Road, Camberwell, Victoria 3124, Australia
(a division of Pearson Australia Group Pty. Ltd.) • Penguin Books India Pvt. Ltd., 11 Community
Centre, Panchsheel Park, New Delhi—110 017, India • Penguin Group (NZ), 67 Apollo Drive,
Rosedale, Auckland 0632, New Zealand (a division of Pearson New Zealand Ltd.) • Penguin Books
(South Africa) (Pty.) Ltd., 24 Sturdee Avenue, Rosebank, Johannesburg 2196, South Africa

Penguin Books Ltd., Registered Offices: 80 Strand, London WC2R 0RL, England

While the author has made every effort to provide accurate telephone numbers, Internet addresses,
and other contact information at the time of publication, neither the publisher nor the author assumes
any responsibility for errors, or for changes that occur after publication. Further, the publisher
does not have any control over and does not assume any responsibility for author or third-party
websites or their content.

PUBLISHING HISTORY
Perigee hardcover edition / November 2009
Perigee trade paperback edition / October 2012

Perigee trade paperback ISBN: 978-0-399-16132-2

The Library of Congress has cataloged the Perigee hardcover edition as follows:

Perozzi, Christina.
The naked pint : an unadulterated guide to craft beer / Christina Perozzi, Hallie Beaune.—1st ed.
p. cm.
Includes bibliographical references and index.
ISBN 978-0-399-53534-5
1. Beer. 2. Brewing. I. Beaune, Hallie. II. Title.
TP570.P38 2009 2009027940
641.6'230973—dc22

PRINTED IN THE UNITED STATES OF AMERICA

10 9 8 7 6 5 4 3 2 1

The recipes contained in this book are to be followed exactly as written. The publisher is not
responsible for your specific health or allergy needs that may require medical supervision. The publisher
is not responsible for any adverse reactions to the recipes contained in this book.

WE'D LIKE TO DEDICATE THIS BOOK TO OUR PARENTS,

WHO ARE SO PROUD THAT THEIR DAUGHTERS BECAME

BEER EXPERTS INSTEAD OF LAWYERS OR DOCTORS.

Acknowledgments

H allie and Christina would like to thank all of the chefs, brewers, and industry experts who generously contributed to this book: Greg Koch, Govind Armstrong, Jacob Wildman, Rob Tod, Brian Thompson, Patrick Rue, Jenn Garbee, Ann Kirk, Larry Caldwell, Josh Loeb, Zoe Nathan, Evan Funke, Samir Mohajer, Chris McCombs, Lucy Saunders, Bryan Simpson, Greg Beron, Andrew Steiner, Matt Accarrino, Michael Saxton, and Randy Thiel.

We would also like to thank the following beer lovers and all-around quality people who helped us along on our own Beer Journey: Mark Jilg, Kevin Kansey, Tomm Carroll, Joe Corona, Mike Smith,

Eric Kremer, Ryan Sweeney, Brian Lenzo, Jason Bernstein, Charlie Farrell, Tracey St. Pierre, Grace and Klaus Gabelgaard, Kirill Taranouchtchenko, Emily Wahlund, Jaime Morrell, Nathalie Balandran, Patrick "Pinch" Merrit, Darren "Jazz 'n Tap" Mann, Brian Ransom, Stacey Piccinati, Mila Becker, Jane and Russell Adams, Kara Slife, the Brewer's Association, the National Beer Wholesalers Association, Thunder, and Enzo. We'd also like to thank everyone at F.O. and the Daily Pint.

A special thank-you to the amazingly smart and talented Erin Tarasi, who was an invaluable asset to us.

Christina would especially like to thank her parents, Bill and Claudia, who have always encouraged her to follow her dreams, even when her dream was to drink a lot of beer. She'd also like to thank her brother, Dan, for always believing in her. She'd like to thank Maury, Kasey, Austin, Karen, the Stefanos, and all her friends around the world for helping with the (ahem) "research" and all the laughs. Mad props to HB.

Hallie would especially like to thank CP; my loving parents, Catherine and Roy, who have given me enormous support in every step of my life; my strong, beautiful sisters, Christine, Holly, and Wendy; sweet little Karter and Kennedy; my loyal and encouraging friends; and Matthew, whose love fills my days with joy.

Last, but absolutely not least, we would like to thank our agent, Michelle Brower, and everyone at Wendy Sherman and Associates, and our editor, Maria Gagliano, and everyone at Perigee and the Penguin Group. We love that you love beer.

Cheers!

Contents

NINE

Brewing at Home 213

TEN

Entertaining with Beer 265

CONCLUSION

Parting Is Such Sweet Sorrow 280

Introduction

Beer loves you.

Do you love beer? Of course you do. It's why you picked up this book. It's why you are dying to try that new craft beer bar down the street. It's why you salivate at the sight of a pint. Most people already have a soft spot in their hearts for beer. Our culture has been embracing this beverage for hundreds of years, weaving it into our celebrations, our sports, our commercials, and our identities. But beer is more than you might think it is. Sure, it's beer, but it's also cultural anthropology. Different beer styles tell different stories: Who made it, where it came from, who drank it, what was happening in the world socially or politically when that beer was first created. Every beer has a story, and for the most part, that story has gone untold. Overshadowed by its mega-brewery cousins, craft and artisanal beer has been underappreciated and undiscovered by the majority of Americans. Until now (*cue choir of angels*).

People seem to love craft beer more and more each day but at the same time are perplexed by its mysteries. If you are not a craft beer believer, we would like to strip away any misconceptions you may have about our favorite drink. Get ready to know beer as it was always meant to be: made from quality ingredients and free from all the bullshit. Cast aside the pasteurized lager for the local Pale Ale. If you do, you can count yourself among a quickly growing group of the public that buys craft beer at the specialty store instead of the twelve-pack of the cheap stuff at the gas station. You know, those people with the huge smiles on their faces, the ones who seem to have found fulfillment in beer. Embrace craft beer, and you can join the devotees who support their local beer makers and who revel in the pride of having the local brewery on tap at the local pub.

Our philosophy of beer has for a long time been one of quality not quantity. As soon as we began to taste different craft beers, we shifted our idea of what beer was all about. No longer would we force ourselves to drink "fizzy yellow water" or focus on drinking just one kind of beer. No longer would we order only wine with fine food. Hell no! We found we'd rather have a balanced Belgian Ale at the end of a hard day than several mediocre or crappy brews. Like anything in life, once your eyes and taste buds are opened to the best, it's nearly impossible to go backward. Your palate wants more. Try as you might, you can't forget how great that Bavarian Hefeweizen tasted, that special tart and refreshing marriage of bananas and cloves. It's a question of the quality of the moment, and drinking a fine beer allows us to celebrate, to partake in a brewer's vision, and to experience what a great beer should be.

Beer Is Funny

We go where the funny goes, and luckily, so does beer. From the hilarious names on the labels (our favorite is Tea-Bagged Furious) to the jokes made between friends in a small pub in Belgium, beer seems to pair best with laughter (loud laughter). We don't like the beer talk to get too serious. Wine has sometimes been accused of this, and we would hate for craft beer to lose its levity. This doesn't mean craft beer deserves any less respect than any other food or beverage. The inspired creations of brewers are to be revered for sure; a great beer is an art after all. We just don't want them to end up behind any velvet ropes or bulletproof glass. We feel that the best way to approach craft beer is by treating it as you would any fine food or drink, tasting and learning and sharing with friends, but never letting go of the wonderfully casual way a group of people can share a bottle of beer. If you find yourself stressing about your beer pairings to the point at which beads of sweat collect over your furrowed brow, you need to pour yourself a nice Tripel and take a breath. And, we hope, when you let out that breath, you'll laugh at your silliness. How serious about beer can you be when you're pairing cheese with a beer called Big Woody Barleywine or Sexual Chocolate Russian Imperial Stout? See, I bet you're laughing right now. Go ahead, let it out. When we look back over our Beer Journey, we find that our best beer memories are set in a background of laughter.

It's Not What You Think

There's a lot of information about beer out in the ether. The difficulty comes in finding what beer knowledge is useful and what knowledge is so esoteric that only a true beer-geek would be interested. We set out to create a new kind of beer book, one that is as accessible and as useful to the novice as it is to the veteran. We want to take you, the reader, on the same journey that led us to our reverent love of beer. This is the same journey on which we've successfully converted hundreds of people from beer neophyte to expert. Yes, even those who, to our shock and dismay, initially uttered the dreaded statement "I'm not a beer drinker" have been converted to full-on beer connoisseurs. In this book, we're not listing beer styles in any strict order of country or provenance but taking an excursion of the palate, focusing on flavor, moving in order from least intense to most intense. This kind of Beer Journey enables you to truly develop your beer appreciation along the way. Beyond beer styles, we also talk about how to welcome beer into your home and incorporate it into your modern dining experience, how to cook with it, and how to take that final step and become a brewer yourself. There's a lot to learn...and it's probably not what you think!

Yes, We're Women and We Drink Beer

As women, we've found that people have been surprised at our love of beer. The truth is, women have been brewing and drinking beer for thousands of years. Women are out there drinking craft beer and brewing and writing about it every day, so there's no reason women should feel that beer is not for the ladies. It's true that the image of women and beer on the tube has generally involved double-D boobs and a wet T-shirt, but we can assure you, our T-shirts are dry. And, though we think craft beer is indeed sexy and are sometimes happy to wear six-inch heels while drinking an Abbey Dubbel, beer is *not* only an afterthought of female stereotypes. We understand that people have been misleading women for years about the caloric content of beer and the necessity of drinking a light beer in order to seem ladylike. But no one really subscribes to this anymore. Women who come to our events are fascinated by the flavors of craft beer. Young or old, once they've had their first sour cherry Lambic or chocolaty Porter, they are on board in a big, big way. And we are thrilled to be a part of this growing community. Let's be honest, what's sexier than a woman who knows her craft beer?

A Final Word

This book is not meant to be the final word on any aspect of beer. We bring you our thoughts as participants in the craft beer community. We love being a part of the dialogue that is present in the craft world today. As the community grows, so do the differences of opinion and the discussion on style and ratings and a multitude of other topics. For us, it's always about being inclusive and sharing the knowledge with anyone who wants it. As you enter the craft beer world, you enter a world that is accessible. The learning curve for beer is quick, and after Beer 101, you will already know more about beer than most people in the bar. We love that the beer world is not a lofty, exclusive one. No one need pass a coolness test to drink this fine beverage. Though beer snobs do exist (and yes, we've been known to raise our nose a few times), we try to bring it back to the fact that craft beer is meant to be enjoyed, not worshiped; not used to alienate, but to bring communities together to toast the events of the day and the changing of the seasons. When the beer talk gets too haughty, we simply excuse ourselves and go open a bottle of Saison. Though we may drink the beer from proper glassware and pair Witbiers with fresh seafood, we never lose sight of our simple credo: *Beer is good.*

Beer 101

He was a wise man who invented beer.
—PLATO

What You Never Learned in School

You've learned many useful things in life. You learned how to walk, how to tie your shoe, how to ride a bicycle without training wheels. In school, they taught you the three R's and how to dissect Dostoyevsky. In home ec, you learned how to make an apple turnover and balance a checkbook. But when it came to beer, the only resource you had was your older brother, whose idea of a perfect evening was shot-gunning a beer and chasing it with a whippet in the local Kmart parking lot. His only concern, when it came to beer, was quantity versus cooler size. Let's be honest, if you dropped him in any craft beer bar today, he'd be considered "that guy"—the one who thinks his mass-produced light lager of choice is the be-all and end-all of beers and the only one he'll drink forever, no matter what occurs. Hey, we're women, we're down with commitment, but even we refuse to be chained to one beer for the rest of our lives.

So let's begin. With Beer 101 you will impress your friends, your date, your bartenders, and your parents (well, maybe not your parents). This will set you on the right path to drinking and loving great beer.

The goal of Beer 101 is to debunk many misconceptions that people have about beer, and to raise it to the level that it deserves as an artisanal and craft beverage. When you graduate from Beer 101, you will have a rudimentary understanding of what beer is. You will know what goes into it, how to describe it, how to taste it, how to order it, and, yes, how to drink it without feeling like a total idiot. In fact, we'll let you in on a little secret: Unlike calculus, the learning curve for beer is quick! After you discover the basics, your knowledge will be far beyond what most people know about this misunderstood beverage. It's part of the beauty of beer.

What the Hell Is Beer Anyway?

Wine is easy to understand. You pick some grapes, you crush them, and then you let them sit around for a while until you get wine. Hell, even the *I Love Lucy* girls understood that. Of course, we realize that winemaking is a much more detailed and complicated process. We know that winemaking concerns the growing of the grapes and the quality of the *terroir*, the wood used in fermenting, varietals of the grapes, AOCs, stems on versus stems off, and so on. But even the most devout winemakers will tell you that when you really get right down to it, wine in its simplest form is fermented grape juice. We get it. You get it. But do you have any idea what beer is? Only a chosen few are in the know. Join us, won't you?

Beer in its most basic form is a *carbonated alcoholic beverage* made from *fermented grains*. It is primarily made up of four key ingredients: malt, hops, water, and yeast. Feel smarter already? You should. You now know more than most people do about beer. (We told you the learning curve was quick.) Now let's take a closer look. What exactly are these ingredients?

Malt

What do Whoppers, Long John Silver's, Ovaltine, and beer all have in common? Well, those chocolate-covered candies, the vinegar you sprinkle on your fish and chips, and that powder you stir into your milk

are made with malt, which just happens to be the basis for all the color, alcohol content, viscosity, carbonation, and subsequent mouthfeel of beer. Malts are cereal grains that have gone through what those in the know call the malting process or, more simply, malting. Sound complicated? Well, it actually kind of is.

Have you ever tried to grow an herb garden that started from seeds? The first thing you're supposed to do is put the seeds between a wet warm paper towel to let them sprout or germinate. Malting starts out with this same germination process. The cereal grains are soaked in water and allowed to just begin to sprout. For your garden, once the seeds sprouted, you'd plant them and watch them grow until you were ready to harvest your herbs. During the malting process, however, the growing process is immediately halted as soon as the cereal grain sprouts by a quick drying. This process allows the starch that exists in the seed to be usable as a fermentable sugar. During the brewing process, yeast consumes that sugar, and the byproducts of that process are carbon dioxide (CO_2), or carbonation (beer bubbles), and alcohol (loud-mouth soup).

Once the grain is dried, it is roasted or baked or smoked or kilned to every degree of lightness or darkness under the sun, from the palest of pale to the deepest black malt. The color to which the malt has been roasted (and the combination of the colors of malt) is *solely* responsible for the color of that beer. (We're going to be emphasizing this point a lot.) The amount of malt used, in conjunction with the amount of yeast used, is *solely* responsible for the alcohol content and carbonation of that beer.

Hops

We like to use the analogy that malts are the male part of beer. You have to encourage them to grow; you have to cajole, manipulate, and control them to make them useful. Hops are the female part of beer. They come in many varieties and can easily dominate, can be quite flowery, can be high maintenance, and are often bitter. (Just kidding...kind of.)

Hops are actually the female flowering cones of the vining hop plant: scientific name *Humulus lupulus*. Hops look like delicate, tiny green pinecones and are in the family of Cannabaceae, which also includes the genus *Cannabis*. That's right, people, another reason to love beer is that hops are a cousin of cannabis, aka Mary Jane, weed, marijuana, grass, la molta, or, as our mothers call it, "the pot."

Water

If you don't know what water is, then we're not sure that we can help you. But what you might not know is that water type and quality are very important in the brewing of beer. The use of soft or hard water affects the flavor of beer in the same way that it affects any beverage, such as coffee or tea.

Yeast

All right, let's just get all the jokes out now. Just get 'em out! It's a completely normal reaction. Believe us when we tell you that *Yeasty Girls* was on our short list of titles for this book just because it made us laugh. We know: Yeast is funny. Ready to move on?

Yeast is a living organism, which forms colonies of single, simple cells. Officially, scientists call this organism a fungus, but in the days of yore, before brewers fully understood the brewing process, yeast was simply called "God is good." Yeasts are hungry little buggers who are responsible for "eating" fermentable sugars, producing CO_2 (beer bubbles) and alcohol (the hooch).

You're probably already familiar with yeast. Maybe you have a packet of it in your cabinet right now. It's that stuff that you sprinkle in your bread machine when it beeps, right? Well, yes and no. The yeast you're probably used to is bread yeast, which has been specifically cultured to make bread and not beer. Beer yeast (scientific name *Saccharomyces cerevisiae*) is specifically cultured for the fermentation of beer. Some bread recipes do call for brewer's yeast, but if you try to use bread yeast for beer, you will be disappointed with the results. And the brewer's yeast that you can find at a health food store is inactive and is meant to be consumed for its high protein and vitamin B content. If you used either of these in beer making, fermentation would not take place, and there would be no alcohol. And that would be sad.

The Birds and the Bees of Beer: Fermentation

Ah, fermentation—it's where the magic happens. Now that you know all of the basic ingredients in beer, you're ready to learn about the birds and bees of beer. We've mentioned fermentation several times already when talking about the brewing process. We're pretty sure that you understand that fermentation is when something becomes alcoholic, but if someone asked you to define fermentation, you might find yourself going numb, with crickets chirping and your pounding heart the only sounds you hear.

So, quickly, what is fermentation? In beer, it's when yeast consumes the sugar provided by the malt and creates the byproducts alcohol (liquid courage) and CO_2 (the bubbles, which produce the carbonation in beer). Thus, the fermentation process is what makes beer, well, beer.

The Biggest Beer Myth

If you listen to nothing else we say, listen to this: The color of a beer has nothing whatsoever to do with the strength, alcohol content, bitterness, or heaviness of that beer. We'll say it again. Just because a beer is dark in color does not mean that it is heavy or bitter.

This misconception stems from the mass beer market, 90% of which are either Pilsner-style or American-style lager beers. Virtually every beer you've bought with a fake ID at the gas station (sorry, Dad), drank in the backseat of your high-school boyfriend's car (sorry, Mom), or pulled from the ice tub during the Super Bowl BBQ falls into this category. They are all light in alcohol, flavor, and color and have virtually no aromatics. Because these are the beers most of us have been exposed to, we wrongly associate the light color with those other light attributes.

Because these beers are not, in our opinion, necessarily good quality or good tasting (when compared to most craft and artisanal beer), many people (especially women) want these beers to be as light tasting as possible, so that they don't experience so much flavor of a not-so-great beer. They don't want a beer with an aftertaste. What they are really saying is that they don't want a beer with a *bad* aftertaste. If something tastes great, wouldn't you want that flavor to linger?

Ordering a beer by its color is like judging a book by its cover. Stand up and fight beer prejudices. Instead, order a beer based on taste. You don't even have to worry about using the correct beer jargon. Who cares about that? We would rather you order a beer using flavor descriptors, like nutty, crisp, lemony, bitter, toasty, sweet, chocolaty, creamy, effervescent, bright, spicy, or fruity. Believe us, you'll get a beer that you might actually *like* versus a beer that you are trying to choke down. You won't just want light, you'll want flavor.

Since we are really examining fermentation, let's take a quick minute to explain carbonation. Of course, a carbonated beverage is one that has bubbles in it. Carbonation, technically, is CO_2 dissolved in liquid. It's what gives beer its bubbly effervescence and plays a big part in the balance of that beer (see Chapter 2). The head on a beer is just the CO_2 being released from that beer. The carbonation bubbles become the vehicles in which the aromatics of the beer ride from the glass to your nose.

Ale vs. Lager: Making a Case for Each

All beers fall into one of two categories: ale or lager. We find that most people don't know the difference between the two. They use the words interchangeably, guessing at the meaning, never realizing what they're talking about. So we're going to break it down for you here. (Please pass the information along to your friends.)

What's an Ale?

An ale is a beer that uses yeast that has been cultured to ferment at the top of the fermentation vessel at high temperatures (60°F to 75°F), resulting in a quick fermentation period (seven to eight days or less). Ale yeasts are generally known to produce fairly big flavors (there are exceptions). You'll often get a lot of aromatics from the whiff of an ale. Ales tend to have more residual sugar, meaning sugar that has not been consumed by the yeast during the fermentation process.

What's a Lager?

The word *lager* comes from a German word meaning "to store." A lager is a beer that uses yeast strains that are cultured to ferment at the bottom of the fermentation vessel at low temperatures (34°F to 50°F), resulting in a long fermentation time (weeks to months). Lager yeast produces fewer byproduct characters than does ale yeast, which tends to create a cleaner, crisper taste (there are exceptions).

Please remember (yes, we know we're being drill sergeants about this), the color of a beer tells you nothing about whether the beer is an ale or a lager. The type of beer has everything to do with the process by which it was fermented. That's it. You can have a very light colored, light alcohol content, nuanced, bright, and crisp ale (for example, Kölsch); likewise, you can have a very dark, high alcohol content, viscous, sweet, and malty lager (like Eisbock). One of the worst things you can do at a craft beer bar is to go up to the bar and order "an ale" or "a lager." These general terms won't get you any closer to a specific beer or to what flavors you crave but will make the bartender sigh.

Flavor Country:
Ingredients Translated into Taste

Malt in Translation

There are several ways to see, taste, and feel malt in beer. First and foremost, malt is reflected in the color of the beer, but the malt can also give off different flavors. When you look at a very light-colored beer, you might determine that you'll taste bready and biscuity qualities that exist in the very pale malts that were used during brewing. If you are looking at a very dark beer, you might expect chocolate, coffee, and roasty-toasty notes that are often present in very dark colored malts. (This does not mean you can judge a beer's entire flavor profile by its color. The type of malt is a hint about the flavor notes you *may* taste but does not tell you about the yeast or hop aspect, so tasting is still important!)

Many people will describe certain beers as malty. What does that mean? Usually they are not referring to the qualities that come from the roasted malt. They are talking about the residual sugars and additional alcohol content that can remain in a beer when an especially large amount of malt is used in the brew. This results in a prominent sweetness of flavor and a viscosity and heat in the mouthfeel.

We've found that when people first start drinking beer, they are unexpectedly drawn to much darker, maltier styles than they could ever imagine themselves liking. They favor the sweet familiar flavors of chocolate, hazelnut, coffee, and toffee that these beers often impart on the palate, rather than the bitter styles that come from highly hopped beers, which are often an acquired taste. Which brings us to our next featured ingredient.

True Hoppiness

Unbeknownst to many, you cannot tell how bitter a beer is by looking at it, as hops are totally invisible in a finished beer (this is part of why you can't determine a beer's taste just by looking at it). After the hops' qualities are extracted through boiling and steaming, the actual hop cones are strained out of the beer. You can detect hops, however, by tasting and smelling the beer. If a beer tastes in any way bitter, if a beer feels in any way dry, or if a beer causes you to feel astringency on your tongue, you are tasting the hops.

Hops contain a chemical compound called *tannin* that contributes to the puckery or cottony mouthfeel that we describe as being dry. You've probably heard of tannins with regard to wine. In wine, tannins come from the skin of the grape. If someone says, "This wine is very tannic," he's saying that he is getting a very dry mouthfeel from the wine. As true *dryness* in a beverage technically means having a lack of sugar, beer is not actually dry (sugar exists in the malt), but the tannins in hops can contribute a balancing dry feeling that is essential to great beer.

Hops also provide major aromatics in beer, and sometimes hops are added only to provide aromatics. These amazing aromas can range from pine tree, grass, citrus, herbs de Provence, and yes, its close relation— the pot. Hops also act as a preservative in beer, due to their antimicrobial properties, which help keep the beer stable (for more, see Chapter 6).

Some brewers like to go further than that balance and create a bold, hop-driven beer, in which the bitterness is dominant. This can often taste like licking a wet pine tree (What, you've never licked a wet pine tree?), married with notes of citrus. New beer drinkers are often initially turned off by this bitter, aggressive flavor, but as their palates grow, they find they crave that bite of hops, just as one craves a sharp shot of espresso. In fact, some people have become so addicted to the hop experience that they have sparked a movement in the craft beer world to push hop bitterness to the extreme. These "hop-heads" are on a beer-quest to find the most intense hop experience out there.

The Importance of Being Earnest: Why Water Matters in Beer

Seems pretty obvious, doesn't it? If beer is liquid, then it has water in it. Water is water. Big deal, right? Well, friends, since beer is about 90% water, just as we are, its origin and makeup play a major role in a beer's ultimate flavor and texture. Whether the water source for a beer is hard, containing a lot of minerals, or soft, containing fewer minerals, will greatly affect the character and the style of that beer. Minerals found in hard water, like calcium, magnesium, zinc, copper, and sulfates, can play an important role in the brewing process and can enhance dry and sharp flavors. Soft water, however, lacks the minerals and is, therefore, generally better for beers with lighter, more nuanced flavors.

In the craft beer world, brewers are considered more honest if they use local water sources. Different regions have water with different mineral components. As a result, different regions are better suited to making certain types of beer. For example, Dublin has a type of hard water that is perfect for making the thick, chalky, dark stout for which the Irish are famous. Plzen (or Pilsen) in the Czech Republic has very soft water that produces a nuanced subtleness in a beer called Pilsner. Overall, there are over a dozen compounds found in water that are significant factors in what that final beer will taste like, so the source of water in each specific beer is of vital importance.

When Yeast Is a Good Thing: Determining Yeast in Beer

Have you ever looked at one of the crappy beers that you've had in the past and thought to yourself, "Well, at least it's clear and shiny"? That's because that beer has been filtered. In other words, the yeast has been physically or chemically taken out of that finished beer, leaving it sparkly and clear. This can be good for crisp, clean beer styles, because they benefit from a fine filtration process.

Some beer styles, however, are not served by having the yeast removed. For example, Belgian and German specialty wheat beers use specific types of yeast that impart very complex flavors. If you held those beers up to the light, you might not even be able to see through them. They would appear cloudy or misty. This is actually a good thing in these beers. Not only is there a fuller, rounder mouthfeel but the unfiltered yeast provides many additional flavors and aromatics in the form of esters.

Maybe the only ester you know is your Aunt Esther in Poughkeepsie, but we're talking about the chemical compounds that yeast emits in beer. There are many different combinations of esters, but simply put, they are chemical compounds that our brains perceive as pleasant flavors and aromas. Brewers can choose these flavors and aromas based on the yeast strain they use. For instance, Hefeweizen yeast gives off banana and clove esters. Esters can be fruity like pears, strawberries, plums, and figs; they can be spicy like cloves, nutmeg, and pepper; they can be flowery like geranium and jasmine; and they can be herbaceous like sage and lavender. These are flavors you want hanging out in a wheat beer.

You Put Coriander Where? Adjuncts and Flavorings

Sometimes a brewer wants to get a little crazy and add something to the mix that is not a basic ingredient. These are called *adjuncts* and *flavorings*. This is a big trend in brewing in America today and makes beer one of the most diverse and interesting beverages on earth. Adjuncts are unmalted grains that are added as a supplement to malted barley. These may be used to provide more sugar or to add a specific mouthfeel or flavor. Flavorings are any herb, spice, flower, and so on that are added to lend a specific flavor to the brew. Here are some examples of ingredients that might be added by creative brewers:

> **ADJUNCTS:** Oats, rice, rye, corn, candi sugar (often used in Belgian beers), and wheat are all common adjuncts used to produce anything from a richer flavor to a specific mouthfeel or head retention.

> **FLAVORINGS:** Fruits (cherry, curacao orange peels, juniper berry, peach, apple, currant, raisin, strawberry) have been used to enhance beer, and herbs, spices, and other crazy stuff (sage, chamomile, coriander, cloves, nutmeg, rosemary, chilies, chocolate, coffee, honey, molasses, nut extracts, spruce tips) have been used as additional flavorings in beer.

The use of additional ingredients underlines our point that the homogenized, industrialized light beer we Americans have been drinking doesn't even scratch the surface of what our beer drinking experience could and should be. If you feel like having a chocolate bar, an orange sherbet, or a licorice whip, you could find it in beer.

There are some purists, however, who don't agree with this new-fangled beer making. The Germans (big surprise) are among the brewers who pooh-pooh the addition of anything other than the original four ingredients—malt, hops, water, and yeast—to make their beer.

Reinheitsge-What?
German Beer Purity Law

 Almost every town and village in Germany has at least one brewery, and some have more than one. In fact, Germany has over 1,300 breweries, more than half of which are in Bavaria in southern Germany. This means that about a third of all the breweries in the world are in Germany.

The Germans don't make and drink just any beer. Like old French wines with their distinct AOC rules and regulations, Germans have rigid and particular ideas about the ingredients, quality, and origin of their beer. For Germans, a beer must have been brewed according to the Reinheitsgebot.

> **REINHEITSGEBOT:** (n) Literally means "purity order." In the 16th century the Bavarian court was concerned about the ingredients that were being used in beer. Brewers used to color their beers with soot or lime, and beans and peas were being used in addition to grains as malt. In 1516, Duke William IV passed a law that restricted the brewing of beer and stipulated that only barley (or wheat) hops and water were allowed to be used in beer (they didn't know about the function of yeast in 1516).

The beer styles in Germany vary greatly, extending far beyond the lagers and light beers that we Americans associate with Germany. (*Note:* Many of us Americans associate this lightness with the beer Heineken, which is *not* German but Dutch, and is an industrialized beer.) Germans make ales and lagers that run the gamut in color, from the lightest of light Kristallklar to the darkest of dark Schwarzbier.

What's Your Type? Beer Styles

Most every beer is given a name based on its general flavor profile, its origin and history, or both. This name is known as the beer's style. The style is usually the first thing you know about a beer, as it's often on the label, so it's helpful to understand the attributes of the various beer styles.

We explained earlier that all beers are either ales or lagers. In addition, ales and lagers are broken down into styles. For instance, a Pilsner is a style of lager, a Dopplebock is a style of lager, a Porter is a style of ale, a Stout is a style of ale, an India Pale Ale is a style of... got it?

Beers are categorized on the basis of historical tradition, ingredients, and sensory characteristics. According to the Beer Judge Certification Program, which is highly respected in the beer world and the go-to for beer style guidelines, flavors that are most important to a beer style are type and strength of malt, yeast strain, strength of bitterness, and type and strength of hops. Aromatics that are most important to a beer style include strength and type of malt aroma, strength and type of hop aroma, and yeast ester aroma. The feel of a beer in the mouth, from the thickness of the liquid to the amount of prickliness from the carbonation, are also important factors in determining a beer style. The visual characteristics that are most important to a beer style are color, clarity, and the nature of the head (for example, the thickness).

Whether the beer is dubbed Bavarian Hefeweizen or Russian Imperial Stout, the name hints at what the aromatics are like, how strong it is, what sort of body it has, how it was brewed, and even what its history is. There are many, many variations of each particular style, and each brewer makes his or her own version of specific styles, but knowing a beer's style gives you a general idea of what to expect.

Here are some examples of common beer styles:

- **AMERICAN ALL-MALT LAGER:** The designation "all-malt lager" means that no adjuncts were used. Though pale in color, these beers will display a broader depth of flavor and a more complex bitterness than the industrialized mass-produced lagers promoted during football games.

- **PILSNER:** A type of lager named after the city in which it was created, Plzen, Bohemia (in what is now the Czech Republic). The beer is crisp, clear, and light straw to golden in color, finishing clean and dry.

- **PALE ALE:** A type of English ale that is usually bitter (hoppy) and higher in alcohol content than your average Pilsner.

- **INDIA PALE ALE (IPA):** A beer created by British brewers who were sending their Pale Ales to India. They found that the ales were going bad on the long journey, so they added more alcohol and hops to help preserve them, creating a bigger brew. IPAs today are generally bitter and higher in alcohol than a Pale Ale.

- **WHEAT BEER:** Simply put, an ale or lager brewed with a portion of malted wheat in the mash. There are two common types of wheat beers: Hefeweizen (light, fruity, unfiltered wheat beer) and Dunkelweizen (darker unfiltered wheat beer).

- **WITBIER:** A Belgian-style ale that's very pale in color but cloudy in appearance both because it is unfiltered (meaning the yeast has been kept in) and because a high level of wheat and sometimes oats are used in the brewing process. These beers are spiced, often with coriander, orange peel, or herbs. The crispness and slight twang come from the wheat and the high level of carbonation. A popular style often replicated well in the United States.

- **BROWN ALE:** Brown Ales are typically rather malty and often full in body. They tend to have a nutty, toasty character, some with lighter notes and others with a heavy malt quality.

- **PORTER:** This is a dark ale and is generally not too high in alcohol content. The name of the style comes from its popularity with the street and river porters of London in the 18th century.

STOUT: Porters were so popular that the English started making Double Porters and Extra Stout Porters, which eventually became known simply as Stouts. These ales are black ales that use deeply roasted barley for their toasty character and dark color. Stouts vary greatly in alcohol content, sweetness, and bitterness. Though these attributes change from stout to stout, the richness of the roasted barley is the common thread.

DUBBEL: A Belgian-style ale that is usually dark in color, with a dark fruit profile of figs and plumbs, and a spice profile of clove, nutmeg, and similar spices. Dubbels have a mild hop bitterness and are effervescent and medium to full-bodied. *Dubbel* refers to the use of up to twice the amount of malt used in a standard Belgian Ale.

TRIPEL: *Tripel* refers to part of the brewing process in which brewers use up to three times the amount of malt used in a standard Belgian Ale. Traditionally, Tripels are yellow to gold in color with a dense, creamy head. The aroma and flavors are complex, often spicy, yeasty, and fruity, with a semisweet finish. Small amounts of spices and herbs are sometimes added as well. Tripels are notoriously alcoholic, and the best crafted ones hide this character, so proceed with caution: sip slowly.

QUADRUPEL: Inspired by the monk brewers of Belgium, a Quadrupel is a Belgian-style ale of great strength, bigger in flavor than its Dubbel and Tripel sister styles. The colors range from deep red to brown. These ales are usually full bodied with a rich malty character. They are often sweet on the palate and rarely bitter, but the alcohol is there all the way; average alcohol by volume (ABV) range: 9% to 13%.

SAISON: These are farmhouse ales that were traditionally brewed in the winter, stored, and consumed throughout the summer months. This is a complex style, and many are very fruity and spicy in aroma and flavor, with earthy yeast tones, and finishing with a tartness or sourness. They are often described as dry, making them perfect companions for food.

○ **BIÈRE DE GARDE:** This ale is usually golden to deep copper to light brown in color. It is moderate to medium in body. This style of beer gives off a toasted malt aroma, sometimes with a bit of fruit in the nose and with a slight malt sweetness and medium hop bitterness on the tongue. Earthy, cellar-like, musty aromas and flavors are possible.

○ **FRUIT BEER:** Any beer (ale or lager) made with fruit. The sweetness, sourness, bitterness, alcohol content, and viscosity depend on the fruit used.

○ **HERBED/SPICED BEER:** This is a style of beer (ale or lager) that is specially herbed or spiced to make anything from the common spiced fall pumpkin beer to Christmas beers with nutmeg and cinnamon to ginger beers to heather ales. Brewers like to get crazy with things like hot peppers, hemp, ginseng, and spruce needles. Many of these beers will blow away your idea of what a beer can be.

Tainted Love: Off-Flavors in Beer

You now know that real beer flavors include a complex array of sweet, salty, bitter, and alkaline. The aromatics of beer also run the gamut from caramel, grainy, and grassy to nutty, roasty, and toasty. But sometimes there are flavors present in beer that aren't supposed to be there. We all know about "skunked" beers, but bad flavors in beer can also vary greatly. These off-flavors can have tastes and aromatics like the burnt qualities of asphalt and sulfur, metallic qualities, aspects of wet moldy newspaper, wet dog, or wet leather. Detecting off-flavors can be confusing because sometimes, except for the wet dog perhaps, one of these flavors might be intended for the beer. For instance, some Rauchbiers can have burnt qualities that work well, and sometimes a Gueuze can have a funky wet-leather earthiness to it that makes it great.

The trick to spotting off-flavors is knowing the variety of flavors that you can expect from the beer style that you're drinking and what flavors shouldn't be there. If these off-flavors are faint, they may go unnoticed by the novice. But an experienced beer taster will be able to tell if a beer he or she had before tastes significantly different this time. When we get to this point in beer school, we actually have our students taste a beer that's off so that they'll be able to distinguish truly bad from an intentional sourness or funky flavor. They forgive us, but they'll never forget that spoiled beer they sipped.

Off-flavors usually come from oxidation, bacterial contamination, an unexpected or accidental spontaneous fermentation, or cork taint. Oxidation is simply when the beer has been exposed to oxygen, possibly from an improper cap seal. Oxidation will generally give you wet-cardboard flavors. Bacteria in beer can produce acid in the beer, which creates sour and tart flavors. As you'll learn in Chapter 6, certain beer styles, like the Berliner Weisse, actually benefit from a fermentation process in which the bacteria *Lactobacillus* is purposefully added. *Lactobacillus* produces lactic acid, which gives the Berliner Weisse its distinctive sourness and citric qualities. A bacteria that is frequently the culprit in producing off-flavors is *Acetobacter*. *Acetobacter* is a bacteria that produces acetic acid in beer and that gives vinegar its sourness and pungency. This organism is great in a Flanders Red Ale, but when it appears in an American Pale Ale, you know something is wrong. If a beer becomes infected by this bacteria, it's usually due to improper cleaning and sanitizing.

Phenols are off-flavors that also come from improper sanitization or from some wild yeast strains. Phenols smell like Band-Aids. Yes, it's true. If you have a beer that smells like plastic or has mediciny, burnt, or smoky qualities, it may contain phenols. Once again, not all phenolic qualities are bad. Wheat beers, many Belgian Ale styles, and Smoked Beers make good use of phenols, but if you're tasting Band-Aids and smoke in your Pale Lager, there might be a problem.

Another fault in beer that can be caused by bacterial contamination or unhealthy yeast is the presence of a compound called diacetyl. Diacetyl gives off buttery and butterscotch aromas and flavors. Again, these qualities might be great in a British Cream Ale, but if you smell buttered popcorn in your Nut Brown, call Houston. Beer can also be contaminated with wild yeast strains that can ferment sugars in beer that normal beer yeast can't ferment. Wild yeast doesn't just exist in the Senne Valley of Belgium. It exists everywhere. If you get a beer that's been contaminated by wild yeast, you could get a super-foamy and bad-tasting mug. Flavors that can come from these accidental and spontaneous fermentations can be the worst of the bunch: sulfuric aromas like rotten eggs and burning rubber. Mmmm... sounds tasty. These flavors usually come from the autolysis of yeast, when the enzymes in the yeast cause it to start eating itself.

One more cause of off-flavors that we'll talk about is a little something called cork taint. Sometimes, with specialty beers, brewers will finish the beer with a cork to allow aging or to be fancy. Cork taint is simply cork contamination (usually by a compound called 2,4,6-trichloroanisole). When a well-stored wine bottle is bad, the culprit is most likely cork taint. We in the industry, who try to limit our use of the word *taint*, call a wine or beer bottle that has gone bad due to cork spoilage "corked." Generally, if a bottle is corked, it will taste musty and moldy like a damp basement. Once again, a great quality in some beers but not so much in other clean, crisp beer styles.

Get Some Digits: IBUs and ABVs

Don't worry. We won't be doing any math here. There are only two numbers you will really need to know in the beer world: IBUs and ABVs. It's important that you know these numbers for a couple of reasons. First, knowing them will aid you in determining what the taste of the beer might be like before you try it. If you don't know that the beer you are ordering has 90 IBUs and you hate bitter, dry beers, you will be in for a shock when you taste it. Second, knowing how strong the beer is will help you steer clear of potential beer goggle incidents and overall whorishness. If you don't know that the beer you ordered is 11% alcohol, you could be ass up in your neighbor's flower garden and doing the walk of shame before you can say "three sheets to the wind."

The first acronym, IBU, stands for International Bitterness Units. The IBU scale provides a way to measure the bitterness of a beer. The number on the bitterness scale is a result of some complicated empirical formula using something called a spectrophotometer and solvent extraction. We don't pretend to understand that, and the good thing is that you don't have to understand it either. The bottom line is that this scale was based on tasting beer samples and correlating the perceived bitterness to a measured value on a scale of 1 to 100. The higher the number, the higher the concentration of bitter compounds in the beer. For example, a mass-produced American lager might have an IBU of 5 on the scale, whereas an extreme Tripel IPA could have an IBU as high as 100.

We encourage you to use your own palate to determine bitterness because the IBU scale can be a bit confusing for newer craft beer drinkers. Some of the more advanced drinkers, and those who are adept at brewing, may begin to pay closer attention to these numbers. Some innovative brewers are starting to put this number on bottle labels, but more often than not, this number is not shown on the beer bottle. If you're worried about bitterness, it will help to know the general range of IBUs for each beer style. You can usually find the IBU number for a beer on the brewery's website. For an IBU range for beer styles, check out the Beer Judge Certification Program's website (www.bjcp.org).

The second acronym, ABV, stands for alcohol by volume and directly relates to how drunk you are going to get. If you're used to drinking mass-produced lagers, the beers you've been drinking are probably between 3% and 5% ABV. When you start getting into craft beers, the ABVs range from the familiar 3% to 5% to big beers that come in at 13% or more (drzunk!!).

If you're going to drink a beer, or a few, you'd better know your ABVs. Believe us when we tell you that there is a *huge* difference between a 5% beer and an 8% beer. A 5% beer can make you friendly; an 8% beer can make you French kiss a tree. Of course, this all depends on how well you can hold your liquor. Can you handle your martinis, or do you get sauced after half a glass of Pinot Gris? It's critical, especially for women, to be vigilant about how much alcohol we are actually consuming. Know your ABVs, and you, your neighbor, and her flower garden will thank us.

The Secret of Beer: How to Get the Beer You Want

Now that you've got Beer 101 under your belt, it's time to take what you know out for a spin in the real world. You now know more than probably 80% of the beer-ordering public, and you have the power to get what you want out of your beer experience. Ordering your first real beer can be daunting. Even we were intimidated the first time we ordered a craft beer. We were dry mouthed and tongue-tied. We thought, "Hey! We know about fermentation, we know our ales from our lagers. What's the problem here?" The fact is that even though we knew what we liked, we didn't know how to communicate it. Communication is a continuing challenge for any relationship, and learning how to ask for what you want from beer can take some practice, but the Universal Law of Attraction and the Secret of Beer is, If you know how to ask for what you want, you just might get it.

We've already told you that beer falls into two types: ales and lagers. But it's not good enough to be this general when asking for beer.

Would you go onto Match.com and describe the person you're looking for as brown-haired, with no other descriptors? If you do, every brown-haired freak under the sun is going to think you have extremely low standards and that he or she may finally have a chance. In short, do not go up to the bar and ask simply for an ale or a lager or, worse yet, "something light."

Ask yourself first what specific flavors you are craving at the moment. We've just given you a vocabulary of styles and a few basic flavor descriptors based on beer's ingredients. Use these to get specific about your desires. You don't have to order any old beer. If you're feeling a bit devilish, ask for a spicy, yeasty ale. If you need a palate cleanser, ask for a hoppy, crisp Pale Ale. As with anything, the more specific you get, the more you will specifically get what you want. And that is true gratification in life.

Try ordering in progression from the flavor you want the most down to the more nuanced flavors. For example, say you want the complex, bigger flavors and aromatics usually found in an ale. Great. Now decide which type of ale you feel like. Use your flavor descriptors. Do you feel like banana? Pine tree? Coffee? Though you know about some major beer styles, you may not feel comfortable asking for a Porter or Stout yet. If that's the case, use the vocabulary for cuisine that you already have. Describe your ideal beer, just as you would describe any other food or spice. Always return to flavors: bitter, nutty, tart apple, and so on. In fact, you could simply list off the herbs and spices you have in your kitchen: cinnamon, pepper, cardamom, and sage, and any great beer bartender worth her salt should be able to find a beer with those flavors.

You may already be fairly comfortable using such terms in conjunction with wine: velvety, peppery, leather, jasmine, cherry tones. We know that if we ask for a Cabernet with earthy, musky flavors, we will get something more uniquely suited to our palate. The same is true of beer! Be specific. Try this equation: Ask for a beer using three descriptors: (1) the dominant flavor you crave + (2) a secondary flavor you would like + (3) a beer style. We hope this will = the beer you want. Examples: bitter + chocolaty + Stout; citrusy + grassy + Witbier; dry + sour + Tripel Belgian.

Like sex, specifics are best. And also like sex, you probably know what you really like but are afraid to ask for it. Beer wants to know how hoppy, how bitter, and how spicy you want it. Are hints of pear good? Is the dry, orange-rind finish working for you? Some people are embarrassed about doing the "dirty talk," so practice in the mirror, look yourself in the eye, and say, "Nutty, chocolaty." Or try it in your car on the way to work, in traffic: "Sour, spicy." The more comfortable you get with the words, the more confidence you'll have the moment the bartender looks at you and says, "What do you want?"

Beer Bar Book of Etiquette

Unfortunately, people new to the beer world have a reputation for behaving badly in beer bars. From ordering to paying to tipping, some people just don't seem to know the right way to conduct themselves. Perhaps there's a disconnect because people feel out of place and are overcompensating. Whatever it is, we are here to put an end to it.

Since neither Emily Post nor *Queer Eye for the Straight Guy* have sections on good beer manners, we've had to step up and fill in the void for beer bar etiquette. Here's a guide of do's and don'ts to help you mind your P's and Q's. *Spoiler alert:* Please be aware that after you read this, you'll no longer be able to say that you didn't know any better. We'll be watching.

ORDERING YOUR BEER

DO ORDER A FLIGHT. It's perfectly good beer manners to ask if the bar offers "beer flights." These are usually found at brewpubs, where breweries want you to get a sampling of their beers. It's also a great way to test your palate. Try tasting the beers without

MIND YOUR P'S AND Q'S

Haven't you always wondered what the warning "mind your P's and Q's" means? Well, here it is: Mind your pints and quarts. This saying was used in England hundreds of years ago. The barkeeps would say this to patrons when they were getting out of hand, knocking over beers or being generally rowdy. It's a nice way to say, "Watch your manners or you'll get a boot in your ass, thanks!"

Oddly enough, mind your P's and Q's also has ties to the sea because it was a method of keeping books on the waterfront. Back in ye olden times, sailors were paid a pittance, so seamen drank their ale in taverns whose keepers were willing to extend credit until payday. Since many sailors were illiterate, barkeeps kept a tally of pints and quarts consumed by each sailor on a chalkboard behind the bar. Next to each person's name, a mark was made under *P* for "pint" or *Q* for "quart" whenever a seaman ordered another draught.

On payday, each seaman had to pay up for each mark next to his name, so he was forced to mind his P's and Q's or he would get into financial trouble. To ensure an accurate count by dubious keepers, sailors had to keep their wits and remain somewhat sober. Sobriety usually ensured good behavior, hence today's meaning of mind your P's and Q's.

looking at the names. Find the flavors and try to guess which one is the Brown Ale, which is the Hefeweizen, which is the Stout, and so on.

DO ASK IF YOU CAN TASTE A DRAUGHT BEER. Many beer bars offer tastes as a courtesy, showing you different flavors and allowing you to find the best beer for your needs. Try to narrow down which beers you'd like to try by looking at the list and talking to the bartender about your favorite flavors. But just like your mom told you at Baskin-Robbins, taking advantage of this tasting courtesy at a beer bar is a no-no. Try to limit your tastes to two beers—three is pushing it.

DON'T DRINK OUT OF THE BOTTLE. Good beer bars serve beer in the appropriate corresponding glass, which varies greatly in size, depending on the beer. When it's served like this, you may think you aren't getting enough of a good thing. But, just as you would not ask for white wine in a Pinot Noir glass, don't ask for your Tripel in a pint glass. Believe us when we tell you that you *are* getting your money's worth. If you had a 16-ounce pint glass full of that 9% Tripel, the beer would be resting too long, causing it to lose carbonation and warm up too quickly for that style. Not only that, but you might find yourself ass over teakettle before the night was through. Pint glasses are perfect for some beer styles but not all beer styles (see Chapter 7).

DO ASK FOR A GLASS IF YOU ORDER A GOOD BOTTLED BEER. We've been to some bars, which shall remain nameless, that dare to bring us a rare specialty Belgian beer, made by monks no less, without even a regular inferior pint glass to pour it into. This would be like ordering a bottle of wine and having it show up without glassware. Would you get the full flavor by drinking out of the bottle? The same applies to good beer. This style of beer should be served in a beautiful goblet or tulip-shaped glass, depending on the beer, just like they do it in beautiful Belgium. If you are a victim of this crime, feel free to ask for a proper glass.

DON'T SIMPLY ASK FOR A LIGHT BEER OR A DARK BEER OR AN ALE OR A LAGER. We cannot repeat or stress this enough. This is like going to a wine bar and just asking for a red wine or saying, "I'll have something white." This is too vague. It will leave your bartender with too much open room to give you a beer that might not match your palate. Again, go with flavors. Or if you are looking for something that is, say, light in alcohol, ask for that, but add some flavor descriptors. For example, "I'd like a low-alcohol, nutty, amber ale." This will get you closer to the happiness you deserve.

DRINKING YOUR BEER

DO **DRINK YOUR BEER LIKE WINE.** We are talking about the kinds of beer that should be treated as well as you would treat a fine wine. Lift your glass up to the light and check out the color. Ask yourself what flavors you can expect from the roast of the malt. Swirl the glass and release the carbonation. Get your nose way down in there and breathe in the luscious aromatics. Finally, take a drink. Swirl the beer in your mouth, over your tongue. Take the time to really taste it. Think about what you are drinking. As with wine, there is the initial flavor, but then there are also secondary flavors and more subtle flavors that are revealed with each new sip.

DON'T **SLAM YOUR BEER.** One misconception that many people have about beer is that it should be guzzled. The Keg Stand, Quarters, Beer Pong, and many other popular pastimes all operate under this assumption. But swilling beer down your gullet without taking the time to savor or appreciate it is an offense to great beer. Unless there's money on the line, or unless it's lite beer that you don't want to taste, or unless you want pictures of yourself barfing on the sidewalk to be spread all over the Internet, don't slam your beer.

DO **TAKE NOTES.** There's nothing worse than having the most amazing beer you've ever had in your life and then not being able to recall it. We've found that if you write down the name of the beer and a few simple tasting notes, you are then able to relive that wonderful experience again and again. Also, writing down your beer experiences will help you refine and define your palate. (Yes, sometimes the notes will be illegible by the end of the evening, but give it a go anyway; if nothing else, they're good for a laugh.)

DON'T **NURSE YOUR BEER.** If you've ever tasted a beer that has been sitting out for a long time, you probably weren't very happy. It was too warm, and the carbonation had released from the beer, leaving it syrupy, sticky, and icky tasting. So don't nurse your beer for an hour. If you've had the same beer for an hour, let it go and order a new one. If you are an extraordinarily slow beer drinker, it might be wise to order your beer in smaller sizes if you can. Which brings us to our next "do"...

DO ORDER HALF-PINTS. If you are planning to taste a lot of flavors and take a little Beer Journey of your own, it's wise to drink half-pints. Other than specialty glasses, the half-pint is actually our favorite beer serving size. There's no shame in ordering a smaller portion. It will allow you to taste many beers without becoming belligerent, and the beer will stay at the proper temperature and carbonation levels. It's true that you'll have to order beer a little more often, but sometimes half-pints are the way to go. The size of your glass does not relate to the size of your anything, so be the person (listen up, guys) who is secure enough to drink out of the half-pint.

DON'T DRINK OUT OF PITCHERS. Most craft beer bars don't even offer pitchers anymore, but if they do, don't order your beer in one. For the same reasons you shouldn't nurse your beer for an hour, you shouldn't drink quality beer out of a pitcher. Not only has the beer at the bottom of the pitcher been sitting around for way too long, but the careful calibration of carbonation is probably off because of the continued pouring and agitation of the pitcher. Draught beer is meant to be poured once: from the tap to your glass. The carbonation of the beer releases too much when it is poured into a pitcher and *then* poured into glasses over and over again. We do realize that pitchers may be cheaper, but usually the price difference doesn't make up for the loss of flavor. Quality, not quantity.

SENDING BACK YOUR BEER

DO SEND BACK A BEER WHEN YOU TRULY DON'T LIKE THE FLAVOR. If it's not what you asked for, or if the beer is totally not want you wanted, or if you hate the taste of it, it's perfectly okay to return your beer.

A Note on the Beer Snob; or, Don't Be a D-Bag

We've been accused on more than one occasion of being beer snobs. And yes, we admit, in the past we have been. In the adolescence of our life with beer, we sometimes used our beer knowledge for evil. We admit that we have used our beer prowess to seem superior to others, take bitchy demanding women down a peg, and belittle arrogant boys. And while that is fun—really fun—it ultimately does not pay off or bode well for good beer. We want to bring people into the craft beer world, not scare them away.

There is a certain amount of snobbery that comes with learning about the finer things. Once you've had an amazing first-growth Bordeaux, for instance, it's tough to go back to enjoying Two-Buck Chuck. That's not your fault. But don't insult someone's beer choice, regardless of how stupid and bad you think it may be. Don't condemn; instead, offer suggestions of a beer that she might like based on the stupid choice you've just seen her make.

But be careful; while you may know more than your friends do, you don't want to become the person no one wants to have dinner with. Realize that knowledge is power. If you're talking more than tasting, telling more than teaching, and insulting more than inspiring, then you're not doing craft beer any favors.

If you know good beer, consider yourself an ambassador for it. Beer knowledge is exciting. You'll want to spread the word. Just do us a favor and do it in the nicest way possible.

DON'T SEND YOUR BEER BACK WHEN YOU'VE ORDERED THE BEER JUST BECAUSE OF THE FUNNY NAME AND THEN YOU DON'T LIKE IT. Ask about the flavors first, then order the Arrogant Bastard because it makes you laugh. Otherwise, you made your beer bed, now drink it.

○ **DON'T SEND BACK A BEER BECAUSE IT'S "TOO FOAMY."** Once you delve into Chapter 6 you will learn that beer is meant to have a substantial head on it. This relates to the aromatics and enjoyment of the beer. In fact, if you are served a pint with no head at all (what we call the dirty dishwater look), you should be suspicious. Beer should have at least a two-finger head, and many Belgian beers have an even thicker head due to the yeast, carbonation, and glass shape.

○ **DON'T DRINK FROM A DIRTY GLASS.** It is perfectly okay to send back a beer if the glass is dirty. Just because beer is often more casual than wine doesn't mean you are supposed to drink your Pale Ale from a dirty glass.

○ **DO SEND BACK YOUR BEER IF IT TASTES OFF.** If you're drinking a beer you are very familiar with, perhaps your new favorite Porter, and it tastes wrong, skunky, or sour, it is perfectly good manners to send it back. There may be something wrong with the keg, or perhaps the draught lines at that bar have not been cleaned in some time. Just like wine, if beer is not kept well, it can go bad. And it's good for the bartender to know that he may have a rotten keg, so that he can send it back as soon as possible.

We can guarantee you that if you walk into a beer bar after taking basic Beer 101, you will outshine every other joker in the joint with your newfound beer manners. Not that this is a competition, but we all like to feel sexy and special, and competing for best outfit in the bar is a bit passé. The best way to stand out is to start dropping your beer lingo, to know what you want, and to ask for it directly. This intelligence and confidence is sexier than the blink of a skirt that model is wearing at the end of the bar.

* * *

Okay, you've passed Beer 101. Easy. How do you feel? You should feel like beer has been demystified a bit. You are now way ahead of most of the drinking public, and as you learn more about the beer styles and can pick out specific flavors, you will see the craft beer list begin to lose its mystery. You will start to group the beers together in your mind based on flavor and style guidelines, and you will know where to go when you want a bitter beer and how to find a sweet one. You've begun the Beer Journey. It only gets better from here...

The Art of Beer

In my opinion, most of the great men of the
past were only there for the beer.

—ALAN JOHN PERCIVALE TAYLOR, BRITISH HISTORIAN

Understanding What Makes a
Great Beer Great

G reat beer is indeed an art form: Part science, part creativity, part perfect palate, and a special dose of a certain *je ne sais quoi*. One must have a strategy to create a great beer. The masterful brewer will lay out quality ingredients, make a specific recipe, and execute each step with great care and attention. She or he must, of course, use what is available, and the brewers from years past did the best they could with their environment, working with and sometimes combating wild yeast, wide temperature variations, failed crops of hops, or disappointing yields of barley. Whatever the circumstances, they brewed on. The great brewer will approach all of these setbacks with a quick change of plan, sometimes leading to unique beers—happy accidents that take on a life of their own. It's important to be able to recognize this great effort when tasting your way through the craft beer world, to know when you are drinking a work of art.

After all, a Beer Journey isn't just about drinking every style, it's also about having a creative approach to your beer choices. It's about understanding what makes certain beers stand out among others and asking yourself why. At this point, you should be forming some opinions and beginning to differentiate between beers based on flavor notes, giving your own personal opinion some gravitas, and anointing your palate to a higher calling. The following chapters break down the flavor profiles and history of different beer styles, from Hefeweizens to Barleywines, and this chapter arms you with the knowledge and skills needed to formulate an approach when evaluating a variety of beers. Now that you have mastered Beer 101, it's time to examine the intricacies of tasting beer—the mouthfeel, the carbonation—to revere beer's great history, and to seek out the deeper questions posed by each pint.

Who Should We Thank? A Little Beer History

Beer is old. We don't mean Sistine Chapel old, we mean *old* old. We're talking people-carving-notes-to-each-other-in-stone old. We're talking sacrificing-goats-at-parties old. Beer is, in fact, arguably one of the oldest of all alcoholic drinks. Scientists have been able to date beer back to around 7000 BCE from remnants in ancient pottery found in what is now Iran. The Sumerians seem to have been the first to have made detailed notes about beer, one of the most famous pieces being "The Hymn to Ninkasi," their goddess of alcohol.

No, the hymn doesn't provide specific malt measurements, but it does mention familiar beer ingredients like water and grain. In fact, beer probably came about from baked grains (a sort of dough, porridge, or bread) that were wetted with water (which released sugars in the grain, making it sweeter) and left out for storage. Enter wild naturally occurring yeasts, and the concoction becomes an early, albeit strange, beer. In those days, there were no hops to be found, so spices, fruit (like dates), honey, and herbs were added to make the funky beer more palatable.

Beer happened all over the globe to many types of grain that were used to make dough or other mash: in China it was wheat, in Japan it was rice. Everyone found a way to turn the gift of harvested grain into a happy beverage.

Beer soon became a thing of ritual throughout history. The beverage is sometimes even given props as the savior of humanity. Without safe drinking water, beer often became the only sanitary beverage around. It was a choice between beer-o'clock around the clock or water that offered a cholera or dysentery bonus. And beer's ingredients made it a substantial food at times. Beer has a lot of minerals, fiber, and antioxidants, which added a huge health benefit to the diet of early civilizations. There is also an argument that beer played a part in people's settling down to plant and harvest instead of roaming and hunting. The idea being that as soon as they found beer, they stopped in their tracks and began planting and harvesting grains for the revered beverage. Sounds logical to us.

Beer even shows up in the first set of laws. Around 1780 BCE, Hammurabi created his code (in which is the origin of the famous "eye for an eye" punishment) and included in it rules for fairly pricing beer. He places responsibility for this on the tavern keeper (sometimes referred to as female). If the beer was overpriced, the tavern keeper would be drowned (Hammurabi was a bit of a hard-ass).

The Egyptians have been praised for their reverence of beer for centuries. Pharaoh Rameses II had a large brewing operation during his reign. Their god of beer was Osiris, and beer became a huge part of ritual in their society. Beer was offered as a fine gift to pharaohs, priestesses, and gods and was included among the possessions of those entering the afterlife ("Here's to your ghost" was a popular toast). It is thought that in Egyptian culture, if a woman drank beer offered by a man, they were then married (think of all the people you'd be married to if that were still true, ladies). Beer was also used as medicine to treat patients and sometimes as payment for laborers instead of money.

Around 330 BCE, beer moved from Egypt to the Greeks, who had mainly been wine drinkers. The Greeks called their beer *Zythos* and were slow to embrace beer with open arms because they associated the drink with less-refined segments of society. The Greeks most likely taught the Romans how to brew. Romans are known for their love of wine, but they happily added beer to their beverage list. Our modern word *beer* comes from the Latin *bibere*, which means "to drink." Pliny the Elder, a prolific Roman who wrote on many subjects, included notes on beer in his works. Julius Caesar was said to be a fan of a good brew, and legend tells that he toasted the crossing of the Rubicon with a cup of ale. The Romans then probably passed their beer recipes on to the Britons around 55 BCE, and the Britons would grow to love it more than wine.

The early Christians really took to beer. The monks got into brewing and found a certain calling, so to speak. The monastery was often the brewery and inn of the olden days. Pilgrims passing through town were offered a pint and a room by the monks as a respite from their journey. Beer in medieval times was a currency, sometimes used as a payment or tax. While good beer was considered a gift from the heavens, bad batches of beer were seen as the devil's work because the science of beer was not yet fully understood. In the 1500s, women were burned if they were thought to be brew witches, satanic souls who were responsible for bad beer (can you imagine a man tasting the beer, declaring it was sour, and then perusing the drinking crowd for a poor lady who would be deemed responsible?).

The Pilgrims included beer among their necessities, and running out of beer was one of the deciding factors for stopping at Plymouth Rock, as we learned from William Bradford's *History of Plymouth Plantation*: "We could not take much time for further search, our victuals being much spent, especially beer." Female Pilgrims homebrewed for the family, using whatever ingredients they could find in the new land. Native Americans introduced corn to the Pilgrims, and this became a useful ingredient when barley was scarce.

During the 1500s, hops started to be regularly added to beer, and recipes began to take on more variety. (Though hops had been used for a long time in certain parts of the world, it wasn't yet commonplace or required.) With hops, beer got better (fewer beer witches were burned, thank God). The hops were revered for their preservative quality, and the hopped beer started to replace the beer made with *gruit*, an herb mixture used to flavor beer. As some countries tried to hold on to the tradition of hop-free beer, the public found new love for the drier drink. The Germans, as we mentioned in Chapter 1, passed the famous Reinheitsgebot, requiring all beer be made with only malt, water, and hops (they didn't know about the details of yeast yet). The Germans also began to lager beers, storing the beer at cool temperatures and creating a style that would become the new favorite. In the 1840s, the first Pilsner was born in Plzen, Bohemia, and the lager style flourished. In America in the 1800s, the influx of German immigrants brought with them new styles, like the Weiss beer and the lagering method of fermentation. Americans soon began to brew these lighter styles instead of the common Porter of the time.

In 1876, Louis Pasteur brought beer forward by describing the basis for fermentation in his work *Etudes sur la Bière* (Studies on Beer). In it, he determined that beer was fermented not by chemicals but by microorganisms—that is, yeast. He noted that bacteria, mold, and wild yeast were often responsible for the sour beer that plagued France and other countries. With this new understanding, he and other scientists began to refine techniques that could contain impurities like bacteria, and thus quality control for beer could be effectively implemented. The process of killing such bacteria and stabilizing beer would come to be known as pasteurization.

As brewers began to understand how temperature and bacteria affected their brewing process, lagers and ales could be shipped, and beer became an even bigger business. When the Industrial Revolution gave birth to improvements in road and railway transportation, and with the invention of automatic bottling, a beer could be shipped far and wide. In the 1870s, Adolphus Busch perfected a design for double-walled railcars that could keep the beer cool using ice.

By 1880, there were more than 2,000 breweries in the United States alone. Compare that to the early 1990s, when five breweries produced almost 90% of the country's beer, and you can see how competition increased and circumstances changed for beer in our country. One of these circumstances was economic. World War I and the Great Depression made quality ingredients for beer hard to come by, and this is when a lot of lower-quality adjuncts like corn and sugar entered the beer scene in a big way. And the start of Prohibition in 1920 didn't help things (everything good is forbidden at some point in time). This forced many breweries to shut their doors due to a lack of business.

After Prohibition was repealed in 1933, only 160 breweries survived in America. The beer that emerged in modern times was the pasteurized lager, and the companies that mass-produced this beer made huge profits. Around 1960, Budweiser was selling around 10 million barrels a year. Pasteurized light lager was popular in many countries other than America; it remained the dominating beer in the business. By the 1970s, about 44 breweries were operating in America.

The craft/microbrew revolution began in 1976 in Sonoma, California,

PROPS TO PLINY

 One of our favorite historical beer-geeks is the honorable Pliny the Elder. Perhaps you recognize his name because of Russian River Brewing's beloved Double IPA of the same name. But have you ever asked yourself, "Why the hell is that beer named after a dead old Roman?" Well, Pliny the Elder, aka Gaius Plinius Secundus (you can see why he chose a street name), was a man of many talents. Born in 23 CE, he was an author, advocate (lawyer), officer, philosopher, botanist, procurator, historian, and naturalist. And in his spare time he wrote an encyclopedia. Pliny wrote about pretty much everything he could, documenting all that he saw and trying to understand in depth the world around him. So what does this have to do with beer?

While he took a break from all of his other exploits, Pliny gave hops its proper botanical name, *Humulus lupulus*, which translates to "wolf among weeds," no doubt in reference to the bitter bite of hops. Russian River pays homage to the man with its super-hoppy beer. It also has a bigger hop-head beer called Pliny the Younger, who wrote about the life of his uncle, Pliny the Elder.

Pliny the Elder was also one of the first people to examine the effects of *terroir* on winemaking, pointing out to many for the first time that the soil affected the vines and therefore the grapes and wine itself. He famously stated, "Truth comes out in wine." Though many of his other findings were not scientifically sound (he was restricted by his times, of course), he made a mark on the history of beer and wine and should be lauded for his attention to these coveted drinks.

Pliny the Elder died in the eruption of Mt. Vesuvius in 79 CE; it is said that he tried to save people from the flowing lava. A great man to the bitter end, so to speak.

at a brewery called New Albion, founded by a passionate homebrewer. Though this brewery lasted only six years, it set fire to other homebrewers, who began to follow suit and open small operations. The 1980s were a time for microbrew pioneers (and big hair and shoulder pads), experimenting with styles far more varied than the light lagers dominating the market. The late 1990s were good for American craft beer, as breweries gained in profit, and by 2000, there were about 1,400 breweries in America.

Today the craft beer world is thriving in America and abroad. Craft beers are available at grocery and liquor stores and are showing up in bars and restaurants all over the globe in big numbers. Though the mammoth breweries still reap high sales of light pasteurized lagers, the business of craft beer sees a steady rise each year, and beer drinking among both sexes and many different age groups grows annually. The history of craft beer's revolution has only just begun . . .

Laying Plans: Criteria for a Great Beer

Now that you are undoubtedly impressed by beer's grand history, it's time to carry that weight by creating your own criteria for evaluating this ancient, beloved beverage. No pressure, we're not requesting an essay of 400 words or less. No need to attempt to write out a five-page outline for beer tasting, or a Haiku about hops (but if you do the latter, *please* send it to us!). We just want you to know a good thing when you drink it. This is up to you and your palate, of course. After all, you are going to have preferences of style and flavor that will differ from those of other beer lovers, but you may find as you go that many agree on what makes for an exceptional beer. Those who have been tasting for years can have wonderful insight into the quality of each brewer's creation.

We're offering up our favorite terms that we use to describe great beer. To us, these are *balance, quintessential, unique, iconic,* and *rare.*

You may come up with a whole different set of guidelines—and more power to you—but we find that most beers we give an A+ to will deserve to be in at least one, if not several, of these categories.

Balance

Balance is admired in food and wine and, yes, beer. This balance is a balance of flavor components. The sweetness of the malt must be balanced by some drying or bitter hops, the alcohol must not be too overbearing, the carbonation should be at a perfect point for the beer. Needless to say, it takes many batches of brew to achieve this kind of success. And it may take brewers years to achieve the kind of balance they want in one particular recipe. Of course, sometimes you crave super-sweet, super-bitter, super-sour, and other extremes; you aren't always necessarily looking for balance in these instances. We're referring to the moments reserved for beers that blend all of the flavors and ingredients together into a seamless experience. It's like when an outfit comes together—when you're wearing the dress, it's not wearing you; when the tie is not too loud but classic. These beers offer a subtlety, in which different flavors are present but one doesn't overtake the other. These are the beers you want when you want the best.

For us, a balanced beer often means it finishes dry, without being bitter, leaving your palate clean and ready for more drink or food. This is somewhat subjective, however, because dry in the wine world has become a description of the best as well. People seem to admire a drink that keeps the sweetness in check, one that has a nice backbone of tannins without being too astringent or bitter. Of course one's sensitivity to bitterness varies widely; sometimes we'll offer someone a beer we would describe as dry, and they find it too bitter. This means their sensitivity to hops is high, either because they are new to the flavor or because they just prefer a sweeter or crisper beer. But even among sweet beers, one can strike more of a balance in comparison to others.

Balance can even apply to a hoppy IPA if the bitterness is married with a nice fruity malty background, balancing out the bitter. Every style can have an element of this balance. Sometimes it means that the complexity of flavors is almost impossible to name, simply because they come together so well. Beers that aren't balanced often present their ingredients separately on your taste buds. The flavor of the malt, hops, and yeast are all present, but they stand apart rather than overlapping with each other. This isn't bad, but it's not balanced and, therefore, not great. Again, there are times when you just want to taste hops or sweet chocolate; although we acknowledge such extremes, we wouldn't count beers like that among the elite. Here are some beers that have achieved balance:

ORVAL TRAPPIST ALE: Brasserie d'Orval S.A., Villers-devant-Orval, Belgium. It doesn't get much better than this: a perfectly balanced, über-complex Trappist beer. Spice, subtle fruit, a touch of sour, earthy, bone dry. 6.9% ABV.

RUDRICH'S RED SEAL: North Coast Brewing Company, Fort Bragg, California. Just the right amount of juicy, bitter hops and ripe fruit. Our go-to beer. 5.5% ABV.

ANVIL ALE ESB: AleSmith Brewing Company, San Diego, California. An American-style ESB that's full of flavor but balanced. Rich toasty malt with just the right amount of a hop backbone. 5.5% ABV.

TROIS PISTOLES: Unibroue, Chambly, Quebec, Canada. A Belgian-style Dubbel with dark raisin, spice, and bread. The alcohol is well hidden, and the hops dry it out perfectly. 9% ABV.

Quintessential

To us, *quintessential* means a beer that perfectly fulfills its style, as in the quintessential Kölsch or the quintessential American IPA. This doesn't mean it's necessarily, though it often is, our favorite within a style, but it is the beer that we think best represents the original intention, the tradition, the history of that style. It represents the essence of the style. This is important to us because we find that many people spit out a beer simply because they are comparing it to a completely different style of beer. Some people will drink a British Pale Ale and call it bland because it is not as hoppy as an American IPA; others try a traditional sour Gueuze and make a mean face because it's not sweet like the Lambics they're used to drinking. Yes, you may have a personal preference, but it's important to recognize that the brewer's intention, based on the style, is different. Otherwise, it's like comparing Pollock to Titian, *The Godfather* to *Caddyshack*, Hunter S. Thompson to Jane Austen—all great, but extremely different and from different genres. If you judge a beer with the style in mind, you may find that your appreciation of the style will grow. Finding a great representation of your least favorite style may change your mind about that style.

Oftentimes the quintessential beer within a style will be found in the country of its origin. The quintessential Rauchbier will most likely be found in Bamberg, Germany; the quintessential Abbey Ale, in Belgium. But because yeast and hops and malt can be shipped around, it is possible that the quintessential beer of a style is far from its origin. All being fair in beer, Americans can replicate an English beer to a tee if they choose to and possess the skill. And comparing one country's creation against the other, within style, is acceptable. Just know the guidelines for a style and be aware of the brewing tradition if you want to find those beers that are quintessential. If the Hefeweizen is a true Bavarian style, look for the traditional banana and clove esters, the touch of sour; don't judge it by the guidelines for a Saison. Speak the truth, find the essence. Here are a few quintessential brews:

> **WEIHENSTEPHANER HEFEWEISSBIER: Brauerei Weihenstephan, Freising, Germany.** The classic German Hefeweizen with traditional notes of banana and clove. 5.4% ABV.

RACER 5 IPA: Bear Republic Brewing Company, Healdsburg, California. Our favorite West Coast American-style IPA; beautifully balanced, fresh bitter hops, wonderful notes of fruit. 7% ABV.

TRAPPIST WESTVLETEREN 8: Brouwerij Westvleteren, Westvleteren, Belgium. The perfect Belgian Dubbel. Flavors of dark fruit, bread, and molasses. Unfortunately, hard to get. 8% ABV.

SAISON DUPONT: Brasserie DuPont spr, Tourpes-Leuze, Belgium. The most famous and often most favorite Belgian Saison or farmhouse ale. Dry and peppery, with a touch of earthy sourness and citrus. 6.5% ABV.

Unique

Unique, of course, means "unlike any other." These are beers that make you sit up and pay attention. They change a night at the bar from average to extraordinary. These are beers that stand out from the rest because they do something different. They may not follow any rules or be the quintessential of the style, but they are almost impossible to replicate. They may use an herb you've never had in a beer or a fruit found only in the area of the brewery. These beers can change your whole idea of what you thought beer could be. They break down barriers and destroy all the rules. These beers often cross over to the rare or iconic section, elevating themselves into the best of the beer world. Some of our favorites from the "unique" category:

CRAFTSMAN TRIPLE WHITE SAGE: Craftsman Brewing Company, Pasadena, California. This could cross over into icon territory for sure. A seasonal beer available only on tap, it can also be counted as rare. This is a Belgian-style Tripel brewed with sage hand-picked by the brewer. 9% ABV.

CHIPOTLE ALE: Rogue Ales Brewery/Brewer's on the Bay, Newport, Oregon. A dark-hued ale brewed with chipotle peppers. Smoky and spicy and surprisingly drinkable. 5.5% ABV.

○ **TRADE WINDS TRIPEL:** The Bruery, Placentia, California. Belgian-style Tripel brewed with Thai basil. Peppery, citrusy, complex. 7.5% ABV.

○ **ROSÉE D'HIBISCUS:** Brasserie Dieu du Ciel, Montreal, Canada. A Witbier brewed with hibiscus flowers. Tropical and refreshing. 5% ABV.

○ **PANGAEA:** Dogfish Head Craft Brewery, Milton, Delaware. A beer brewed with an ingredient from *every* continent—for example, crystallized ginger from Australia, water from Antarctica, and Basmati rice from Asia. (This brewery gets the gold for making the most ambitious, unusual, history-laden beers.) 7% ABV.

Iconic

Madonna, Jack Kerouac, Oprah, and Robert Redford have all become icons. A beer that becomes an icon is one you may see on posters, something you've heard talk of in craft beer circles; its reputation precedes it. These are beers that tend to have the highest ratings within their style. They don't have to be quintessential or balanced; they are famous because of the populace, and popularity doesn't necessarily require the brew to be balanced, unique, rare, or anything else, just favored by the public. Chimay Tripel (White) is a great example of this. To some people, it is the quintessential Belgian Tripel; to others, not at all, but everyone has heard of it, and most bars have Chimay posters adorning their walls. It's famous, not rare; balanced to some but not others; and loved by thousands. An iconic beer is a must-have beer:

○ **CHIMAY TRIPEL:** Bières de Chimay (Abbaye Notre Dame de Scourmont), Baileux (Chimay), Belgium. The largest Trappist Belgian brewery and the most popular. A staple of every craft bar. 8% ABV.

○ **SIERRA NEVADA PALE ALE:** Sierra Nevada Brewing Company, Chico, California. The most popular West Coast Pale Ale. Many attempt to copy this style, but few get it so right. Every bottle boasts the same constant quality hop bite. 5.6% ABV.

- **ANCHOR STEAM:** Anchor Brewing Company, San Francisco, California. The one and only American Steam beer. Dominates the waterfront piers of San Francisco. 4.9% ABV.

- **BUDWEISER:** Anheuser-Busch Inc., St. Louis, Missouri. Let's admit it, it is a beer icon. 5% ABV.

- **GUINNESS (ORIGINAL):** Guinness Ltd., Dublin, Ireland. Perhaps the most beloved beer of all time. A classic dry Irish Stout. Best in Ireland. 6% ABV.

- **PILSNER URQUELL:** Plzensky Prazdroj, a. s., Plzen, Czech Republic. It made true Pilsners famous in America. 4.4% ABV.

- **PABST BLUE RIBBON:** Pabst Brewing Company, Woodridge, Illinois. Even among craft beer drinkers, this little can gets props. A beacon for the working man and still quite popular. 4.7% ABV.

- **FAT TIRE AMBER ALE:** New Belgium Brewing Inc., Ft. Collins, Colorado. The first craft beer for many beer drinkers. Beloved brewery with a green focus. 5.2% ABV.

Rare

The beer people buy on eBay. The beer that has been aged a few years. The beer that has a number on its bottle because there are only a few in the world. The beer that was brewed only once. The seasonal beer. The beer that you can get only in that little town in Belgium because they make it only for the monks. Like anything—diamonds, French perfume, truffles, honest politicians—the more rare, the more coveted, the more expensive. Those obsessed with beer know when something is rare. They know that their favorite Porter is more rare on cask than on tap or in the bottle. They know that a certain local brewery offers its aged Cherry Sour Belgian only in February, and when it's gone, it's gone. It's wonderful to drink a special beer like this. It seems to capture the fleeting aspects of life, to force you into the pleasure of the moment. These aren't beers you can find at any store; they come around once in a while, and drinking them becomes a celebration of craft beer and its creative components. These beers aren't always even the best, but finding them often provides such excitement that you can appreciate them even if they don't get on your top ten list. A few of the extremely rare:

- **ANY BEER FROM THIS BREWERY:** Brouwerij Westvleteren (Sint-Sixtusabij van Westvleteren), Westvleteren, Belgium. The most elusive Trappist brewery, they allow only a limited amount of beers past their doors and do not sell them to American craft bars (see Chapter 5).

- **THE ABYSS:** Deschutes Brewery, Bend, Oregon. An extra-special Russian Imperial Stout. Super complex, great for aging, sublime. 11% ABV.

- **SAMICHLAUS BIER:** Brewery Castle Eggenberg, Eggenberg Austria. This is a Dopplebock that is brewed only once a year and aged for several months. Rum flavor, deep molasses, and dark fruit. A whopping 14% ABV.

- **TEMPTATION:** Russian River Brewing Company, Santa Rosa, California. The brewery sells only a certain number of bottles of this complex, sour, Belgian-style brew aged in French oak Chardonnay barrels. Well balanced for such a sour Belgian, if you see this hiding in a bar's fridge, grab it! 7.25% ABV.

These guidelines will help you discriminate between beers as you delve into a variety of styles and eventually begin your beer pairings and tastings, and finally start brewing your own. Of course, favorite beers are certainly subjective, and no one can really tell you you're wrong about your favorite beer. It's like one's taste in music. You may love Kenny G, and who's to stop you? (Well, *we* would if we could!) But in music, there is *some* general agreement on what is great, what is well written, what is musical, what is unique: Beethoven's Ninth, Sinatra singing "New York, New York," U2's "One," The Beatles' "Hey Jude," Led Zeppelin's "Stairway to Heaven," Devo's "Whip It." So how do we, the drinkers of beer, detect this greatness? How do we participate in this art? Surely the consumer is as important a participant in the beer world as the audience is in the theater world. Without the eyes of the audience, is there really a show? We are the audience for great brewers. We are where the beer ends up; our taste buds, its stage (what, too much?). So it *is* important that we create some personal guidelines for a great beer, a barometer of greatness, if only for our own Beer Journey. Graduating Beer School means fulfilling this art requirement.

Celestial Bodies: Understanding the Mouthfeel of Beer

As the word implies, mouthfeel is the sensation of how a liquid or food feels in your mouth. The term refers to its body, its consistency; how it feels on your tongue, how it hits the sides of your mouth, the back of your throat, your nasal passage (sexy, isn't it?). It is a textural, tactile descriptor that encompasses the experience of a beverage or a food. It is subjective and varies from person to person. We've all used many familiar words to describe the mouthfeel of whatever we are consuming; a cup of coffee is sharp, a soup is heavy, a glass of Champagne is refreshing, a Pinot Noir is dry, a soda is crisp, a Chardonnay is creamy. These descriptions are extremely popular in the beer world, and *mouthfeel* is a common word found in beer reviews. A beer's mouthfeel is influenced by all of its contents: carbonation, hops, malt, alcohol, water, yeast, and adjuncts and flavorings. You know about these ingredients by now, so let's consider how they affect the mouthfeel and experience of the beer. Let's work it out.

Carbonation

You've all had this experience with a bottle of soda: You open it, it's prickly (almost unbearably so), and it tastes refreshing, light, crisp, and sweet. Leave that bottle out for a while, and we all know what happens: The loss of carbonation brings out more of the sweetness in the soda, it gets syrupy and loses some of that refreshing feeling, and it becomes weighty, almost a dessert. This is because those little soda bubbles break up that syrupy sweetness; they balance out a heavy feeling, lifting up the flavors and the sugar. Sweetness in beer is affected in a similar way by the carbonation. The bubbles of carbonation in beer often balance out the sweetness of the malt, giving a lift to the alcohol and sugar. In a hoppy beer, the carbonation can keep the beer from tasting too bitter, enhancing the crisp and astringent feeling of the hops in the mouth. And the bold fruity aromatics of many hops are carried to the nose by those little bubbles. Beers with a high ABV can mask the alcohol with a good amount of carbonation. Think of how the soda in a whisky and soda masks some of the heat and high alcohol of the liquor.

On the flip side, Cask Ale or Real Ale (see page 94) tends to have less carbonation than other beers, and this can be a benefit. In fact, some beer experts will tell you to let the beer open up (yes, just like wine) and lose some of that carbonation to allow more flavor to come through. Think of carbonation as a distraction; sometimes it helps divert your attention away from an unwanted mouthfeel of potentially cloying malt or the heat from high alcohol. Other times, excess carbonation could hinder you from tasting the nuanced, toasty flavor of a subtle British ESB. Whether the distraction is a good or bad thing depends on the beer style and what the brewer thinks brings out its best components.

Hops

As you know, the brilliant tiny cone-shaped hops flowers do a lot for a glass of beer. As we said in Chapter 1, the hardworking hops can add dryness or bitterness, right? Well, think of how you determine if something is dry or bitter. When you suck a lemon, your whole mouth is involved; you make that crazy pouty face and feel a shock throughout your taste buds, in the back of your throat, and in your nasal passages. This is the total mouthfeel experience of astringency. In beer, usually most of the same puckery astringency comes from the hops and can affect your mouth in a similar, if not so extreme, fashion. If the beer is simply dry because of the hops, it can have a clean, crisp mouthfeel, leaving the taste buds without any residual flavors and cloying sweetness. The dryness can also balance out high alcohol or sweetness in the same way carbonation can. This is often the primary function of hops, offering a balance to sweetness in the same way that tannins in wine offer a balance to the sugar. Tannins are contained in hops as well, and the astringency they offer is a gift to beer, which would otherwise be all sweetness and no balance. When you taste beers, pay attention to any dryness, astringency, bite, and zing you get in the mouthfeel; this can often be attributed to the hops.

Malt

You know that malt provides the sugar for the yeast to consume and create CO_2 and alcohol. You also know that more malt means more sugar. More sugar means more for the yeast to eat, which means more viscous, weighty, and coating alcohol and more effervescent, prickly, and cleansing CO_2. Because malt is the instigator of many of these effects, it is a key contributor to the mouthfeel of the beer. The amount of malt directly relates to the warming alcohol in your mouth or the prickly CO_2. Beyond that, the mouthfeel of the beer can be affected by the amount of malt, or sugar, that still remains in the brew after the fermentation process is finished. This lovely stuff is called *residual sugar*. In addition to a sweet flavor, residual sugar can give off an oily viscosity on the tongue, an almost syrupy quality that adds weight to the beer.

Alcohol

A shot of bourbon, a snifter of sambuca, a little whisky in your coffee; we all know how these drinks feel going down. They create great warmth, coating our throats and leaving us with a waft of the liquor in our mouths. Nothing warms one up in the snow like a nice Scotch. Similarly, high-alcohol beer can give us that warming sensation. Beer lovers often describe this warmth in their beer reviews, and whether the alcohol is present on the tongue or well hidden is an important aspect of the mouthfeel of that beer. A beer with big bitter chocolate and coffee flavors, like a Russian Imperial Stout, can support a nice warm alcohol, and this style does indeed boast an ABV anywhere from 7% to 10%. Well-crafted beers have perfected the art of hiding alcohol in beer, hitting your mouth first with complex flavors of roasted malt, dark fruit and spice, or sour earthy tang, followed by a bit of warmth at the end. This can be quite dangerous (don't forget to check the ABV!). When you taste beers, try to detect the alcohol by mouthfeel. You'll learn a lot from trying to estimate the ABV. When you guess that the ABV is low and it's actually high, you will be in awe of the brewer's know-how.

Yeast

Oh, magic yeast, how we love ye. You do so much for beer. Yes, this includes affecting mouthfeel. Yeast is the eater of malt and creator of alcohol and CO_2, so it would follow that the type and amount of yeast used in a beer affects the creation of these things, which in turn affect the mouthfeel. But beyond that, yeast can have other textural effects on your beer-drinking experience. If a beer is unfiltered, like a Bavarian Hefeweizen, it will be cloudy due to the yeast hanging out in the brew. This adds a coarseness to the liquid, a fullness, a texture on the tongue. Yeast can also give sourness to beer (see page 79), and like a sour candy in your mouth, this is a full mouthfeel experience, similar to bitterness but not quite the same. It hits you all over, sometimes balancing a sweetness or a funky earthiness, other times just making you pucker up and say Howdy!

Adjuncts and Flavorings

As we said earlier, adjuncts and flavorings are special little things often added to beer and can have quite an effect on mouthfeel. The effect depends on the adjunct or flavoring itself. Here's a little breakdown of a few of them and their general effects:

- *Chipotle peppers* or *jalapeños* can add a hot spiciness.
- *Oats* can give a silky smooth texture.
- *Chocolate* can make for a weightier beer or dry and bitter brew, depending on the type of chocolate used.
- *Rice* can lighten the body.
- *Candi sugar* can make the alcohol higher and the beer weightier, more viscous.
- *Rye* increases head formation.
- *Lactose* adds to the body and sweetness of the brew.
- *Fruit* can give a sour sensation or sweet, syrupy weight.
- *Wheat* has a lot of protein and can add silkiness on the tongue and a foamier head.
- *Corn* can add to the sugar content, putting a weight in the liquid.

When you start to review beers, be sure to include descriptions of mouthfeel. It will train your palate to stay active as you taste your way through your Beer Journey. Take the following terms along with you so that you can get specific about mouthfeel:

Weighty	Dry, clean finish
Syrupy	Crisp, refreshing
Heavy	Tangy
Chewy	Prickly
Viscous	Puckery
Warm, hot, high-alcohol	Effervescent
Creamy	Astringent

The Philosophy of Beer: To Draught or Not to Draught?

Draught or bottle? That is the question, isn't it? For many people, the answer becomes the deciding factor when choosing a beer. Of course draught beer is obviously better, right? Draught beer must be fresher, and fresher is better, right? It is true draught beer is wonderful. Many people sidle up to the bar to peruse the tap handles, eager to taste a freshly tapped beer. But is draught beer the be-all and end-all of beer service? Some say that certain beers are actually much better out of the bottle. First of all, sometimes an American craft brewery is so small it doesn't even have a bottling line, or sometimes a brewery only bottles its beer, so in these cases you have no choice between a draught and a bottle.

Second, some people think that beers out of the bottle are a little more trustworthy. When you drink a craft or artisanal beer right out of the bottle, it's as if the brewer handed it to you himself. With beer on tap, you add the risk of draught lines. Draught lines need to be properly and constantly cleaned and maintained, or they can contaminate your beer. If draught lines aren't cleaned on a regular basis, gunk like sugars, proteins, hop resins, yeast, bacteria, and microflora can build up and make even the best beer taste like crap. Most beer bars are pretty vigilant about this, but if you start tasting funky off-flavors (see page 24) from a keg that is not otherwise bad, you may want to start drinking beers from bottles at that particular establishment.

So what is the answer?

Because there are many varied answers to this question, we thought we'd go straight to the top. We asked Randy Thiel, former brewmaster at Brewery Ommegang in New York and current director of quality control at New Glarus Brewing Company in Wisconsin. Oh, and he's also the first American ever to be inducted into the Knighthood of Brewers Mashstaff by the Belgian Brewers Guild in Brussels. (We're not messing around.) Randy says, "The quality of a conditioned beer should not differ based on the volume of beer. Albeit bottles can be conditioned to higher carbonation levels than kegs or tanks, for example, high carbonation does not dispense well from draught. Carbonation has a big impact on flavor, but that's not necessarily a quality differentiation as it is a personal preference."

Wow, "personal preference"—now there's an interesting concept. Here's a little example of how it works. In Los Angeles, we can get the Abbey Ale Maredsous 10 both on draught and in bottle. Maredsous 10 is a Tripel, with 10% ABV. It has big malty sweetness; a doughy richness; and spicy, peppery notes. Now, personally, we like this beer better from the bottle than on tap. Why? The whole carbonation factor. To us, the higher carbonation that's only possible in the bottle provides a better mouthfeel, lifting up what could be a cloying beer. On tap, that crisp, effervescent snap, that balance we like, is lessened. Now, that's just our opinion. Perhaps someone else would prefer the different flavor and mouthfeel that comes from Maredsous 10 on tap; maybe she likes a less carbonated Maredsous 10 and thinks it's better balanced. Who are we to say that she's wrong?

So, in the big draught versus bottle debate, you have to take a lot of factors into consideration. You have to think about what style of beer you're drinking. You have to think about the quality of the draught lines

THE WAITING IS THE HARDEST PART: BOTTLE CONDITIONING

Some beer labels will include the phrase "bottle conditioning." Okay, what the hell is that? Simply put, this is the process of an additional fermentation in the bottle, which can add flavor complexity, CO_2, and more alcohol to a beer. Sometimes this is accomplished by filtering the beer and adding fresh yeast and sugar to the bottle to allow some further magic to happen. This may add another layer of flavors in the form of more alcohol and CO_2. Other times the beer is left unfiltered, allowing the original yeast to work away, usually on an additional sugar added to the bottle. The effects of bottle conditioning can be slight or quite pronounced depending on the amount and type of yeast and sugar.

Bottle conditioning is a bit tricky, since brewers can only control a certain amount of what happens in the bottle. Knowledgeable brewers will know which and how much yeast and sugar to add to a bottle to produce certain effects, but once the bottle is sealed with cap or cork, the yeast does what it likes. This may mean that more CO_2 than desired will occur, and the opened beer may shoot like a geyser. In fact, many bottle-conditioned Belgian beers boast a ton of foam. Or perhaps the complexity from the yeast has added unbelievable fruit and spice flavors that the brewer hadn't even considered possible. The thing to remember is that bottle conditioning can produce higher alcohol and CO_2 but usually it's primary function is to add to the complexity of the flavor profile. We love bottle-conditioned beers; they may take a little more time but are always worth the wait.

and system, you have to consider the brewer's intent with the beer, but most important you have to make your own decision based on your personal preferences. We defer to Sir Randy's credo and New Wave band Devo's lyrics: "Use your freedom of choice."

We hope you are now inspired to go forth and taste the artful creations in craft beer. You are about to get into different styles and details about each brew, but keep your criteria for evaluating beer close at hand. Don't judge a beer by its label or its color, but by your palate. These criteria will no doubt change with every new beer style, as one's palate tends to embrace flavors it once abhorred. After you've examined every style, come back to the Art of Beer and see how much you've changed. You may laugh at what you once thought was a quintessential Hefeweizen. By the time you're brewing your own, your list of favorite beers will have varied greatly and your philosophy of beer will have deepened.

THREE

The Neophyte

A fine beer may be judged with only one
sip...but it's better to be thoroughly sure.

—CZECH PROVERB

Walk Before You Run

We envy you, the newly converted, the Neophyte, just setting out on your Beer Journey, with all those beautiful beers ahead of you, just waiting for you to taste them for the very first time. You are standing on the precipice of your journey, and with Beer 101 under your belt and a respect for the Art of Beer, you're ready to make your taste buds ridiculously happy. But this moment is tenuous. Don't get ahead of yourself. Many of the newly converted tend to take their beer info and run with it. They go to the bar and demand the strongest craft beer with the highest ABV. Yes, once you have a taste of quality, you, too, may have the overwhelming desire to go huge! But believe us when we warn you that there have been many potential beer aficionados who have been foiled by an overconfident headfirst dive into the deep end of the beer ocean. You are in danger of sampling beers that are way too big and powerful for a young craft beer palate. While we appreciate and sometimes exhibit this kind of bravado ourselves, and while this kind of maverick beer experimentation *can* lead to a happy accident, it's more likely to lead you to a bad beer incident that could leave you doubting yourself and, even worse, doubting the goodness of beer (The Horror!). That's not a risk that we are willing to let you take.

We believe that the right path to fully assimilating your palate means starting out with lighter, more delicate beers. This will train your palate to recognize the most delicate of flavors, from the dry to the bitter hop, from the biscuity to the nutty malt profile, and from the fruity to the buttery yeast esters. And don't forget the extreme difference between the mass-produced and the artisanal craft brews. These beers are the same style as the mass-produced lagers, but they have more interesting, fresher flavors. This will teach your palate to pick up on nuance and quality.

These lighter beers are also great for your friends who say they don't like beer and don't know what to order from a craft beer list. It's important to understand, and for you to tell them, that *light* should not equal *flavorless*. This is one of the greatest misconceptions about beer. *Easy drinking* implies that you should bypass your taste buds, but this shouldn't be your mantra where craft beer is concerned. Start with the beers discussed in this chapter and savor their refined profiles. You will begin to acquire a taste for the true flavors of a lager, the fruity notes of a real Bavarian-style Hefeweizen, and the tartness of a deliciously sweet and sour Lambic Ale. When you begin to distinguish the lies from the true flavors, you'll be able to carry that knowledge with you throughout your entire life of beer drinking. These are lessons you can really use in your beer life. No more drinkin' for the man; burn those corporate beer logos and begin to live! Reclaim your beer freedom!

Tastes Great, Less Stupid

Pale Lagers are the most common beer style attempted by the giant beer corporations. So in some ways, you may be most familiar with this style, but sadly most of us are familiar only with the crappy kind. Drinking a mass-produced lager and then tasting a true Pilsner from the Czech Republic is like eating waxy Halloween chocolate as a kid and then, years later, tasting a bar from Italy made with 80% cacao. It's as if you'd never had chocolate before. You laugh at your childhood notions of chocolate. One is a taste of your youth, when getting more Halloween loot than your friends was more important than the quality of the candy. Similarly, the beers of your youth were made for plentiful consumption (chug, chug, chug!) but lacked taste. The beers that we want you to begin your journey with are still often lighter in alcohol and lighter in body (and yes, still chuggable, if you must), but they give your brain some flavor to mull over. It will be as if you'd never had beer before. Trick or treat.

Pilsner, I Hardly Know Her

THIS BEER'S FOR YOU IF YOU LIKE: CRISP TASTES. CLEAN FINISHES. REFRESHING DRINKS. READING KAFKA IN PRAGUE. LOW ALCOHOL. LOW BITTERNESS. NO FRUIT, NO FRILLS. BRIGHT AND CLEAR BEVERAGES.

As we said earlier, the majority of beer produced and consumed in America today—particularly mass-produced, industrialized beer—is made in the Pilsner style. We should know what that is then, shouldn't we? Wait, so what is that?

A Pilsner (or Pilsener, or Plzen), which means "green meadows," is a type of lager named after the city in which it was created, Plzen, Bohemia, now the Czech Republic. The Bohemians, who had created a brewers' guild called the People's Brewery to improve the quality of their beer, were fed up with cloudy, funky, heavy, dark brews that seemed to turn sour. They recruited genius Bavarian brewer Josef Groll, who produced the first batch of Pilsner in 1842. Pilsner beer was a revelation and completely free of the funky look of the darker, sometimes murky ales because Groll used the German lagering method (brewing with lager yeast at a low temperature) to ferment only pale malted grains (instead of a mélange of darker malts). He also mixed in a good dose of Czech Saaz hops. This, combined with the native soft water, produced a beer that was crisp, clear, light straw to golden in color, biscuity, clean, and dry. To this day, good Pilsners still have those same qualities. So don't be fooled by mass-produced Pilsners that claim to be light and clean but are mostly flavorless and drinkable. Yes, Pilsners are light, but they should not remind you of water.

Note: Sprechen Sie Tschechen? Wait a minute. Couldn't you have sworn that Pilsners were German beers? And what about all the American Pilsner styles that everyone's been drinking? WTF? Czechs may have been the Pilsner originators, but they are not the only masters of the Pilsner. Not to be outdone, the Germans, seeing the popularity of the sparkling, clear, and clean beer, created their own version of the brew. Theirs has a similar flavor profile to the Czech style but is even more pale in color and often more effervescent. The German Pils also boasts a heftier dose of hops, with a bit more spice and citrus.

So if you want a Czech-style Pilsner, make sure to order a Bohemian Pilsner, and if you want a German-style brew, then order a German Pilsner. There's quite a bit of confusion regarding American craft brewers and Pilsners because often American brewers will make a Pilsner in the Czech or German style or create an amalgamation of the two. An

THE BUD WARS

If you know nothing about beer, at least you can be certain that you know that there is only one Budweiser "The King of Beers," right? Well, think again. There is a little town in the Czech Republic called Budweis, which, just like the city of Plzen, has its very own style of clean, bright lager beer that is sometimes called, you guessed it, Budweiser, which, literally translated, means, "of Budweis" or "from Budweis." This is a style of beer and not necessarily a particular brand of beer that had been proudly brewed in the Budweis area since 1265. But in the late 1800s, German-born American Adolphus Busch (yes, of Anheuser-Busch), wanting to conjure ideals of history and excellence in brewing, decided to name a clear, light, bright lager beer from St. Louis, Missouri, Budweiser. It was to be the start of much controversy and legal wrangling in the beer world.

Several Czech breweries were already brewing Budweiser beers, and as Anheuser-Busch got bigger, the use of this moniker became

American-made Pilsner might not be as authentic as the beers from Das Mötherland, but the craft creations are much more delicious and complex than the mass-produced Pilsner styles that most Americans are used to. Here are some of our favorite Pilsners and Pilsner-style craft beers that are perfect for taking baby steps:

- **KROMBACHER PILS:** Krombacher Brauerei, Kreuztal-Krombach, Germany. Quintessential German-made German Pilsner from a family-owned brewery. It starts hoppy and herbaceous with a longer malty finish. 4.8% ABV.

- **REALITY CZECK:** Moonlight Brewing Company, Fulton, California. An American made Czech-style or Bohemian Pilsner. Toasty and quite an issue. For almost a century, the Czech Budweiser brand made by Budejovice Budvar Brewery and Anheuser-Busch have been butting heads over who has the right to use the Budweiser name around the world. Anheuser-Busch won out in the United States, and Budvar must call their beer Czechvar in the States. Internationally, however, the right to use the Budweiser moniker is relegated on a country by country basis. So both companies use the name throughout Europe, causing a lot of confusion and, we're not going to lie, some hurt feelings as well. And around and around we go as the trademark debate still continues.

The question as to who is the original Budweiser may be up for grabs, but we can say for sure that the Czech Budweiser is an excellent, well-balanced beer, a little creamier and a little sweeter than the American version. But why don't you decide? We suggest you buy both Czechvar and American Budweiser, gather your friends together, tell them the story, and wage the war at home with a taste-off!

biscuity up front and finishing with a nuanced, crisp hoppiness. 4.8% ABV.

PRIMA PILS: Victory Brewing Company, Downingtown, Pennsylvania. An American made German-style Pilsner with a nice maltiness up front and a mild, dry, hoppy finish. Subtle sweetness in the front with clean, dry, crisp hop bitterness at the back end. Superb! 5.3% ABV.

CZECHVAR (BUDWEISER BUDVAR): Budweiser Budvar/B.N.N.P., Ceske Budejovice (or Budweis), Czech Republic. A Bohemian Pilsner with a light malt sweetness, creamy head, and floral grassy dry hops. 5% ABV.

What's in a Name? Helles and Blonds

THIS BEER'S FOR YOU IF YOU LIKE: BLEACHING YOUR HAIR. GERMAN LAGERS. A TOUCH OF SWEETNESS. LOW ALCOHOL. THINGS THAT ARE EASY.

When we were new to beer, we were shocked at the multitude of light, crisp, clean styles out there. Just like the Bavarians who fell in love with the crisp clean Czech Pilsner style and made one of their own, many other European countries started brewing beers in a similar style. Some added a little more hops, some added a bit more malt for sweeter notes, some relied on the water source of their region to put their distinctive stamp on the beer, creating a general style called European Pale Lagers that serves as a kind of umbrella title for this style of beer. The great thing about this variety is that even if you never move from this stage of beer drinking, preferring only light, clean, and subtle beers, you will still have a plethora of beers to choose from.

One of these styles is Helles Bier (*helles* means "pale"), created by taking only pale malts and brewing them with the lager method. Helles Lagers are generally a bit more malty and therefore a touch sweeter than Pilsners, but they're still light and nicely hopped. Helles Bier is common in Germany but relatively rare in the United States, so if you see one, grab it and try it.

Another light style that fits under the Pale Lager umbrella is blond (or blonde) beer. This can be a vague and confusing category. Blond beer is one of those modern inventions—a style named because of what it brings to mind: something that is easy on the palate. Many people order a blond because it sounds light. Some brewers do officially call their beer a blond, typically showing a beer that is pale in color, low on the hops, low in alcohol, with subtle fruit or honey and biscuity flavors, and a fairly clean finish on the palate. However, other brewers, especially

Belgians, can call their beer a blond even when it has quite a bit of alcohol content and maltiness. We've found that Belgians are generally referring to a paler malt when they calls their beers blond, and American blond beers tend to relay attributes that we Americans often apply to blond people, like bubbly, bright, light, and easy. So if you want a lighter style of blond beer, you might want to make sure that you are drinking an American version. Here are some great pale beers with which to while away your Neophyte days:

- **WEIHENSTEPHANER ORIGINAL:** Brauerei Weihenstephan, Freising, Germany. A Bavarian Pale Lager. Biscuity with a clean touch of sweetness. 5.1% ABV.

- **AYINGER JARHUNDERT BIER:** Privatbrauerei Fanz Inselkammer KG/Braurei Aying, Munich. A light honey and citrus, with grassy hops and a dry finish. 5% ABV.

- **SAMUEL SMITH'S ORGANIC LAGER:** Samuel Smith's Brewery, Tadcaster, UK. Described by some as "Britain's best lager"; gentle, smooth, and clean. 5% ABV.

- **GRIMBERGEN BLONDE:** Brouwerij Alken-Maes, Alken, Belgium. A delightful Belgian Blond with honey notes. Bready and dry with nice carbonation. 6.7% ABV.

Unfiltered and Unfettered: The Wide World of Wheat Beer

We frequently get requests for a good wheat beer. Many people ask for a wheat beer because they think of it as light and refreshing, mainly because they are used to seeing it with a big fresh lemon wedge attached. But the lemon doesn't make it a wheat beer, so what does? Simply put, a significant quantity of the grain used as malt should be wheat, typically between 30% and 70% wheat malts and the remainder is regular barley malt, usually of a pale variety. Though there are many different styles and substyles that can be called wheat beers, they all share certain characteristics. Wheat has a lot more protein in it than barley, which contributes a cloudy haze and creates a thick, long-lasting head on the beer. Wheat has very little flavor, sometimes a sourness, but it does contribute a distinctively silky mouthfeel.

A lot of people think that all wheat beer tastes the same or that wheat beer is one style of beer. These are major falsehoods. Even though wheat beers do share some common characteristics, they can also vary a great deal in color and flavor. For instance, one of the most popular wheat beer styles in the world is called Hefeweizen. We're sure you've heard of this beer style before. Most people use the terms "Hefeweizen" and "wheat beer" interchangeably, but the truth is, a Hefeweizen is one *substyle* of wheat beer, and not all wheat beer is Hefeweizen.

True Bavarian-style Hefeweizens taste very different from American Hefeweizens. Belgian Wheat beers (called Witbiers) taste quite different from any Hefeweizen. There are also several beers and beer styles that use some wheat as a malt source for flavor and for the creamy mouthfeel attributes, but these beers wouldn't be considered wheat beers because they don't use a high enough percentage of wheat or don't have the flavor attributes of a quintessential wheat beer. We know it's all a bit confusing, but we're here to help point out the differences. Many wheat beers are a great jumping off point for beer Neophytes because they are light on the palate and offer different flavors than a Pilsner.

Here are some wheat beer styles that we think you could get down with.

It's Hefeweizen, Not Hefeweizer

THIS BEER'S FOR YOU IF YOU LIKE: BANANAS FOSTER. HIDDEN SPICE. HONEY. SUNNY DAYS. LOW ALCOHOL. FRUITY ESTERS. CLOVES. NO LEMON. A TALL GLASS. WHEAT.

The most commonly consumed and mispronounced wheat beer in the world is the famous Hefeweizen. (Say it with us now, HAY-FAH-VIZEN—not Hefferwizer or Heffenweizen.) *Hefe* means "with yeast," and *weizen* means "wheat." Hefeweizen is a style of beer that originated in Bavaria, which is the southeast area of Germany. A true Hefeweizen is an ale that is brewed with a majority of wheat, usually 50% to 70%, and a special weizen ale yeast strain that is left unfiltered in the beer. Hefeweizens—or Hefes, as they are sometimes called in the United States—are low in hop bitterness and high in fruity flavor. Now, this is going to be hard to believe, because most people associate Hefeweizens with a citrus flavor, but the quintessential aromatic and flavor attributes of any great Bavarian style Hefe are bananas and clove. What? Yes, these rich flavors are a result of the specific type of yeast used and left to hang out in the brew, producing a cloudy, carbonated, beautiful beer. Note that if you are drinking a beer that claims to be a Hefe and it has no fruit and spice to it, you are not drinking the true German style. People love to drink this beer with a lemon wedge squeezed into it, but true Hefes are so full of flavor because of this yeast that they should really be consumed naked—that is, sans lemon. Try some of our favorite Hefeweizens and Hefe-style beers:

- **HEAVENLY HEFE:** Craftsman Brewing Company, Pasadena, California. Our local Hefe and one of our favorites. True to its Bavarian roots, with amazing fresh banana aroma, clove bite, and a slightly sour finish. 5.2% ABV.

- **WEIHENSTEPHANER HEFEWEISSBIER:** Brauerei Weihenstephan, Freising, Germany. A true Bavarian Hefe that's bright and fresh. Clean tropical fruits and banana, with a waft of cloves. Super dry and light. 5.4% ABV.

- **DANCING MAN WHEAT:** New Glarus Brewing Company, New Glarus, Wisconsin. Spicy clove and cinnamon, sweet banana bread, tangy lemon peel, and wheat. 7.2% ABV.

NFL Draught

Although we could be discussing the way Tom Brady's ass looks in his uniform pants, the NFL we're talking about here does not refer to the National Football League. We're talking about a phrase that we beer drinkers should embrace: NFL—No fucking lemon!

Because American-style wheat beers tend to be more citrusy, you'll often find a bartender mistakenly putting a lemon on the edge of a Bavarian-style Hefeweizen. Don't do this. We know, we know...perhaps you like the citrusy goodness of a lemon or a lime squeezed into your beer. But we're telling you right now that if you are drinking good craft beer, you are most likely ruining that delicately balanced brew by adding citric acid to it, killing the head and masking the flavor that was skillfully achieved by the brewer. Using wheat as an ingredient in beer was the first exception made to the famous beer purity law, Reinheitsgebot (see Chapter 1), and that exception was specifically made so that the nobility could continue to enjoy this style. As we mentioned,

PAULANER HEFE-WEISS BIER NATURETRUB: Paulaner Salvator Thomasbraeu AG, Munich, Germany. Classic Hefe with banana, citrus, and clove; well balanced. 5.5% ABV.

A Whiter Shade of Pale: Witbier

THIS BEER'S FOR YOU IF YOU LIKE: SPICE RACKS. CITRUS. HERBAL TEA. DRIED FRUIT. CREATIVITY. LOW BITTERNESS. CORIANDER. CURACAO ORANGE PEEL. PALE MALTS. THINGS BEING SERVED WITHOUT FRUIT.

Witbier (or White Beer) is a cloudy, unfiltered ale like Hefeweizen. It gets its name from yeast clouding up the light-colored beer, making it look almost white. If you see the word *white* on a beer in any language

Hefes use a special strain of yeast left unfiltered in the beer, producing a flavor that shouldn't be messed with.

How the "tradition" of using citrus in beer came about is a point of contention. Most likely, the reason is that many mass-produced beers suffer some kind of spoilage between the brewery and the consumer, especially beers that are in clear or green bottles, which can easily allow light to skunk the unprotected beer. Skunkiness in beer doesn't come from age but is actually the chemical byproduct that happens when light interacts with the hops in beer. In fact, the chemical reaction that happens when light strikes beer is identical to a skunk's spray! Now that *would* be a reason to put a lemon into a beer: to mask the skunky, gross aroma and flavor of a light-struck beer. But putting a lemon in a quality Hefeweizen is like putting Heinz 57 on filet mignon. Go ahead and do it if you like it. But, as your friends, we have to tell you that you're making a big mistake.

(*blanche*, *blanco*, etc.), chances are that it's a Witbier, though, in truth, these beers tend to be a pale straw to yellow color, with a lot of carbonation and good head retention. Brewed with a majority of wheat malts, these beers fall under the category of a wheat beer. Like Hefeweizen, Witbiers are also low in hop bitterness, but unlike Hefeweizens, Witbiers have a different flavor profile and don't have to adhere to any purity laws that restrict the ingredients used.

Wits were first created in medieval times, when they were brewed without any hops at all, using instead a blend of spices and other plants to add flavor and balance out the sweet malt. The blend was called *gruit*. Witbiers today often use a spice/fruit combination in the brewing, inspired by the ancient gruit. That combination usually consists of coriander, orange rind or other fruit, and some form of hops. Brewers can go crazy with this beer, using grapefruit rind, pepper, lemongrass, Curacao orange peel, clove, and so on. With these flavorings, Witbiers generally have a little more going on than Hefeweizens. They also offer layers of complexity due to the use of specific yeast strains that produce a variety of fruity notes, such as pear, apple, lemon, vanilla, orange, and sometimes even a bit of a sour taste. The subtlety of the fruit and spice varies, as does the dryness and the alcohol content, but most Wits stay between 5% and 7% alcohol.

Sadly, the Witbier is another style of beer that has been bastardized with a lemon or an orange wedge squeezed into it. Now we love fresh lemon or orange juice, and maybe you just want to add that to your Wit to create something new, but we are encouraging you to take a sip first. Understand what the beer's nuances are, and you may find that the beer is great on its own. Give the brewer a chance to show you his or her creation (see "NFL Draught" on page 72). Here are some Witbiers that we dig:

- **ST. BERNARDUS WITBIER:** Brouwerij St. Bernardus NV, Watou, Belgium. A quintessential true Belgian Witbier with subtle orange peel and spice. Nuanced, clean, and dry. 5.5% ABV.

- **ALLAGASH WHITE:** Allagash Brewing Company, Portland, Maine. An American craft version true to style. Subtle coriander and bitter orange peel. Well balanced, dry, and complex. 5% ABV.

- **LOST COAST GREAT WHITE:** Lost Coast Brewery, Eureka, California. A White Ale brewed with lemongrass. Citrus, herbs, and fruit with a dry finish. 4.8% ABV.

- **HITACHINO WHITE:** Kiuchi Brewery, Ibaraki-ken Naka-gun, Japan. Like biting into a crisp pear; from a great Japanese brewery (originally a sake brewery) specializing in Belgian styles. 5% ABV.

- **ORCHARD WHITE:** The Bruery, Placentia, California. Hailing from a wonderful small brewery in Orange County, brewed with coriander and lavender. Notes of wheat, oats, and citrus peel. 5.7% ABV.

All-American: Wheat Beers Born in the USA

THIS BEER'S FOR YOU IF YOU LIKE: ADDING FRUIT TO BEER. APPLE PIE. FOOTBALL AND SOUVENIRS. CITRUS FLAVORS. CLOUDS. BREAD. BEING LOVED BY ALL AMERICANS.

If you just can't let go of the idea of putting a lemon into your wheat beer, then the American Wheat beer styles might be more to your liking than the traditional Hefeweizen. The American version of the wheat beer still uses the unfiltered, cloudy goodness of a traditional wheat beer, but instead of using a yeast style that adds banana and clove to the mix, American Wheats use a different kind of yeast that is much cleaner, if you will; in other words, this brewing method is missing the esters that are present in the German and Belgian versions. This is why many Americans are often surprised by the fruit and spice present in the Bavarian, German, and Belgian styles of wheat beer. They are used to American Wheats, which do not give off such distinct flavor notes.

American Wheat beers (some of which are confusingly labeled Hefeweizen) are medium bodied, super subtle, and refreshing, with a hint of citrus and biscuit, and a very mild hop presence. Because of this, American Wheat beers are often served and sometimes even marketed with a lemon or an orange wedge perched on their rim. While we generally pooh-pooh the use of fruit as a beer garnish (see "NFL Draught" on page 72), if you are going to do it, now is the time. You are much better off squeezing lemon into an American Wheat than a German one. The fruit will still kill the head and deaden the aromatics, but at least it won't necessarily clash with any strong flavors in the beer. American Wheat beers are a good gateway beer for any beginner looking for something simple. Try some of these:

 GUMBALLHEAD: Three Floyds Brewery, Munster, Indiana. Brewed with a touch of lemon, nice grapefruity hops, and some heft on the tongue. 4.8% ABV.

CRACK'D WHEAT: New Glarus Brewing Company, New Glarus, Wisconsin. An interesting take on the style; cinnamon and clove mixed with definite citrus notes. Hybrid style that uses both Bavarian and Wisconsin wheat. 5.9% ABV.

BLUE STAR GREAT AMERICAN WHEAT BEER: North Coast Brewing Company, Fort Bragg, California. A fine example of a no-frills American Wheat. This beer boasts unfiltered lemon notes. Very light fruit on the nose, with a dry hop finish. 4.5% ABV.

SIERRA NEVADA WHEAT BEER: Sierra Nevada Brewing Company, Chico, California. Simple in the best way, with big citrus on the nose and hints of spice; a mild bitter but nonassaulting finish. 4.4% ABV.

Are We Clear? Kristallklar

THIS BEER'S FOR YOU IF YOU LIKE: SHINY CLEAR THINGS. LIGHTER HEFEWEIZENS. SUN-TANNING. CLARITY. WAFTS, HINTS, TOUCHES OF CLOVE AND TROPICAL FRUIT. BEING UNOBTRUSIVE. LOW ALCOHOL.

In the craft beer world, authenticity is always appreciated. So if you're not big on the bananas and spice in your traditional Hefeweizen but you still want to enjoy a true Bavarian Wheat beer, you actually have a great option in a rare but tasty beer style called Kristallklar. As we've reminded you ad nauseum, most wheat beers are unfiltered and cloudy. This style, however, is one of the only German wheat beers that *is* filtered. There's not much mystery in this style, but Kristallklar (or *Krystal Weizen*, "crystal wheat" in German) is what you would imagine: a nice, crisp, clean ale that tastes like a lighter version of a Bavarian Hefeweizen. The filtration removes the residual yeast that contributes to the bananas and cloves in the beer's flavor and character. Kristall Wheat beers are much lighter in body, are pale straw to light amber in color, and come in at around 5% ABV. You generally won't find a lot of these beers on tap in America, but if you're lucky, you may come across one. If you do, pick it up if only for the experience. These are perfect beers with which to lie out in the sun, and they make great summer refreshers. It's a shame that this style isn't more available in the United States. But if you like the Hefe, the banana, and the spice but want just a hint of those flavors, it would behoove you to hit the pavement and seek out this style. We like these two Kristallklars:

○ **WEIHENSTEPHANER KRISTALLWEISSBIER:** Brauerei Weihenstephan, Freising, Germany. Light and lemony with light banana and clove. Crisp and refreshing with a hint of wheat. 5.4% ABV.

○ **ERDINGER WEISSBIER KRISTALLKLAR:** Erdinger Weissbrau, Erding, Germany. Crisp and clean grain with a touch of banana. Simple and mild. 5.3% ABV.

What about advanced wheats? Yes, there are other great styles of wheat beer, and don't think that we're leaving them out. There are dark, strong, intense wheat beers called Dunkelweizen and Weizenbock. There is even a super-sour and complex wheat beer called Berliner Weiss. We talk about these beers later on in this book; however, for the Neophyte, these beers might be a bit much. Remember, we are taking baby steps here. But if you have become a wheat-o-phile and are curious about other wheat beers out there, please refer to Chapter 4, where we talk about these amazing styles.

Believe It or Not: Beers That Don't Taste Like Beer

Every once in a great while, we will run across a person who has been so harmed by bad beer or so turned off by the marketing of said bad beer that they decide to turn away from beer forever. In these instances, more beer therapy than baby steps is needed. These people need shock therapy. They need to be awakened to the possibility that beer can taste like nothing they've ever imagined before.

While this therapy has been wildly successful, it's also a bittersweet method for us because of the reaction that it invokes, which almost always is, "This doesn't taste like beer at all!" No, no, no! We don't want that reaction! We don't want you to like this beer because it *doesn't taste like beer*! We want you to love this beer because it's representative of the variety of beer flavors that exist, the imagination that brewers have, and the skill with which they apply their knowledge and art. We've said it before and we'll say it again: There is a beer out there for every person, even the haters. These are beers that "don't taste like beer" but do indeed taste like beer.

Fruity Wheat Beers

THIS BEER'S FOR YOU IF YOU LIKE: CHERRIES. PLUMS. LEMONS. BLUEBERRY PANCAKES. STRAWBERRY PIE. WHEAT.

Because wheat contributes so little to a beer's flavor while producing some much-desired qualities—such as head retention and a smooth, full mouthfeel—it is the perfect style to use as a base for many fruit beers. There was a time when virtually every brewpub we walked into was serving a wildly popular Raspberry Wheat Beer. Though this isn't the case now, there are still quite a few of these fruity wheats. But fruited wheat beers aren't limited to berries. Virtually every fruit and quite a few spices have found their way into a wheat beer recipe at some level. Although none has had the staying power and popularity to earn a separate style distinction, there are simply too many fruited wheat beers on the market to not acknowledge them.

Blueberry, apricot, and raspberry wheat are popular with the new-to-beer crowd. The fruit is right there in the name and draws in those looking for a fruity flavor profile. Instead of leaving the fruit flavor to the esters in yeast, these brews usually add some fruit or fruit concentrate or syrup to a wheat beer. Here are some of the fruity wheat beers that we imbibe on a regular basis:

- **LOST COAST APRICOT WHEAT:** Lost Coast Brewing, Eureka, California. Sweet and fruity, lots of bubbles. 5% ABV.

- **HE'BREW ORIGIN POMEGRANATE ALE:** Schmaltz Brewing Company, San Francisco, California. Malty sweet, with a sour pomegranate flavor. High alcohol, but the fruitiness makes it a good choice for Neophytes. 8% ABV.

- **WATERMELON WHEAT BEER:** 21st Amendment Brewery, San Francisco, California. Light candy watermelon flavor mixed with biscuit wheat, served in a can. 5.2% ABV.

- **SEA DOG BLUE PAW WHEAT BEER:** Sea Dog Brewing Company, Bangor, Maine. A refreshing wheat beer made with wild Maine blueberries. Delicious and subtle. 3.5% ABV.

Into the Wild Beer Yonder: Lambics, the Secret Yummy Beer

THIS BEER'S FOR YOU IF YOU LIKE: TART RASPBERRIES. FRESH PEACHES. CANDY. STINKY CHEESE. HISTORY. BEERS WITH FRUITY NOTES. SOURDOUGH BREAD. PRETTY GLASSES. AIRBORNE YEAST. LOW ALCOHOL. NO BITTERNESS. SOUR FUNK. SWEETNESS. ACIDITY.

Lambic is an extra-special style of ale created through an unruly process called spontaneous fermentation. This refers to the magic of the yeast used in Lambics, which is in fact the wild, naturally occurring yeast that floats around in the air waiting to turn liquids into beer. Yes, it's true; these yeasts drop in on the brew and create a crazy, often sour beer that is sometimes combined with macerated fruit. Lambic hails from the Senne River Valley in Belgium. This region naturally holds the magic bacteria and airborne yeast essential for this beer. The word *lambic* comes from the village of Lembeek, which is in the municipality of Halle, Belgium. This style gets extra props because it is the oldest style of beer and is the only style still fermented wildly. The magic of spontaneous fermentation is the way beer was made way, way back in the day, when people didn't even know about the effect of airborne yeast; they just knew that the liquid left out made them happy. So know that when you are sipping a Lambic, you are tasting history (*pause for effect*).

Lambics are brewed with a good amount (30% to 40%) of unmalted wheat and have the hazy look of other wheat beers. Lambic brewers use aged hops instead of the fresh hops used in all other styles. These aged hops impart none of the typical bitterness. Brewers use them for their tannic and preservative qualities. To ferment wildly, Lambic wort (the liquid extracted during the brewing process) is poured into "cool ships," which are large vessels designed to cool down the wort before the yeast is added. Though brewers in olden times making other styles of beer hoped none of the airborne yeast would get into their wort and make the beer sour and funky, Lambic brewers desired the opposite. Everyone is welcome into the fermentation process, even dust and cobwebs. Nothing should be too clean because it might upset the life of the natural yeast.

After the fermentation is in full swing, Lambics are put into wooden casks (or barrels), usually left over from port or sherry production, and left to make it happen. Here, even more little friends can get into the ale, such as bacteria in the wood—anything to funk it up, just like Lambic likes it. The Lambic is left to age for months, even years, depending on the brewer's choice. Lambic brewing embraces the wildness in nature, lets go of the control and lab-like process of many brews, and appreciates whatever may come.

Once in the casks, Lambics are then blended, because each cask has something different to offer. A newer Lambic—bright, sour, and acidic—may be blended with an older one to balance it out. Most Lambics are a blend (called *gueuze*, pronounced GOOZE or GER-ZER; see Chapter 6), though straight, unblended Lambic can be found if one looks hard enough.

Sour-tasting Lambics are often softened by the addition of sweet macerated fruit. The sugar in the fruit gives the yeast something else to eat and creates a complex drink full of fruit character. Because Lambics can be quite funky, the fruit sweetens up the brew, making it approachable and almost dessert-like. Cherries, raspberries, peaches, black currants, and apples have all been used in Lambics. Note that the fruit is usually written in French or Flemish on the label—for example, peach = *pêche*, cherries = *kriek*. Like a good fresh fruit, fruited Lambics should be both sweet and tart. Some tend toward the sweet side, some are drier. This may be due to the blend or the age of the brew. Most are served in a flute-type glass and are, in fact, reminiscent of Champagne. That's right, we said *Champagne*. You ladies who think you know beer and hate it, don't quit. Try a Lambic and allow your mind to be blown and your palate to be pleased. We are big fans of these Lambics:

- **LINDEMAN'S PÊCHE LAMBIC:** Brouwerij Lindemans, Vlezenbeek Belgium. Sweet and sour, and deliciously peachy. Great for dessert, bubbly like Champagne. 4% ABV.

- **CANTILLION BLABAER LAMBIK:** Brouwerij Cantillion, Brussels. Brewed with Danish blueberries; purple color with tiny bubbles. Complex, tart, and funky in a good way. 5% ABV.

- **SELINS GROVE THE PHOENIX KRIEK:** Selin's Brewing Company, Selinsgrove, Pennsylvania. Rich with balanced sour and sweet cherries. Nice warmth with a touch of vanilla. 8% ABV.

- **WISCONSIN BELGIAN RED:** New Glarus Brewing Company, New Glarus, Wisconsin. A favorite Lambic style. This gem boasts over a pound of Door County cherries in each bottle; super bubbly and intense cherry. 5.1% ABV.

Your Beer Is Neither an Ale Nor a Lager...
Discuss: Hybrid Beers

Sometimes a beer is more than just one beer. It is two beers. Well, maybe not, but some beers dance between the definitions of lager and ale. This is because they are either fermented with lager yeast at high ale temperatures or vice versa. The "hybrid brews," as we like to call them, can be hard to pin down in the beer world, but they help remind us that a beer should ultimately be judged by flavor, not by name alone. These are great gateway beers to the bigger styles in the following chapters. They still have a fairly light and delicate profile but begin to introduce darker malts and slightly bigger flavors of fruit and nuts. Here are some hybrid styles that may cross your path and please your palate.

Catch a Kölsch

THIS BEER'S FOR YOU IF YOU LIKE: GERMAN ENGINEERING. CYLINDRICAL RODS. THE RHINELAND. AOC. NUANCE. CRISP, CLEAN FLAVORS. SLIGHT FRUIT UNDERTONES.

Not many people have heard of Kölsch beer, but if you aren't ready for the more bitter, bigger brews or if you have staunchly decided that you want something a bit softer than a German Pils, then Kölsch may be your baby. Kölsch is a hybrid beer made using top-fermenting yeast (making it an ale), but it then undergoes a cold fermentation, or lagering, which creates a beer that is super clean and light in body but with slight fruity and vinous undertones. Kölsch beers traditionally used a bit of wheat in the malt, but today, they're one of Germany's only all-barley pale beers, using mostly light Pilsner-style malts. They are sparkly clear with a frothy head and are known to have a pale straw color and low alcohol (between 4% and 6%). They should be clean and dry on the finish. Because these beers are lagered, a Kölsch has very slight but perceivable aromatics of biscuit and sourdough on the nose.

Despite its hybrid status, Kölsch is called the German Pale Ale by some and is another one of those beer styles that is named after its place of origin: Koln, in the Rhineland of Germany (Cologne to us Americans), just northwest of Bavaria. As a matter of fact, just like the French AOC denominations in wine—by which geographic regions govern and certify the quality of wine, cheeses, and other products—a Kölsch can be officially and legally labeled "Kölsch" only if it has been brewed by a member of the Koln Brewers Union in the city of Koln. Considered a female-friendly beer in Germany (that doesn't mean that dudes don't drink it!), Kölsch is traditionally served in a tall, skinny, cylindrical, 6.75-ounce glass called a *Kolner Stangen*, or *Stange*, German for "stick" (we were told by a leering drunken German ex-pat that it means "pole" or "rod," to which we did not comment).

Kölsch beers are often overlooked, discounted as run-of-the-mill light beer. But because a Kölsch is so soft and delicate, it is essential that the brewer have great craft and skill; there are no powerful flavors to cover a mistake or an inferior ingredient. This style has a smallish distribution in the United States, but if you happen to see it in a store or bar, we strongly encourage you to try one! Try to grab one of the following:

- **REISSDORF KÖLSCH:** Brauerei Heinrich Reissdorf, Cologne, Germany. A Kölsch with a cult following. Smooth, light, yet complex. Hints of jasmine and a cedar-like woody finish. 4.8% ABV.

- **HOLLYWOOD BLONDE:** The Great American Brewing Company, Chatsworth, California. Light-bodied, tasty American-made beer that is more biscuity and corny than the authentic version, but just as good. 4.5% ABV.

- **NEW HOLLAND FULL CIRCLE:** New Holland Brewing Company, Holland, Michigan. Brewed with a single malt (Pilsner) and a single hop (Saaz); light-bodied and rich in flavor but simple in its delivery. 5.25% ABV.

The Alternative Route: Altbier

THIS BEER'S FOR YOU IF YOU LIKE: TRADITION. ANTIQUES. NUTS. A SPLASH OF COLOR. LOW ALCOHOL. BITTERNESS. LIGHT BODIES.

Okay, we bet that you will love Kölsch because, well, we haven't met anyone who didn't, but are you feeling randy, baby? Have we earned your trust enough yet to take you to the next destination on your Beer Journey? Well, travel just 25 miles down the Rhine River from Cologne and you'll be in Dusseldorf and in the land of the Altbier. *Alt* (German for "old") harkens back to an old style of brewing in Germany. Just like Kölsch, the Altbier is one of the few indigenous German beers. And also like Kölsch, it's another example of a hybridized beer style. Most Germans will tell you that an Altbier is definitely an ale. But once again, this is a beer that uses ale yeast and then ferments at cooler temperatures and is lagered, or stored fermenting for anywhere from one to two months.

Originally brewed in Westphalia, this kind of beer is a great foray into drinking a darker-colored beer for those beer drinkers who prefer lighter styles. Because of the lagering process, this beer has low hop aromatics, but instead of using the same Pilsner-style malts that Kölsch does, Altbier uses much darker malts, creating a deep amber, orangey, and copper-colored beer. Altbier does have some hop bitterness on the tongue, but it's very subtle and is balanced by caramel, toasty flavors with a dry and nutty finish. This is a beer that is full of flavor yet still considered light bodied. It is generally low in alcohol (yes, there are exceptions). Because of its color, this beer frequently gets lumped into the Amber Ale category (see Chapter 4). But to us, Altbier has its own identity and deserves mad props. Here are some of our favorite Altbiers:

ALASKAN AMBER: Alaskan Brewing Company, Juneau, Alaska. Nutty, sweet, with roasted caramel. Light bodied, dry finish. 5.3% ABV.

OTTER CREEK COPPER ALE: Otter Creek/Wolaver's. Middlebury, Vermont. Nutty and dry with notes of caramel. Well-balanced and true to the style. 5.4% ABV.

DIEBELS ALT: Brauerei Diebels, Issum, Germany. Complex and balanced, with dried fruit, tobacco, and cocoa. Finishes with nice hop bitterness. 5% ABV.

Steam Punk: Steam Beer and California Common

THIS BEER'S FOR YOU IF YOU LIKE: AMERICAN HISTORY. SAN FRANCISCO. THE OLD WEST. PANNING FOR GOLD. LOW ALCOHOL. MEDIUM-ROAST MALT. SUBTLE NUTTINESS.

Steam beer is another ye olden style of beer but was born in the good old U.S. of A., most likely during the gold rush. It is basically another ale-lager hybrid because of the use of lager yeasts fermented at high ale temperatures. This was an attempt to make a refreshing lager-style beer without the use of refrigeration, as ice, cold water, and other ways to cool down water was often unavailable in the gold-rush era. It gained popularity in California and is still associated with San Francisco and its giant brewery Anchor. The beer was originally made cheaply (thus the lack of refrigeration) and probably tasted like crap back then—yes, it's true. As with many beers from ye olden times, there wasn't much control over the brewing environment, especially in the makeshift situations of the Old West. Now, of course, the style has been refined. Today, Anchor's brewery is nothing to sneeze at, with copper kettles, quality ingredients, and pristine walkways.

The derivation of the name "steam" is much debated. Some claim it is because the CO_2 pressure built up in the brew kettles and had to be released slightly before transfer, thus letting off "steam." Others believe that the word comes from *Dampbier*, which is German for "steam beer," an ale that German Americans would have been familiar with. Anchor Brewing subscribes to the belief that the name came from the brewery's old practice of cooling the hot wort in large open bins on the brewery's roof, sending up clouds of steam. Whatever the origin, this style typically has a nice nutty malt character, notes of fruit, with low to medium bitterness. They are low-alcohol beers, coming in at around 5%.

A relative of the steam beer is California Common. This style boasts the same flavor profile of steam beer, but has had to be renamed because of Anchor Brewing's trademark of the name "Steam" (they're no dummies). California Common has the same flavor notes of a steam and is fermented at high temperatures using lager yeast. But any craft brewer who wishes to re-create this style, often from California, must use "Common" on the label or face a good-old American legal battle. Here are our favorite uncommon Commons:

○ **ANCHOR STEAM (STEAM BEER):** Anchor Brewing Company, San Francisco, California. The classic. Nutty and lightly bitter, touch of sour and citrus. 5% ABV.

○ **LUGNUT LAGER (CALIFORNIA COMMON):** Skyscraper Brewing Company, El Monte, California. Nutty malt, hint of caramel, citrus hops, balanced. 5.2% ABV.

○ **UP-IN-SMOKE ALE (CALIFORNIA COMMON):** Bear Republic Brewing Company, Healdsburg, California. Earthy and crisp, with some floral and fruity hops. 5.9% ABV.

* * *

Okay, Neophyte, we've given you enough to drink for most of the rest of your life. Trust us, the quest for rare Lambics alone could fill the remainder of your beer days. Though you may feel the need to dare to drink different, bigger brews, and we encourage this rock 'n' roll spirit, we want you to recognize the vastness of the craft world within even one style of beer, the pleasure that can come from comparing Kölschs and weighing in on Witbiers. The Beer Journey is not just about trying every different style in the world or about everyone else's top 10 (except ours, of course); it's about getting in deep, even when you're in the shallow end of the beer ocean. The nuance of your palate depends on your ability to distinguish between even the tenderest of flavors and the most subtle of spices. This, beloved Neophyte, is what keeps the journey alive.

The Sophomore

A quart of ale is a dish for a king.
—WILLIAM SHAKESPEARE

Still So Young

At this point you're looking to move up in the system. You've lost any reservations you may have had about becoming a craft beer drinker, and you're going to go the distance. Now that quality beer is making your life a lot happier, you're ready to push the envelope. Being a Sophomore on the Beer Journey is something to revere. You know enough to feel more mature than the cute little Neophytes you once related to, but you know that you're not far enough along to carry the weight of a true beer sommelier. Many beer Sophomores think now that they've learned about beer and found their favorite Pilsner, it's done and their journey has ended. But don't suffer this Sophomore slump. You're young in your beer life, revel in it. Don't worry about the responsibility of a beer expert—embrace mistakes and laugh them off. Visit the beers of different countries, go to the pub often, taste everything.

Now you can take your next not-so-baby steps. Many of the beer styles that we describe in this chapter use darker malts than the styles in the previous chapter. Now don't judge them ahead of time because of their color; we think they're the perfect next step, but not as steep a step as you may think. These beers are a little bigger, have a little more intensity, and are perhaps a little scary right now. But, fear not, young Jedi. We wouldn't lead you astray. We think you're ready. Drink or drink not...there is no try.

Study Abroad: Across the Pond

A bit of tea and some fish and chippies—brilliant! But what about that pint at the pub? Are the Brits so different from us when it comes to beer? I mean, we share the same language, we both appreciate steak and potatoes, David Beckham, and rock 'n' roll. Hell, we Americans get many of our brewing and beer drinking traditions from the Brits. After all, it was the Brits who popularized pubs (the public house) as a meeting place where most of life happened. This tradition remains a lively force in any English, Irish, or Scottish town. Going "down the pub" is as essential as the daily bread. The very word *pint* comes from an old British quantity that was used for corn and over time became the desirable amount for a glass of ale all over the world.

British, Scottish, and Irish beer culture differs from the general American beer culture in that it favors the nuanced top-fermenting ale. This means that their beer quest is not for the ice-cold lager or the especially bitter IPA but for the nuttier, more delicate, amber-colored ale or, especially in Ireland, the rich, dark Stout. The United Kingdom likes to hold on tightly to tradition, and the British were skeptical of hops when they first appeared on the beer scene in the 15th century. The ingredient was for a time banned in England, the public not yet used to the bitter hop bite. And Scotland was not able to produce many hop yields and thus created ales with a more sweet smoky flavor than a dry bitter taste. Once hops became the norm in England and were grown on British soil, ales took on the familiar dryness that we taste in pubs today. But even British IPAs are not too bitter, and the ales from this region still have a more subtle flavor profile than many American craft beers.

These traditional styles encourage a well-seasoned palate that can pick up on subtle fruit, caramel tones, spice, and hops. With this palate, beer drinkers go down the pub expecting the barkeep to pour them a true, quality brew, often made in-house. This respect for a proper pint has kept big breweries from dominating the UK beer scene.

We can learn a lot from drinking in a British pub and seeing what they favor and then comparing what we learn to the typical American bar. Craft brewers in the United States have embraced Britain's love of these ales with open arms. Most American craft breweries offer a Bitter, or Nut Brown, and a Porter or Stout. Though the American beer world tends toward extreme beer styles, we can trace our craft brew roots back to the United Kingdom.

But much of the beer-going public fears the differences between British traditions and American beer practices. You may still be pondering the story your cool cousin Peter told you about being served warm beer in the United Kingdom and how he could hardly drink it. And what about that period piece you got dragged to where they pumped the beer by hand with a very unsanitary-looking old-timey gadget you didn't recognize? Gross! Or is it?

You need to respect British beer and customs before you suffer the stink eye from a surly British bartender. Stop before you ask for ice cubes

Lukewarm, at Best?

Okay, let's get it out there: the Brits drink warm beer, right? Or do they? British beer is traditionally served at cellar temperature. Do you know how cold a cellar is in England? Let's just say, you wouldn't want to strip down to your skivvies and let it all hang out in there. This temperature is actually about 55°F. Sound warm? Perhaps to our readers in Alaska it does. It's true that traditional British beer drinkers stay away from the ice-cold beers many seem to revere in America. Why? The British want to keep their beers from being too cold because this allows the flavor nuances to be present rather than hidden by low temperatures. The nuttiness of an Extra Special Bitter (ESB) doesn't come through as well at super-cold temperatures. Think of an ice-cold glass of wine versus one served at the correct temperature. The latter allows more fruit and floral notes to come through. The practice of serving beer at cellar temperatures does have its roots in tradition and, like many traditions, came from the practical circumstances of the time—a time before refrigeration existed (much less the kegerator). Yes, it's true, when these beer styles were created, cellars were the only option, but this is still arguably the best temperature for beer. So don't sneer at British beer—learn to love the perfect temp.

for your beer (The Horror!). The Brits do indeed value different flavors, styles, and ways of drinking beer from those that we do, but their customs are not to be sneered at. They have evolved to enhance their delicious and decidedly British styles. The Brits love beer as much as we do. Their passion for the pint is legendary, so let's examine what lies behind their taps.

Amber and Red: Different Shades of Ale

THIS BEER'S FOR YOU IF YOU LIKE: RED HAIR. NUTTY THINGS. DRY FINISH. GENERALIZATIONS. IRELAND.

Many people ask for an amber beer. But because *amber* can mean anything from yellowish to brownish to orange-ish, most beers can be considered amber in color. Therefore and thus, this *style* is a bit vague. Don't be fooled by color; as we've said earlier, a beer's color tells you *nothing* about its taste. Amber in the lager category usually means an amber to copper-hued beer around 5% ABV. These beers often have a caramelly, nutty profile with a varied degree of hop bitterness. If you feel like you want to order an amber beer, you are probably craving something a bit nuttier than a Pilsner and not super fruity like a Hefeweizen. That's fine, but you'll have to be more specific. Just as ordering a blond beer can be a challenge for a craft beer bartender, ordering an amber can have him wondering what it is you really want: a beer with amber in the name? A nutty lager? A Brown Ale? A slightly bitter beer? So be ready to use your newfound skills and communicate whether you want a beer that is bitter, sweet, or smoky. While some beers have their color in the name, it's always better to use specific flavors rather than hair colors when you are ordering your beer.

Red beers are a shade deeper than the amber, but to us, this color is slightly more specific as a style and is a fair request at a craft establishment. The red beers are so called because of a deep ruby hue and often have a sweet toffee caramel quality that's a bit bigger than what most refer to as an amber ale. Perhaps the most famous red beers are Irish Reds, which have a malty, toasty, tea-like quality and very low hop presence. American-made red styles, on the other hand, have a pronounced bitterness and are sometimes grouped with American Pale Ales, which tend to have a bigger hop presence. Red beers have become quite a popular labeling for American brewers and can vary greatly in intensity, ABV, and bitterness. Try these great ales to get right with reds:

BROOKLYN LAGER (AMERICAN AMBER LAGER): Brooklyn Brewing Company, Brooklyn, New York. Lightly nutty, bready, with a good hop bite. 5.2% ABV.

○ **REUDRICH'S RED SEAL ALE (AMERICAN RED ALE):** North Coast Brewery, Fort Bragg, California. Well-balanced, refreshing citrus, rich malt, crisp, spicy, piney hops. 5.5% ABV.

○ **GREEN FLASH HOP HEAD RED (AMERICAN RED ALE):** Green Flash Brewing Company, Vista, California. Bright citrus hops, bold bitter flavor. 6% ABV.

○ **SMITHWICK'S IRISH ALE (IRISH RED ALE):** Smithwick's Brewery/Irish Ale Breweries Ltd., Kilkenny, Ireland. Caramel, grain, and mild hops with a dry finish. 4.5% ABV.

Note: This red ale is not to be confused with Flanders-style red ale, which is an altogether different thing (see Chapter 6).

Nuts to You: Browns and Nut Browns

THIS BEER'S FOR YOU IF YOU LIKE: BROWNIES WITH WALNUTS. HAZELNUT LATTES. SESSION BEERS. ENGLAND. LOW ALCOHOL. NUTTY FLAVORS. LOW BITTERNESS.

Brown, or Nut Brown, beer originated in England around 1600, and the Brits are still great producers and fans of this style. Brown Ales are a great showcase for malt in the same way that Hefeweizens and Witbiers are a great showcase for yeast. Drinking Nut Browns is a good way to test your palate on the different styles and roast levels of malt used in an ale. Of course there is a presence of both yeast and hops in this style, but they are meant to add a nuance of butterscotch or balance the sweetness of the malt, respectively. Describing a Brown Ale is a test of your nutty vocabulary: hazelnut, peanut, almond, filbert (wait, isn't that a hazelnut?). As we always say, use words that you know when searching your brain for a way to describe the malty taste of these ales. Much of the malt itself is named after common foods: biscuit malt, chocolate malt, coffee malt, and so on. Other, more daring descriptors that pop up with

What's the Deal with Real Ale?

 You may hear a lot of chatter in the pub from beer lovers about Cask Ale or Real Ale. So does that mean that the Pale Ale in front of you is an illusion? Are all the beers on tap just pretending? And isn't cask that beer you heard about in England? What's the deal?

Real Ale (or cask-conditioned ale) is a term coined by Campaign for Real Ale (CAMRA), a voluntary group formed by four British beer devotees in 1973 in an attempt to protect the quality of English ale. This was a reaction to the spread of highly carbonated, pasteurized, boring beers taking over the pubs of Europe at the time. Traditionally, Real Ale is beer left to mature in an 11-gallon cask, where it undergoes a secondary fermentation (this is what is meant by *conditioned*). It is then served to the public from this same cask. It is understood that this beer will not be filtered or kept super cold (though it is kept cool) and therefore has a shelf life, meaning it is meant to be consumed fairly quickly and is not for the mass beer market. Because it is not filtered or pasteurized, and the yeast is still alive and fermenting, it is considered a living thing.

Typically, Cask Ale is served without the addition of the CO_2 pressure that is usually used to propel beer through modern draught systems. The CO_2 pressure added to modern beer kegs keeps the existing CO_2 in the beer from being released until it hits your glass. In Real or Cask Ales, the beer is preserved in its native state without this pressure.

Brown Ale flavor profiles include crème brulee, toffee, caramel, brownies, fudge, chocolate-chip cookies... (okay, now we're just naming our favorite desserts).

Nut Browns are ales that use brown or dark malt and have relatively low bitterness, leaving the malt free to express its nutty characteristics. The alcohol is generally low, and these ales are often described as sweet. We find a lot of ladies respond well to the hazelnut, chocolate, caramel,

Because of this, Cask Ales tend to be flatter than typical draught beer, but this isn't a bad thing; this is beer in its natural state, with as many bubbles as God intended.

Cask Ales favor some beer styles over others. Beers that are meant to contain their carbonation and be quite sparkly, such as Hefeweizens, may not be best on cask, whereas others that go well with a creamy, less-carbonated mouthfeel, like Brown Ales and Stouts, tend to show well on cask. In fact, the nitrogen taps, or "creamer faucets," used for beers like Guinness were created in part to re-create the creamy mouthfeel of a Cask Ale. The lower carbonation allows different flavors to come through that may not be as present if the same beer is on a traditional tap.

Cask beer in the American craft beer world has become a highly desirable thing among its devotees, though still relatively rare in bars. In England, any respectable pub will have at least one cask tap, but American pubs aren't used to the pump, and the general public isn't savvy to the pleasures of cask. Those who are in the know actively seek out cask offerings. Cask beer lovers trade e-mails and constantly call specialty beer bars searching for Real Ale. A craft beer on cask can have quite a different flavor profile from that same beer on a regular tap, and this makes the experience desirable to beer lovers searching for the best and most rare.

toasty character of these ales, especially if they want something sweet but not necessarily fruity. Here are some great Brown Ales that can start you down that nutty road to happiness:

⟳ **SAMUEL SMITH'S NUT BROWN ALE:** Samuel Smith Old Brewery, Tadcaster, North Yorkshire, England. Creamy and nutty, buttered bread, dry finish. 5% ABV.

How Does a Keg Work?

A keg—or, more appropriately, a half barrel—has a stainless-steel tube inside of it that goes all the way to the bottom. At the top is a spring-loaded ball valve that opens when you tap the beer. The beer keg has added CO_2 pressure to contain the carbonation until tapping. Once tapped, the CO_2 pressure mixed with the pressure of the gas in the beer line will force the beer through the line all the way to the pint glass. The top of the keg is attached to something called a coupler (a device used to tap the keg), which is attached to the beer line (a long plastic hose that hooks up to the tap system in the bar) and a CO_2 line (a line that hooks up to the gas system).

Now if you have ever gotten a keg for a party at home, you may remember that these have that hand pump thing (are you having high school flashbacks?). This pump pushes air into the keg, forcing beer to come out of the hose in the same way the CO_2 gas forces the beer out of the keg in a bar.

○ **NAUTICAL NUT BROWN ALE:** AleSmith Brewing Company, San Diego, California. Roasted almonds, caramel, bitter hops. 4.8% ABV.

○ **HAZELNUT BROWN NECTAR:** Rogue Brewery, Newport, Oregon. Sweet American Brown, super hazelnutty, not bitter. 6.2% ABV.

○ **SIXPOINT BROWNSTONE:** Sixpoint Craft Ales, Brooklyn, New York. Chocolate, toffee, grassy bitter hops. 5.8% ABV.

Mild Ale: Better Than It Sounds

THIS BEER'S FOR YOU IF YOU LIKE: MELLOWNESS. DRY BISCUITS. LOW, LOW ALCOHOL. NOT GETTING WASTED. NUANCE.

Mild Ales are low-alcohol (around 3%), low-bitterness beers that origi-nated in England around the 1600s. *Mild* originally meant "young beer," meaning it had not been aged (as much of the beer of the time was), but the term now defines a low-bitterness beer. Mild Ales have been described as "running beers," referring to the fact that the beers were served just a few days after they were brewed; they became popular in the pubs of the late 19th century. This was probably because the aged beers had a bit of a sour taste due to the stability issues with the yeast used. The idea of drinking a freshly brewed beer is still popular among British pub-goers. Mild Ales were also often mixed with other English Ales, like Browns, to create a unique, complex brew. Mild Ales tend to be nutty and mellow, with subtle fruit, molasses, toffee, and caramel notes. Their low alcohol and full flavor make them perfect for a session (see page 98). The style is extremely rare in America, where the idea of a session is a bit foreign and where using the word *mild* as an advertisement wouldn't sell a cheap hooker to a salty sailor. Here are a few tasty Milds:

- **SURLY BREWING MILD ALE:** Surly Brewing Company, Brooklyn Center, Minnesota. Toffee flavor, caramel malt, mild hops. Served in a can, but don't let that keep you away. 4.2% ABV.

- **THE TAP MERRIMACK MILD ALE:** Haverhill Brewery Inc., Haverhill, Massachusetts. Roasty sweet caramel, hint of coffee, mild hops. 3.4% ABV.

- **VICTORIAN RUBY MILD:** Dark Star Brewery, Haywards Heath, UK. Just slightly bitter. Nutty, mild, mixed with aged dark beer. A bit high in alcohol for its style at 6% ABV.

Bitter, but Not Angry: Bitters

THIS BEER'S FOR YOU IF YOU LIKE: BEING SURLY BUT NOT MEAN. LONG DISCUSSIONS ABOUT SHAKESPEAREAN THEMES. NOTES OF TOFFEE. STAYING ON YOUR STOOL. EVENINGS AT THE PUB.

British Bitter is one of the most popular styles in Merry Ole England. Bitters are almost synonymous with Pale Ales, but were coined "bitter" by drinkers who wanted to differentiate these beers from other popular brews like the Mild Ale and Porter. The Bitter has a higher hop profile

than the others and is thus described by its taste. Bitters gained popularity around the mid-1800s and are still a common request by Brits. Bitters have a nice wide range of alcohol, anywhere between 3% and 7%; a malt roast level of golden to deep brown; and a variety of bitterness. The most important thing, we think, to remember about a bitter is this: *It's not that bitter!* This is where the British accent on beer is something we Americans need to decode; the bitter in England is *not* the bitter in America. When a British fellow walks up to the bar and asks us for a Bitter (BITT-AH), we know he doesn't mean an American IPA or even a bold

American Pale Ale. He means bitter as opposed to mild, light amber, dark Stout, or Porter. To the American craft drinker, these beers may simply taste dry, not bitter. To the British, these beers benefit from a subtlety that is appreciated by their countrymen. Some Bitters are popular session beers, being fairly low in alcohol but flavorful enough to enjoy pint after pint.

Bitters have several different titles, as it were. These titles are general categories of Bitters, usually giving information about the alcoholic strength of the ale. Here they are in loose order of strength, from mellow to high: Session Bitter, Ordinary Bitter, Regular Bitter, Best Bitter, Special Bitter, Extra Special Bitter, Strong Bitter, and Premium Bitter. British IPAs will often be found around the session section of the Bitter scale. This is again quite contrary to our American IPAs, which would be somewhere way past the Premium Bitter on the way to "Holy shite!" for most Brits. Perhaps the most common British-style Bitter found in the states is the ESB. It is one of the biggest styles of Bitter, referring to a higher-alcohol brew with slightly bolder flavors of a fruity, roasty, toasty nature. ESBs sometimes use darker malts in the mash, leading to a deeper copper- or brown-colored beer, and may have more hops in an effort to balance out a higher malt content, but they are still not . . . what? Yes, you guessed it: bitter. Here are some Bitters that make us happy:

○ **ANVIL ESB ALE:** AleSmith Brewing Company, San Diego, California. An American-style ESB with bold toasted malt flavors and a good dose of hops; well balanced. 5.5% ABV.

○ **FULLER'S ESB:** Fuller Smith & Turner PLC, Chiswick, London, UK. A famous British ESB; earthy, caramel sweetness; bitter end. 5.9% ABV.

○ **MORLAND OLD SPECKLED HEN:** Greene King Brewery, Bury St. Edmunds, UK. Nutty, caramelly, touch of bitterness. 3.5% ABV.

○ **OAKHAM ASYLUM:** Oakham Brewery, Peterborough, UK. Bitter with bold grapefruit and bitter, resiny hops. 4.5% ABV.

TOGETHER IN PERFECT HARMONY: THE BLACK AND TAN

 You're probably familiar with the black and white cookie of beer: the Black and Tan. This is usually a combination of a Pale Ale or English Bitter with a Porter or Stout. Sometimes a Pale Lager is used in lieu of the Pale Ale, but either way, the tan part of the concoction is a beer that is low in bitterness and alcohol. The most popular combo for this drink are the Irish beers Harp and Guinness; however, Black and Tans are not actually consumed often in Ireland and are much more popular with Brits and Americans. In fact, in Ireland the term *black and tan* refers to the Royal Irish Constabulary Reserve Force, which was engaged in the 1920s in active suppression of the revolution in Ireland. Employed by the queen of England and made up of World War I vets from England and Scotland, the force was supposed to focus on fighting the infamous Irish Republican Army (IRA), but instead they were famous for attacking Irish civilians. The point of this history lesson is that *black and tan* can be an offensive term in parts of Ireland; in fact, Ben & Jerry's ice cream had to pull their black and tan flavor made in honor of St. Patrick's Day in 2006 due to Irish feelings about the association.

Black and Tans are made by slowly pouring the tan portion into a pint first and finishing with Guinness (or whatever Stout is used) on top. The Stout is often poured over an inverted spoon, or "brolly," which hooks onto the pint glass, preventing a mixture of the two beers. The perfect

Get Deep

This is where we delve a little deeper into a world ruled by a Dark Lord. Okay, maybe we're going too far with that, but we definitely want to turn you on to a beer style that doesn't get as much play in America as it should: the Bavarian-born Dunkel (pronounced DOONK-ELL).

Black and Tan is pleasing to the eye and counterintuitive because the dark portion floats above the light. The reason the Stout hangs above the lighter beer is because the Stout is actually less dense than lager and Pale Ale. Wow for physics.

In addition to the Black and Tan, here are some other 50/50 splits from around the globe:

- **HALF AND HALF:** Half warm Guinness and half chilled Guinness. Some Irish claim that this produces the perfect temperature Guinness.
- **BLACKSMITH OR PINT OF SPECIAL:** Half Smithwick's Irish Red Ale, half Guinness. This is the way to order a Black and Tan in Ireland if you don't want to get kicked out of the pub.
- **SNAKEBITE:** Half lager, half hard apple cider. This is a common choice for new beer drinkers because of the sweetness.
- **SHANDY:** A percentage (50% to 60%) of beer (lager or lighter ale) and lemonade or lemon-lime soda.
- **BLACK AND GOLD OR BLACK APPLE:** Half hard apple cider and half Guinness.
- **BLACK BASTARD:** Half Stone's famous Arrogant Bastard Ale and half Guinness.
- **BLACK AND BLOOD:** Half Guinness and half Ribena (a popular black currant juice abroad).

Even though these beers are deep in color, there's no deep, dark mystery here. *Dunkel* is just German for "dark." That's it. Now, Dunkel can be a little confusing because the word *dark* can really be applied to almost any darker beer. As you know, we don't like to judge a beer by its color; in this case, it's the flavor profile of these Dunkels that really sets them apart from other dark beers, like Porters or Stouts.

We talked about Pilsners in Chapter 3 and how they were met with such acclaim and popularity. Well, that's because up until the 1840s all beer was pretty much dark, or Dunkel. However, because the brewing process wasn't necessarily understood, those beers were dark, muddy, murky, and questionable in flavor at best. These aren't the Dunkel beers we're talking about here. The Dunkels of today are clear dark lagers that aren't necessarily heavy, charred, or smoky. Dunkels traditionally also use a method called decoction (a word that makes us giggle). The decoction method concentrates a portion of the beer and aids in a process that creates nice, malty, sweet, caramelized characteristics: a revelation in dark beers at the time.

Because of the popularity of Pilsners and light sparkly beers, Dunkel styles pretty much took a back seat to them and became less frequently made. But Dunkels are seeing a resurgence in popularity, and we've decided to honor the style and bring 'em back big-time, baby, yeah.

München mag Dich (Munich Loves You): Munich Dunkel Lagers

THIS BEER'S FOR YOU IF YOU LIKE: SAYING FUNNY WORDS. CRUNCHY BAGUETTES. MAHOGANY. COMPLEXITY AND RICHNESS. CARAMELS.

Munich Dunkels are the classic dark lagers and are made using a majority (and sometimes 100%) of the rich and complex Munich malt, which lends sweetish notes like caramel and bread crusts, nuts and cocoa. For the most part, Munich Dunkels are not intense or bitter beers and usually ring in between 4.5% and 6% ABV. They should be approachable, comfortable, and medium bodied. Because these beers are not cloying or overpowering, they are great steps in acclimating you to the truth that dark beers are not bitter or heavy. (Yes, we said it again.) In fact, this beer style should have none of the big burnt, super-smoky, or bitter flavors that its darker cousins Porters and Stouts have. Lest you think that this style might be too sweet for your liking, there is usually a nice hop presence in these styles that isn't necessarily bitter but provides a clean, not too astringent finish to the sweetness. Sound good? Try some of these rad Dunkels:

- **AYINGER ALTBAIRISCH DUNKEL:** Brauerei Aying, Aying, Germany. Amazing balance, clean, toasty. A classic representation from one of the best breweries in the world. 5% ABV.

- **LEINENKUGEL'S CREAMY DARK:** Jacob Leinenkugel Brewing Company, Chippewa Falls, Wisconsin. A great American version of the Bavarian classic. Smooth and rich; nutty with hints of chocolate. 4.9% ABV.

- **NEGRA MODELO:** Grupo Modelo, Mexico City, Mexico. This Mexican version of a Munich Dunkel is pretty darn good. Caramel and brown sugar with a clean finish. 4% ABV.

May the Schwarzbier with You

THIS BEER'S FOR YOU IF YOU LIKE: THE COUNTERINTUITIVE. HINTS OF SULFUR AND SMOKE. ASPHALT NOTES IN WINE. COFFEE AND CHOCOLATE. AN UNEXPECTEDLY LIGHT BODY.

Schwarzbier (SHVARTS-BEER) means "black beer" in German. Upon hearing that, many beer drinkers head for the hills, thinking that a black beer must be stronger and bigger than even the most imperial of Stouts. As a matter of fact, Schwarzbier is a lager that is actually much lighter bodied and much less intense than even typical Porters and Stouts.

Traditionally brewed in Saxony and the surrounding areas in what is now eastern Germany, Schwarzbier is becoming very popular among craft brewers and drinkers alike. Using chocolate, caramel, and Munich malts, Schwarzbiers are usually opaque, super-dark beers that can range from auburn to an ebony tone. Clean, light- to medium-bodied beers with typical flavors of coffee, chocolate, and licorice and just a waft of smoke,

Schwarzbiers can range in intensity and can sometimes be so surprisingly light-bodied that they are referred to as Black Pils. The hops used in this beer style help create roasted and toasty notes with a medium dryness that lingers at the finish, sometimes with a nice sweetness. Drink these Black Lagers so the Schwarzbier can be with you:

- **SAMUEL ADAMS BLACK LAGER:** Boston Beer Company, Boston, Massachusetts. A little bit sweeter than your typical Sam Adams beer, with notes of caramel and singed grain. 4.9% ABV.

- **SPRECHER BLACK BAVARIAN:** Sprecher Brewery, Glendale, Wisconsin. Aromas of coffee, caramel, and chocolate. Smooth and complex. 5.86% ABV.

- **KÖSTRITZER SCHWARZBIER:** Köstritzer Schwarzbierbrauerei, Bad Köstritz, Germany. Light bodied, crisp, and clean, with just a touch of coffee and a waft of smoke. 4.8% ABV.

- **DEATH & TAXES:** Moonlight Brewing Company, Fulton, California. Chocolate truffles and espresso with nice spicy hops. Great balance and truly delicious. 4.2% ABV.

Word to the Weizen: Dunkelweizen

THIS BEER'S FOR YOU IF YOU LIKE: YOUR NANA'S FAMOUS BANANA BREAD. CLOUDS IN YOUR COFFEE. A LIFE LESS ORDINARY. SKOR BARS.

Another famous substyle of the Dunkel dynasty is the delicious Dunkelweizen, which translated from German means "dark wheat." And, you guessed it: this beer is a style that, like a Hefeweizen, uses a substantial amount of wheat as part of its malt profile. Unlike a Hefeweizen, however, a Dunkelweizen also uses chocolate, caramel, and Munich and several other tasty darker malts that give this beer a coffee, toffee-like quality. However, the Dunkel version Weizen also uses the yeast styled for banana and clovey Hefes. So you end up with flavors of delicious banana nut bread or a delectable bananas Foster. The hops in this style of beer are present in their spiciness more than their bitterness or dryness. Get a load of these tasty Dunkelweissens:

- **WEIHENSTEPHANER HEFEWEISSBIER DUNKEL:** Brauerei Weihenstephan, Freising, Germany. Fairly light bodied for a Dunkelweizen, big banana in the nose but mild on the palate; spicy and fruity. 5.3% ABV.

- **CRAFTSMAN DUNKELWEISSE:** Craftsman Brewing Company, Pasadena, California. Dark sugar and molasses and banana. Classic flavors from a great American brewery. 5.8 ABV.

- **NATIVITÉ ROUSSE:** Dieu du Ciel!, Montreal, Canada. Focused on the spice versus the banana. A red Dunkelweizen; lightly roasted wheat with a touch of clove. 5% ABV.

Note: Dunkel Lagers and Dunkelweizen beers should not be confused with a style of beer that exists in some parts of Germany called Dunkelbier, which does indeed taste sweet and malty but has no alcohol (The Horror!).

I Wanna Bock with You: Bock Beers

THIS BEER'S FOR YOU IF YOU LIKE: GETTING KICKED IN THE HEAD. GOATS. FREEZING THINGS. TOFFEE AND CHOCOLATE. FULL-BODIED RICHNESS. THE ZODIAC.

Like much of the beer history in the world, the origin of the name of this beer style, Bock, is a point of contention. One theory is that the style got its name vaguely from the city in which it was invented, Einbeck, Germany. Others think that the moniker was given because this beer style was traditionally brewed in winter months during the sign of Capricorn, whose zodiac symbol is the goat. "Billy goat" in German translates to *Geißbock* or *Ziegenbock*, and many Bock beer brewers have even taken the goat (which is also a customarily satanic symbol) as a mascot for their beer. Personally, we like the theory that the name was based on the German phrase *einen bock schießen*, which means "to commit a blunder" or "to pull a boner." (Look it up!) Regardless, it's true that if you drink too much of these strong beers, you might end up feeling like you got kicked in the head by a goat the next morning.

The Bock, or Bockbier, style was traditionally a seasonal beer, sometimes brewed in the winter and consumed in the spring during Lent and Easter, and other times brewed for the winter holidays. Today, Bock is pretty much available year-round. Bockbiers were beers of celebration, meant to be consumed after toasts of better days to come. Most Bocks are bigger and stronger than most lagers. They range in color from dark copper to auburn to deep chestnut, and have a rich mouthfeel, bold malty characteristics, and a restrained hop presence. They usually come in at 6.6% to 7.5% ABV, although some are much higher. Now, even though these beers have robust flavors and high alcohol content, Bockbiers and most of the substyles of Bock (with the exception of Weizenbock) are lagers! What? Are you still thinking that lagers are light in color, body, and alcohol? Not so, young Padawan. These beers are bottom fermented over a long period of time and lagered for months in cold temperatures, which mellows the flavors and creates a smooth-drinking, well-balanced brew.

Some of our favorite beers are Bockbiers, and there are several different substyles of this masterful brew. There is Weizenbock, which as you know by now means "strong wheat"; it breaks from Bock tradition and is an ale rather than a lager. This style is usually a bigger, fuller-bodied Dunkelweizen, with many of the same characteristics of bold bananas and cloves. Dopplebocks, or Double Bocks, are even stronger Bock beers. Not literally double the strength, these lagers are deliciously strong with dark fruit, roasted chocolate qualities, a lush sweetness, and a heat in the finish due to the 6% to 9% ABV range. As an homage to the first beer made in the style, Paulaner Salvator, many Dopplebocks are sometimes named using the suffix "-ator," like Captivator, Celebrator, Decimator, and Detonator.

On the other end of the Bock spectrum is the style called Maibock, which refers to the month of May and is a style that is traditionally brewed for spring holiday celebrations. Another very similar and sometimes interchangeable style is Helles Bock (or Heller Bock), which means (as you know from Chapter 3) "pale." Both Maibocks and Helles Bocks tend to be lighter in color and have more assertive hop aromatics and bitterness than other Bock beers. However, the lighter color doesn't mean that these beers are any lighter in alcohol content. In fact, in addition to the hoppiness, Maibocks and Helles Bocks also have a noticeable maltiness, viscosity, and depth.

The beer world is full of happy accidents, and one of these ended up creating a delicious style of Bock beer called Eisbock. As the story goes, a German barkeep or a Bavarian brewer (depending on who is telling the story) left casks of Bockbier outside in the winter, and they partially froze. Not wanting to throw the beer away, the ice in it was discarded and the beer was tasted. What they discovered was a concentrated, fractionally distilled, strong, and delicious brew that they called an ice beer, or Eisbock. Now, this style of ice beer is not to be confused with the mass-produced American style of ice beer, which is usually light in alcohol, color, and body. Eisbock is dark, malty, and hearty with a significant alcohol content. Get kicked in the head with some of our favorite Bock beers:

- **SHINER BOCK:** Spoetzl Brewery, Shiner, Texas. This one is a heart pick. Full-flavored, deep-amber-colored beer, with an inviting smooth taste without excessive bitterness. 4.4% ABV.

- **SCHNEIDER AVENTINUS WEIZEN EISBOCK:** G. Schneider & Sohn, Kelheim, Germany. Full-bodied, with big roasted bananas and clove on the nose, and caramel, nutty, woody notes on the finish. 8.2% ABV.

AYINGER CELEBRATOR DOPPELBOCK: Brauerei Aying, Aying, Germany. Dark and rich, with complex fruitiness and roasty, toasty malt. Full-bodied with a semidry smoky finish. 6.7% ABV.

KULMBACHER EISBOCK: Kulmbacher Brauerei, Kulmbach, Germany. Concentrated malt sweetness but exceptionally clean tasting. A deceptive 9.2% ABV.

SIERRA NEVADA PALE BOCK (MAIBOCK/HELLES BOCK): Sierra Nevada Brewing Company, Chico, California. Famous for its Pale Ale, this brewery produces other great beers, including this bready, rich, and assertive Helles Bock. 6.5% ABV.

The Darker the Berry: Beers with Some Deep Color

Some people think darker beers are a black hole into which they don't want to fall. They say they are too heavy, too strong, or too much for their palate to handle. Okay, well, how do you like the sound of this: chocolate, espresso, cinnamon, tobacco, licorice, tar. Sounds like a perfect deep red wine, a nuanced cigar, an haute chocolate bar from Italy, but in fact, it is the darker side of beer. On the flip side, there are those of you who crave a deep dark mass of ale in a glass. Those who seek it out for the same reasons others avoid it, wanting to look tough, drinking dark brew as a dare to anyone who may question your edge. But you don't have to have the need to prove anything to drink dark beer. And though you have all heard tales of Porters and Stouts consisting of an entire meal of calories or those with a high alcohol content, know that this is not true of all Porters and Stouts.

You have probably tried at least one Stout, if not a Porter. It is a well-advertised style owing to one well-known brew: Guinness. Yes, this is the star of Stouts, the king of the Irish, the creamy ale. We acknowledge the devout following of this classic beer and are humbled by its history, but we would like to introduce a little variety. If you are one of the thousands who crave the chocolate milkshake flavors in this beer, there is a whole world of dark-malt-based beer to try.

A Broad Definition: Porter and Stout

Porters and Stouts are similar, if not the same. Porters were named such in the 18th century due to their popularity among the river porters of London. They emerged as an attempt to copy a common practice of mixing several ales, like Mild Ale and Brown Ale. These combinations were called *entire* and were unique to each pub. Porter became the most popular beer in England, Ireland, and America for a time. This lasted until Prohibition and war made brewing various styles impossible. They are again popular today, especially among American craft brewers, but are still fairly rare in England.

PORTER

Porter is made from dark roasted malts, though its flavors vary rather widely. The stronger versions were often called Strong Porter, Extra Porter, Double Porter, and Stout Porter. In fact, Guinness started out as Guinness Porter. The name Stout would end up on its own later when the Porter designation would be dropped for some ales, similar to the way that Scotch whisky is generally called just Scotch. This would lead us to believe that a Stout is in fact a stronger version of a Porter. Although arguably true, this is not always the case—especially today, when the terms are pretty much interchangeable. It is actually up to the brewer to pick which name to use for his or her beer within this range of style. This is ripe for debate, of course, and if you are a beer-geek, you will go through many pints of Porter discussing this issue with brewers; if you are newer to the beer world, you'll think those beer-geeks are losers and will go about your merry drinking way.

Because Porters have a wide range of flavor (like Stouts), they leave room for the brewer to add notes of coffee or chocolate; some brewers even age the beer in whisky barrels. Porters can range from 5% to 9% ABV, depending on the brewer's desire. Their hop bite is hugely varied as well. Their common trait is the featured flavors of the dark roasted malt, but not much else.

Porters generally fall under three substyles. First is Brown Porter, a fairly mild British style that is low in bitterness, with a chocolate, nutty, toffee flavor. Brown Porters tend to stay away from any burnt ash flavors and will generally be lower in alcohol. Another is Robust Porter. This style can also have some chocolaty toffee notes but will boast a burnt flavor. Robust Porters may or may not be bitter and can vary in ABV, though they're typically higher than Brown Porters. And finally, there is Baltic Porter, which is a complex Porter originating in the countries from the Baltic Sea region. Baltic Porters tend to be high in alcohol, anywhere from 5% to 9.5%, and thus have a pronounced warmth in the mouth from the alcohol. They are usually brewed with lager yeast. If one is made with ale yeast, the beer is then fermented at cold temperatures, making this a sort of hybrid beer. These Porters can have flavors of dried fruit, licorice, coffee, and spicy hops. They are typically less burnt in the mouth than Robust Porters and are much more complex than Browns. Dive into these Porters:

- **BLACK BUTTE PORTER:** Deschutes Brewery, Bend, Oregon. Chocolaty with notes of burnt sugar, nice dose of hops, complex, and well balanced. 5.2% ABV.

- **GREAT LAKES EDMUND FITZGERALD PORTER:** Great Lakes Brewing Company, Cleveland, Ohio. Roasty chocolate and bitter coffee, bold hops. 5.8% ABV.

- **ANCHOR PORTER:** Anchor Brewing, San Francisco, California. Chocolate, licorice, burnt brown sugar, dark fruit, dry finish. 5.6% ABV.

- **FULLER'S LONDON PORTER:** Fuller Smith & Turner PLC, London, UK. Molasses, tobacco, lightly bitter, dry. 5.4% ABV.

STOUT

As we mentioned earlier, *Stout* was originally a general term for a strong dark beer. Stouts today range from chocolaty and smooth to bitter and intense. They are often the beers found on nitrogen taps at pubs, benefiting from a creamy mouthfeel and dense head. The implication of strength is really no longer applicable, because the ABV can be quite low. Too many people turn away Stout because they think it is too heavy or too high in alcohol; others feel a sense of overwrought pride because they were "man enough" to drink a Stout. Most people don't realize that a Guinness is as low in alcohol, often lower, than a Pale Ale. In fact, Guinness, which is classified as a Dry or Irish Stout, is considered light in the realm of Stouts and Porters. This may come as a shock. The rich color, along with the coffee, toffee, and sometimes bitter notes, have confused drinkers for years. Dry Stouts tend to have that coffee, chocolate flavor that Guinness has, ranging from sweet to bitter chocolate or even sour.

On the opposite end of the Stout continuum are Sweet or Milk Stouts—full-bodied English-style Stouts with the same chocolaty/coffee notes but quite low on bitterness and higher on sweetness, due to the addition of lactose sugar. This sugar is not fermentable and therefore hangs out in the brew and imparts a sweet milky flavor. This beer is quite rare these days. Most of you have heard of Oatmeal Stouts, another classic style. Yes, these Stouts do have oats in them—an excuse to have them with breakfast? Why not? The oats are added to the mash, lending a grainy complexity to the flavor and silkiness in the mouth. They are anywhere from sweet to bitter, depending on the brewer's recipe.

Stouts from other countries that aren't quite of the Irish Dry or

British variety can fall under the term Foreign Extra Stout. This is a fairly general style that includes many versions of Stouts from many countries. These Stouts can range from about 6% to 8% ABV. They can be sweet, bitter, toasty with notes of dried fruit, sour, and dry. Basically, they are all over the place.

Our domestic American Stouts tend to have a bold coffee flavor with chocolate notes. They can stand apart from other Stouts by using cascading down the glass. These are the nitro bubbles. The creamy taste is not just pretty but gives us a weighty mouthfeel, which complements some styles of beer. This is meant to re-create the mouthfeel of a cask-conditioned beer. The widget that has been invented for cans of Guinness Export serves the same purpose. By releasing some nitrogen into the can, the creamy mouthfeel comes through, if not authentically.

Stouts in particular, with their chocolate and coffee notes, handle the weightier, creamier feel quite well. Nutty English Ales become a thing of beauty when the cream is added to their subtle flavor notes. But remember that the creaminess comes from science: it is not actual cream, it does not mean that the Stout on a nitro tap is a meal, it is not higher in calories than it would be if it were on a regular tap. It may seem like a meal because of the perceived milkshake mouthfeel, but it does not have any more calories because it is heavy in nitrogen bubbles.

Nitro taps drive home the fact that the carbonation in a beer has a huge effect on the flavor and entire taste experience of a beer. Try a Guinness on a creamer faucet next to a Guinness from a regular bottle; compare the experience and marvel at science.

American-bred hops, which have a piney, citrusy, resiny flavor. Breweries may add some oats to these Stouts as well. They range anywhere from 5% to 7% ABV.

And last, for dessert, we have Chocolate Stouts. These have become quite popular among craft brewers, extending the natural chocolate flavors dark malt can give a Stout by adding actual chocolate. This can be of the sweeter variety or in the form of a cacao powder or bitter baking chocolate. A Chocolate Stout after a meal can be heaven. Similarly, brewers have been putting coffee into Stouts for some time as well. They can be an interesting ride, with the alcohol and caffeine giving you a nice freak-out. Both Stouts and Porters stand up well to these additions, and even spices like vanilla can show up in these styles. Succumb to some of these Stouts:

- **SHAKESPEARE STOUT:** Rogue Ales Brewery, Newport, Oregon. Roasted chocolate and coffee, sweet and bitter. 6% ABV.

- **BARNEY FLATS OATMEAL STOUT:** Anderson Valley Brewing Company, Boonville, California. Bold coffee, resiny bitterness. 5.7% ABV.

- **BELL'S KALAMAZOO STOUT:** Bell's Brewery Inc., Kalamazoo, Michigan. Bittersweet chocolate, licorice, burnt sugar. 6.5% ABV.

- **MACKESON TRIPEL XXX STOUT:** Whitbread PLC, London, UK. Rich caramel character and smooth hops. 4.9% ABV.

- **YOUNG'S DOUBLE CHOCOLATE STOUT:** Wells & Young's Ltd., Bedford, UK. Sweet, rich, dark chocolate milkshake flavors; a perfect dessert. 5.2% ABV.

* * *

All right, Sophomore, hit the showers. Actually, no, hit the pub. Get specific and try some of these darker brews. Embrace the varied and international flavors of beer. We find that once beer lovers cross this threshold and find a roasty, toasty beer they can love, their apprehension dissipates and they are game for anything. Perhaps this is because dark beer suffers the most stereotypes. But once male and female drinkers alike find the nuance of flavor in beers that aren't pale in the glass, they feel altogether well-educated in brew. So take hold of this confidence. Down a Dunkel or a Stout, wink at the Neophytes, and keep on the fast track to graduation. Who says you can't be a beer sommelier?

The Devout

But if at church they would give some ale.
And a pleasant fire our souls to regale.
We'd sing and we'd pray all the live long day,
Nor ever once from the church to stray.

—WILLIAM BLAKE

The Spiritual Side of Beer

What is that thing that can make some beer greater than the sum of its parts? It's something we can only explain as the beer's chi, prana, spiritus, élan vital—whatever you want to call it, the vital life force or essence that elevates a beer to atmospheric heights. At some point, every person searches for it: The Perfect Beer. (*Insert choir of angels here.*) You can't always point to it, and you can't always prove it, but you can feel it deep down in your special place. Sometimes magic occurs in certain beers, and we lowly drinkers are left with a sense of wonderment and awe, not to mention the happiness we feel after a couple of these greats. We remember both the beers that blew our minds and the beers that spoke to us and nourished our souls. We vividly remember the beers that made us want to get down on our knees and say amen! The brewers behind them seemed to be touched by God; they convinced us to close our eyes and trust their vision.

It's these kinds of religious experiences that have turned us into believers and fueled our quest for discovering what makes a great beer so great. Once we understand what to look for on a deeper level, we can appreciate beer in a way that we never could have before. The following beers are an inspiration in the beer world. They are often considered the cream of the crop and the beers that newer craft brewers attempt to replicate. Some, the Trappist Ales, are actually made by holy men. So when we say "religious experience," it's not just a figure of speech. You are ready to taste these magical brews that some crown as the most balanced, complex beers out there. We know some of these brews will have you giving thanks. Once you have a transcendental awakening like this, you become a part of the Devout. So, are you ready to get religion? Are you open to the spiritual side of beer?

Is It Sinful? Counting Calories and Carbs in Beer

Your body is a temple. So before you can devote yourself to beer and have a truly ethereal experience, you're going to have to baptize yourself of any residual feelings of guilt related to beer's original sin: calories. Beer gets a bad rap for being filling, fattening, and heavy. Weight-conscious drinkers assume that they have to wave the beer away. The mega-mass-produced beer world has reinforced these stereotypes by kowtowing to these worries. Instead of trying to teach the public that when it comes to calories, beer isn't as bad as many other alcoholic beverages, they feed the fear. By doing so, they create lowest common denominator beers that tout calories in the 60s and pervade our bars and restaurants (curses!).

First of all, let us say that beer has *no fat*! But we're not going to deny that there are calories in beer. And hey, if there were an amazing beer out there that wasn't watered down and had great flavor and no calories, we'd be drinking that beer, too. Unfortunately that's not the case with low-calorie and low-carb beers. The flavor simply isn't there. Just because we are talking about beer doesn't mean that we have to settle for less in terms of quality or taste. Would any true wine connoisseur in her right mind order a wine by the calorie content (shudder!)? It's time that we looked at the truth about beer and calories, and the truth shall set us free.

Let's start with alcohol. If you are going to drink any alcoholic beverage, you are going to swallow calories. The more full-bodied and the more alcohol a beer has, the more calories are going to be in that beer. Alcoholic drinks harbor lots of calories and inhibit the body from burning fat. It's true, we know it's true. But beer is not the demon here, and we refuse to let it take all the blame! First of all, beer is unfairly associated with lots of unhealthy foods. People think of buffalo wings and onion rings, ribs, and a juicy burger. Okay, those things are yummy and damn good with a beer to wash them down, but one does not *need* to eat fatty food while drinking beer. And beer is not more guilty than most of the popular beverages out there. Most people just don't realize how many calories are in their favorite cocktail, soda, or a glass of great Pinot Noir. Google it!

So now let's talk about carbonation. Some people say that they don't like beer because it's too filling and makes them feel, you know...a little gassy. Once again, it's true. Beer does have carbonation, but carbonation does not equal carbohydrates. Bubbles in beer are not secret fatty things filling up your belly. Yes, you may belch a bit, but why do people sneer at beer bubbles and then happily drink a glass of Champagne, 7-Up, Diet Coke, or Perrier and call them refreshing? Again we think the mass beer companies are to blame for fanning the flame of obsession with light beer, teaching us that all other beer, if not light, is heavy, and that beer is inherently weighty. Carbonation's function in beer is to lift the beer—to lighten up the sweetness of the malt, the bitterness of the hops, the heat of the alcohol. It is there to add a refreshing balance.

It comes down to this: If you are so concerned with calories and carbs in beer, we'd rather see you give up drinking alcohol altogether than see you drink the lite and low-carb versions of "beer" that are out there today. Sometimes you gotta use tough love.

Have you cast out your notions of beer and sin? Can you now relax and let go of any negative associations with this fine beverage? It's important to enter into the world of the next few beers with a clean conscience and a prepared palate.

Hear the Calling

The following beers are worthy of praise. If Trappist beers are the breathtaking ancient church of beer, then these next styles are the surrounding beauteous grounds (we'll withhold the *Sound of Music* reference for you). They achieve a balance that plays well with food and your palate. These austere beers are a perfect entrée into the elite world of specialty beers. They are not too high in alcohol but they are über-complex, challenging your palate without stabbing it with huge flavors. Once you can appreciate these fine, balanced ales, you will be ready to enter the heavenly world of Trappist brews.

Spirit of the Saison

Originally brewed around the town of Liège in French-speaking Belgium, Saison beer was almost extinct until fairly recently, but it is now seeing a revival in the craft beer world. Saison, which means "season" in French, was traditionally a beer brewed in the winter and meant for summer consumption. Saisons are now brewed all year round. Usually 6% to 8% ABV, this beer style is considered a farmhouse ale, and is called so because of the rustic, earthy, almost sour quality that it's famous for. Sometimes overlooked and underrated by extreme beer fans, Saison could quite possibly be our favorite beer style. Straw golden to amber in color, these beers have amazing complexity and a completely unique flavor profile. They are almost a cross between a high-alcohol Belgian Witbier, with its herbaceous, citrus qualities, and a Bière Brut, with its malty sweetness and peppery dryness. The spice and dryness make this a great beer style for food pairing (see Chapter 8). Green grassy, biscuity, and fruity on the nose, with a woolish dryness and sour finish, this beer style's unassuming nuanced goodness always surprises and delights us. Taste our favorite Saisons and be delighted, too.

- **SAISON DUPONT:** Brasserie DuPont, Tourpes-Leuze, Belgium. The quintessential Saison. Perfectly balanced, with spicy hops, high bitter citrus, cloves, and cardamom. 6.5% ABV.

- **SAISON D'ERPE-MERE:** Kleinbrouwerij De Glazen Toren, Erpe-Mere, Belgium. Foggy straw yellow, sparkly and bright, zesty and floral, with a dry burlap finish. 7.5% ABV.

- **SAISON RUE:** The Bruery, Placentia, California. Deep rich amber; unique with peppery spicy notes, tart *Brettanomyces*, and toast owing to the addition of rye. Nice dry finish. 8.5% ABV.

HENNEPIN: Brewery Ommegang, Cooperstown, New York. Earthy, dry, nutty, and grassy. Good hop presence with more bitter than sweet notes. 7.5% ABV.

Keeping the Faith ... in My Stomach!
Bière de Garde

THIS BEER'S FOR YOU IF YOU LIKE: KEEPSAKES. NORTHERN FRANCE. FARMS. WOODY FLAVORS. ANISE. THE MONTH OF MARCH.

The French are known for their winemaking abilities, but as we learned while eating bean soup and sausages in northern Italy with not a noodle in sight, European cultures aren't necessarily defined by hard and fast borders. Take Bière de Garde, for instance. Originally a beer style from the Pas-de-Calais region of France, Bière de Garde, which means "beer for keeping," is a beer born from an area in France that was too far north to grow grapes but perfect for growing hops. Just like Saison, Bière de Garde was brewed in the cold months, cellared in the warmer months, and meant to last (or keep) throughout the summer. And, just like Saison, this beer is considered a farmhouse ale, having many of the same earthy, rustic characteristics. But Bière de Garde is different from Saison in a couple of significant ways. Bière de Garde usually has a pronounced sweetness and uses darker malts and a different yeast strain, which produces less pepper and citrus and more deep, woody flavors. This style has complex herbal characteristics, such as anise and fresh rosemary, and lacks the tartness of a Saison.

Currently made year-round, this style has several substyles and is featured as Blonde (blond), Ambrée (amber), or Brune (brown). There is also another seasonal variation, a style called Bière de Mars (Beer of March), which isn't meant for keeping but meant for drinking immediately. (Yeah, now we're talkin'!) The alcohol content of Bière de Garde is about the same as that of Saison: 6% to 8% ABV. Keep some of these in your stomach:

CASTELAINE BLOND BIÈRE DE GARDE: Brasserie Castelaine à Bénifontaine, Bénifontaine, France. Lighter colored with definite Saison characteristics. The pepper and citrus are there but are much less intense. Reminiscent of spring air. 6.4% ABV.

LA CHOULETTE AMBRÉE: Brasserie La Choulette, Hordain, France. A great example of a French amber. Full-bodied with notes of caramel apples and cinnamon. Dry effervescent finish. 8% ABV.

CRAFTSMAN BIÈRE DE GARDE: Craftsman Brewing Company, Pasadena, California. Deep copper brown, with old-school charm. A good malt profile, warm sweetness, and a pronounced earthiness. Great balance. 7.5% ABV.

OMMEGANG BIÈRE DE MARS: Brewery Ommegang, Cooperstown, New York. Fine Belgian-style amber with a bit of magical space dust woven in: *Brettanomyces bruxellensis*, a wild yeast that imparts added tartness, extra zing, and a touch of funk; dry-hopping enhances the hop aroma. 6.5% ABV.

Those Monks Sure Know How to Live!

D amn, these brothers can brew. Devoted monks, in order to support their way of life, have modestly created what are, in our humble opinion, some of the best beers in the world. In fact, these are the only beers in the world for which we'd be willing to don brown robes, forgo makeup, and impersonate men. Brewers the world over have attempted to duplicate the style and grace of these beers, some with great success, but Marvin Gaye and Tammi Terrell said it best when they sang, "Ain't nothing like the real thing, baby." While our staunch reverence for these beers is sometimes mocked, our admiration will never die. The time has come for us to give you Trappist Ales.

The Brothers: Trappist Ales

THIS BEER'S FOR YOU IF YOU LIKE: PRAYING. FASTING. VOWS OF SILENCE. *THE NAME OF THE ROSE.* WEARING A ROBE. AOC. *LADYHAWKE.* SECRETS. TRADITION. LISTENING TO ENIGMA.

If you are studying wines, one of the first things you learn about is something called an AOC, the Appellation d'Origine Contrôlée, which is basically a law that protects the place of origin of the wine and sets geographical boundaries and guidelines for style, quality, and flavor. For instance, you've heard of a Burgundy wine. Well, Burgundy is the name of an AOC in east-central France that is the home to delicious and famous super-high-quality Pinot Noirs and Chardonnays. According to the law, you cannot call your wine a Burgundy unless the grapes in your wine come from that particular established geographic region. In the beer world, there is something similar called Trappist or Trappiste beers.

How will you know that a beer is a Trappist? It's all in the logo. These beers have an official logo/seal on the label that says, "Authentic Trappist Product" in white, with a red-brown background contained within a white-rimmed hexagon. If you see this sign, be sure to drink the brew and begin your religious experience. Trappist Ales have strict regulations, which are constantly monitored by an organization called the International Trappist Association (ITA). First of all, the beer must be brewed within the walls of a Trappist monastery, not contracted or farmed out to anyone else but on the actual premises of the monastery. Second, the beer must be brewed by the monks *themselves* or by someone who is under their complete control. Either way, the beer must be brewed to the monks' age-old exact specifications, and no one else's. Third, the brewery must not overshadow the fact that the monks are men of God first and brewers second. The making of beer and all brewery business take a backseat to the monastic way of life. Along those lines, there is a final rule governing Trappist breweries: the credo that the monks are not to brew beer for profit. What? That's right, even though it might go against our sensibilities, the ITA's rule says that the money that comes from selling Trappist beer is to go only toward living expenses and sustaining the monastery; the rest is to go to charity. Wow...those guys must live like monks!

The ITA is not messing around. You could be the strictest monk, making great beer, but if the ITA says that you don't qualify as a Trappist brewery, then you aren't one, and all the self-flagellation and fasting in the world won't get you there. And if you say you are a Trappist brewery and you haven't been approved by the ITA, you might possibly get sued for using the name and logo. In addition, if you already have the Trappist seal of approval from the ITA, and you let secular people take control of the brewery or you become too commercialized or slack in sustaining the quality of the beer, the ITA can yank that name and logo right away from you. And don't think they won't do it. Like the French with their wine, the Belgians take their Trappist Ales *very* seriously.

With all of these rules and regulations, wars, revolutions, lawsuits, and strife, only seven Trappist breweries exist today. Yes, seven. That's it. Six are in Belgium, and one is in the Netherlands. And they still create amazing beers with centuries-old recipes and traditions. The seven Trappist breweries are (drumroll please) the following:

- **WESTMALLE:** The brewery at Abdij Trappisten van Westmalle is known as the originator of the Belgian beer style known as the Tripel (see page 130). The abbey, whose full name is Our Lady of the Sacred Heart, began making beer in 1836, although it wasn't commercially available to us peons until 1920.

- **ORVAL:** Originally established over 900 years ago, the Abbaye Notre-Dame d'Orval was destroyed and rebuilt several times until its most recent renewal in 1931 as a Trappist brewer. This brewery makes just one beer, simply called Orval, which means "valley of gold." And it is one of our favorites (see page 126).

WESTVLETEREN: The smallest producer of all the Trappist breweries, Westvleteren is located at Abdij Sint Sixtus. These monks adhere strictly to making and selling only enough beer to sustain their brewery, shunning commercialism and brewing only once a week. Founded in 1831, Westvleteren doesn't ship their beer or sell it to distributors. So if you want some, you'll have to get yourself to Belgium and drive to the actual abbey or to the café in de Vrede across the street (the only venue that the monks say can resell Westvleteren). It's illegal to sell or buy this beer in the United States.

ROCHEFORT: With a history that dates back to 1230, Rochefort beers are brewed at the Notre-Dame de Saint-Remy (Rochefort is a nearby town). This monastery has also gone through much strife and rebuilding as a result of war. The area also suffered famine and plague and the abbey was sold and demolished before finally being resurrected in the late 1800s. In 1899, the brewery began producing beer again, although not enough was available for sale until 1952. Rochefort arguably makes some of the best beer in the world.

ACHEL: Achel, or the Brouwerij der Sint-Benedictusabdij de Achelse Kluis, has a storied history that dates all the way back to the 1600s. Destroyed and rebuilt several times, this brewery was last dismantled in 1917, when the Germans wanted to use the copper from Achel's brewery in their war effort. Revived in 1998 (with help from monks of Westmalle and Rochefort), Achel is the newest Trappist brewery.

CHIMAY: Brewed at the Abbaye Notre-Dame de Scourmont, Chimay is the Trappist brewery that you most likely recognize. Established in 1850, it is the most commercial and the most widely distributed of all the Trappist beers. Chimay has clearly put a lot of their revenue into production, advertising, and distribution.

Trappist Mind Trick

Knowledge is power. It's great to remember the names of all the Trappist breweries so that you'll recognize them on menus, but in our experience, being able to recite all of the Trappist breweries on the spot is actually an awesome way to impress your beer-loving friends and pick up people in bars. But are you having a hard time remembering them all? Our friend and colleague actor Charlie Farrell came up with a mnemonic device to remember them that, he says, pays homage to us, his beer tutors. That device, embarrassingly enough, is "WOW, what a RACK," and it is pure genius:

Westmalle
Orval
Westvleteren
...what a...
Rochefort
Achel
Chimay
Koningshoeven

Some may see this as a bit of selling out in the monk world, and others accuse the brewery of brewing beer outside of its monastic walls. But whatever the case, Chimay produces three high-quality, respectable ales.

KONINGSHOEVEN: Brewing since 1886, Koningshoeven (the Abbey of Tilburg and the Abbey of Our Lady of Koningshoeven) has had a bit of a controversial relationship with the International Trappist Association. With the pressures of production and declining numbers in the brotherhood, the monks decided to contract their beers to a Dutch Bavarian brewery that brewed the beers under the "La Trappe" moniker. Because of that, the ITA brought the smackdown and took away the brewery's right to use the Authentic Trappist Product logo. However, the monks appealed, claiming that even though the brew is being made by secular people, the brewery is still entirely on the monastery grounds, and its operations are still under the monks' complete control. In October 2005, the ITA reconsidered and granted Koningshoeven the right to use the logo.

It is a badge of honor for any beer aficionado to have tasted some or all of the Trappist beers. They are becoming more and more popular (sometimes to the monks' and our chagrin) and, as a result, are becoming more available in the United States. However, Trappist monasteries still regulate the amount of beer sold, sometimes making them extremely hard to get and notoriously hard to stock in craft beer bars and specialty shops. Sometimes an importer or distributor may get only one or two shipments a year of certain beers. On the other hand, we just saw four different Trappist Ales at Whole Foods. Yes, the times they are a changin'. But it is still feast or famine with these special beers. Our modus operandi is that when we see a Trappist beer, we buy it. These beers are great to have on hand and are fantastic as collector's items because many Trappist Ales are even better after aging (see page 173). It's amazing to explore the different ales from these highly respected breweries. Here are our favorites from each of the holy Trappist breweries:

○ **WESTMALLE TRIPEL:** Brouwerij Westmalle, Malle, Belgium. The Tripel that started all Tripels. This is an amazing beer with a great balance; lemon on the lips, sweet and dry with floral and fruity esters, and a lovely lingering finish. 9.5% ABV.

○ **ORVAL TRAPPIST ALE:** Abbaye de Notre-Dame d'Orval, Belgium. The only beer made by the Trappist brewery at Orval. This beer is wonderfully unique. Earthy, rustic, and super dry, with notes of flannel, dirt (in a good way), and grass. 6.9% ABV.

- **WESTVLETEREN BLONDE:** Abdij Sint Sixtus, Belgium. This exclusive Trappist brewery is famous for its Westvleteren 12 Quadrupel, but our favorite is this Belgian Pale Ale. Reminiscent of a Witbier, this pale straw beer is bright, spicy, herbaceous, and perfectly bitter. 5.8% ABV.

- **TRAPPISTES ROCHEFORT 6 (RED CAP):** Notre-Dame de Saint-Remy, Belgium. The lightest bodied of Rochefort's three dark ales; beautifully restrained and dry but still has the raisiny, spicy goodness of this brewery's bigger beers. 7.5% ABV.

- **ACHEL 8° BRUNE:** Brouwerij der Sint-Benedictusabdij de Achelse Kluis, Belgium. Delicious Trappist Dubbel that pours a super effervescent deep orange with hints of figs, vanilla, green apple, brown sugar, biscuit, and a touch of pepper. An amazing balance and finish. 8% ABV.

- **CHIMAY GRANDE RÉSERVE (BLUE):** Abbaye Notre-Dame de Scourmont, Belgium. A Trappist Dubbel (sometimes called a Belgian Strong Ale) that's much different from the Achel and will give you insight about the varieties that can exist in one beer style. Deep and dark with notes of Old World fruits and spices. Plums and persimmons, cloves and cardamom. 9% ABV.

- **KONINGSHOEVEN QUADRUPEL:** Abbey of Tilburg, The Netherlands. Creamy caramel, cocoa, sweet fruit, and some citrus notes, all followed by a warming viscous finish. Delicious and dangerous at 10% ABV.

Other Cloistered Beers: Abbey and Abbey-Style Beers

THIS BEER'S FOR YOU IF YOU LIKE: DRESSING UP AS A MONK FOR HALLOWEEN. BORROWING NAMES. PROPRIETARY YEAST STRAINS. COMPLEX SPICE AND FRUIT. LESS RIGIDITY.

Now wait just a minute. Haven't you seen a million beers out there with a monk on the label? You know that there are way more than seven beers that were brewed at the Abbey of Such and Such and made by Father or Pater or Brother So-and-So! These beers sport a figure of a monk, or the outline of a robe, or a picture of an abbey. So why aren't these Trappist breweries?

Well, even though there are only seven Trappist breweries today, there used to be a lot more. And many of the monasteries that brew beer aren't necessarily of the Trappist order. Over time, these monastery breweries stopped production for whatever reason and, in many cases, were taken over by secular breweries that have bought the rights from those monks and are licensed to use their abbey and beer names, brewing methods, recipes, proprietary yeast, and sometimes even the equipment and brewery buildings. Affligem and St. Bernardus are examples of breweries that have these kinds of arrangements. Beers brewed under these circumstances, based in true monastic breweries, are called Abbey Ales.

There's another category of Abbey Ales that aren't necessarily brewed under a monastic license. Many of these breweries are named after defunct monasteries that perhaps never even had a brewery. Some Belgian breweries are also named after saints and other religious symbols but have never been under the control of any religious organization. Most beer connoisseurs call beers from these breweries Abbey-style ales instead of Abbey Ales, to denote the difference. Even lower down on the name-game ladder (not to us, but to some) are the American beers that are made in the monastic style. These beers, no matter how skillfully crafted, are relegated to being called Belgian-style beers. Try these amazing beers and see if the Trappist stamp really makes the difference to you.

ST. BERNARDUS PRIOR 8: Brouwerij St. Bernardus, Watou, Belgium. A Dubbel; sweet with notes of caramel, raisins, and chocolate. Nice esters and a good kick. 8% ABV.

AUGUSTIJN GRAND CRU: Brouwerij Van Steenberge, Ertvelde, Belgium. Surprisingly delicate and complex. Herbaceous, with hints of mango and passion fruit and a hoppy dryness. 9% ABV.

MAREDSOUS 10: Brouwerij Duvel Moortgat, Breendonk, Belgium. A Tripel; big citrus, lemon, and orange on the nose, with slight vanilla and a tart bitter dryness. 10% ABV.

The Holy Grail: Dubbels, Tripels, and Singles

THIS BEER'S FOR YOU IF YOU LIKE: MONTY PYTHON. COOL GLASSWARE. MONKS. TRADITION. COMPLEXITY. SECRET RECIPES. HIGH ALCOHOL. OLD WORLD TRADITION.

Although the Trappist name does represent a paramount level of quality and craftsmanship, it doesn't necessarily define a beer's style. They fall under the Trappist name because, as we said earlier, they are made by monks. Trappist beers come in many different styles, colors, and ABVs. All of the Trappist beers are bottom-fermenting ales and are famously higher in alcohol content than your average pint. But while Belgians obviously respect and honor their traditional brewing methods, they have also historically allowed a certain amount of creativity. They have taken some of the brewing traditions from the Trappist breweries and created their own versions of strong Belgian Ales, often called—you guessed it—Belgian Strong Ales. Many of these beers are so complex or unique that they can't simply be pigeonholed into a single style, thus the rather large umbrella-style name. (That's fine with us; we'd prefer to let our palates decide.) However, some Trappist Ales have developed a huge following and have been so highly lauded and so often imitated that a style has arisen from those particular beers. These are styles that tried to stay quite close to the flavor profiles of the Trappist Ales. Two such beer styles are Dubbels (Doubles) and Tripels (Trippels or Triples).

Again, like many things in the beer world, a lot of speculation surrounds how these beer styles got their names. Many people wonder what a Dubbel is and assume that it is a beer that is twice the strength of a mysterious original beer. Although it might be true that the term *Dubbel* was used to imply a certain relative beer strength, there's little proof that this is the true definition. Many people assert that a Dubbel is a beer that has been fermented twice, and while that is sometimes true, the term refers mainly to style parameters. A Dubbel is a dark, relatively high alcohol content beer (6.5% to 7% ABV) that is fairly malty and sweet, with a spice profile that can have notes of clove, nutmeg, allspice, and cardamom. Dubbels usually have secondary flavors of dark, Old World fruit, like figs and plums. Fruity yeast esters should definitely be present in the nose. These beers are typically medium bodied, and while they have the potential to be fairly cloying beers, the skill and quality of the style comes through in their dry finish and high effervescence level, which should lift the ale off the palate.

Tripels were made popular by the Westmalle Tripel, and this beer style, too, suffers the same misunderstandings that Dubbels have. People assume that *tripel* means that the beer is three times stronger than some mysterious original ale or that it is a beer that has been fermented three times. However, once again, it comes down to the style parameters. A Tripel is a complex, lighter colored beer that has distinct citrus and herbal characteristics. This relatively full-bodied beer should have slightly higher alcohol content than a Dubbel, ideally running between 7.5% and 9.5% ABV. Again, fruity esters should be present from the yeast strain used, and there should be a dry and mildly bitter hop presence along with sparkling carbonation to assist with a long but lean finish.

This does beg the question though, If there be a Dubbel and a Tripel, wherest is the Single? Does the Belgian Single exist? Is that the elusive "original" beer? The answer is yes, but it's very unlikely that you will get your hands on an authentic one (and if you do, call us). These

Single Abbey Ales are the beers that the monks make to drink themselves. It's often their table beer. Though these beers are much lighter bodied than their brethren, they still have complexity and spice. This is a great style for the monks, who could drink the ale with their meal and still concentrate on their meditations and their work. Many beers today are made in this style under many titles. Sometimes they are called Belgian Pale Ales, sometimes simply Belgian Ales, and sometimes (but *rarely*) called Single-Style Ales. The following are a few of these styles we praise:

- **WITKAP PATER SINGLE:** Brouwerij Slaghmuylder, Ninove, Belgium. Unfiltered earthy Single with light fruitiness like grapes and pears. Light spice and floral hop finish. 6% ABV.

- **LOST & FOUND ABBEY ALE:** The Lost Abbey, San Marcos, California. A great American version of a Dubbel. Dark and malty with notes of figs, plums, and dates. Nutty, with raisins and cloves. 7.5% ABV.

- **GOUDEN CAROLUS TRIPEL:** Brouwerij Het Anker, Mechelen, Belgium. Noble hops balance this clean and strong Tripel. Estery hints of tropical fruits, ginger, and honey. 9% ABV.

You're So Golden, Baby: Belgian Golden Ales

THIS BEER'S FOR YOU IF YOU LIKE: GOLD. YELLOW. A THICK HEAD. SPICE. A NICE DOSE OF ALCOHOL. SEQUELS.

We can't talk about the Devout without talking about another Belgian beer style that got its roots in the Trappist tradition but then became its own style because it was so often imitated. This delicious treat is known as a Strong Golden Ale. A famous example is Duvel, brewed by the Moortgat brewery. Duvel, which is Flemish for "devil," is one of the top-selling beers in Belgium and has become a beacon for many other

Beers to Drink Before You Die

It's good to have life goals. People often make a mental note of Wonders of the World they want to see with their own eyes before they shed this mortal coil. We all have our secret wish lists: things we want from love, places we want to visit, foods we want to try, people we'd like to meet. Beer lovers almost always have a secret list, or perhaps a documented public one, of the beers they must taste before they die. This list is often a guide for a life's Beer Journey. If one of the beers is available only in Germany, they must plan a trip there; if a beer is not available in the bottle except in one U.S. state, that will determine their next flight.

We, too, have a little list of beers we would highly recommend and beers we have yet to taste but are destined to meet. The list keeps growing, of course, as new beers are made every day, and this keeps things lively in the beer world. No one has ever finished their Beer Journey; no one can check everything off of the list. There are beers that are but an apple in some master brewer's eye at this moment but that someday will be added to lists by beer-geeks all over the globe. Here is our present offering of beers we won't miss out on in this lifetime, and you shouldn't either! We've picked these beers for a plethora of reasons; these beers are artful creations and all fall into our Art of Beer categories. Some of these beers are rare, some are unique, and some are quintessential—but the common ground for all of them is that they taste amazing!

The Abyss, Deschutes Brewing Company

Aecht Schlenkerla Rauchbier Marzen, Brauerei Heller-Trum

Allagash Curieux, Allagash Brewing Company

Allagash White, Allagash Brewing Company

Anchor Steam Beer, Anchor Brewing Company

The Angel's Share, The Lost Abbey

Ayinger Celebrator Doppelbock, Privatbrauerei Franz Inselkammer

Beer Geek Brunch, Mikkellar

Black Butte Porter, Deschutes Brewing Company

Black Chocolate Stout, Brooklyn Brewery

Black Orchard, The Bruery

Boon Oude Geuze Mariage Parfait, Brouwerij Boon

Cantillon Iris, Brasserie Cantillon

DeuS Brut de Flanders, Brouwerij Bosteels

Edgar's Ale, Craftsman Brewing Company

Firestone Twelve, Firestone Brewing Company

Girardin Faro 1882, Brouwerij Girardin

Girardin Gueuze 1882 Black Label, Brouwerij Girardin

Hitachino Nest Japanese Classic Ale, Kiuchi Brewery

La Roja, Jolly Pumpkin Artisan Ales

Lion Stout, Lion Brewery Ltd. / Ceylon

Maracaibo, Jolly Pumpkin Artisan Ales

Masala Mama India Pale Ale, Minneapolis Town Hall Brewery

Nogne Klin Kokos, Nogne o

Oaked Arrogant Bastard, Stone Brewing Company

Older Viscosity, Port Brewing Company

Old Rasputin Russian Imperial Stout, North Coast Brewing Company

Orval, Abbaye d'Orval

Pangaea, Dogfish Head Craft Brewed Ales

Pêche Mortel, Dieu du Ciel

Pliny the Elder, Russian River Brewing Company

Quelque Chose, Unibroue

Racer 5 IPA, Bear Republic Brewing Company

Reality Czeck, Moonlight Brewing Company

Red and White, Dogfish Head Craft Brewed Ales

Reissdorf Kölsch, Brauerei Heinrich Reissdorf

Rochefort Trappiste 10, Abbaye Rochefort

Rodenback Grand Cru, Brouwerij Rodenbach

continued

Saison DuPont, Brasserie DuPont

Samichlaus Bier, Eggenberg Castle Brewery

Schneider Aventinus, Weissbierbrauerei G. Schneider and Sohn

Smoked Black Lager, Craftsman Brewing Company

Tea-Bagged Furious IPA, Surly Brewing Company

Temptation, Russian River Brewing Company

breweries, defining an Abbey-style ale that is light golden to amber with big but rounded flavors. This beer style usually sports a huge cotton-like head and has soft tropical and stone fruit notes in the nose. The spice comes through in the end of this beer along with a welcoming warmth that comes from a high alcohol content. Here's some gold for you:

- DUVEL: Brouwerij Duvel Moortgat, Breendonk, Belgium. Green apples, bitter orange peel, lemon zest, and a spicy hoppiness help make this beer the defining example of this style. 8.5% ABV.

- DAMNATION: Russian River Brewing Company, Santa Rosa, California. A hoppier choice with notes of bananas, pear, and pepper. Nice dry finish. 7% ABV.

- DELIRIUM TREMENS: Brouwerij Huyghe, Melle, Belgium. Fruity, flowery, and sweet. Great balance, with orangey citrus rind, clove, and coriander notes. 9% ABV.

- DON DE DIEU: Unibroue, Chambly, Quebec, Canada. A great Belgian-style example and nod to the quintessential Golden Ale, Duvel. Bright and spicy, with good fruit and a boozy finish. 9% ABV.

* * *

You once were lost but now are found, and your Beer Journey has led you to this spiritual place. All the hard work that you've put in, drinking many different beers and learning about their history, is paying off in spades. You've experienced the ecstasy in a Trappist Ale. You've sought

Thiriez Xxtra, Brasserie Thiriez

Trappist Westvleteren 12, Brouwerij Westvleteren

Tripel White Sage, Craftsman Brewing Company

Vanilla Bean Aged Dark Lord RIS, Three Floyds Brewing Company

Weihenstephaner Hefeweissbier, Brauerei Weihenstephan

Wisconsin Belgian Red, New Glarus Brewing Company

out the quintessential Dunkelweizen. Look at you. You now have an appreciation for the beers that can touch your soul. You can now fully experience the rapture that these beautifully crafted beers bring to you. In the next couple of chapters, we'll show you how to further your devotion by deeply integrating beer into your life. Beer will become a part of you. Now, give thanks.

The Promiscuous

Do not cease to drink beer, to eat, to intoxicate thyself, to make love, and to celebrate the good days.

—EGYPTIAN PROVERB

Turn Down the Lights...

The following beers will make you want to slip out of your things and say howdy. They put the s-e-x into b-e-e-r. Even the most seasoned beer drinker can't help but salivate over these babies. These are beers you can have with the finest food at the fanciest restaurant with your best shoes on, and they will fit right in. Yes. We've given you a lot of great beer to choose from so far, now we're taking you to a whole new level of happiness. The beers in this chapter are rich and complex, nuanced, and complicated. They are beers that benefit from a seasoned and mature palate. If you are looking to impress a wine snob, these are your beers. If you are ready to take your date back for a little naked Twister, these are your beers. If you want to celebrate because you finally told your boss to stick it where the sun don't shine, these are your beers. With a bit of James Bond, a touch of Shaft, and a dose of Mrs. Robinson, these beers will make you feel especially debonair and like you've got some game.

Going All the Way: Bière de Champagne, or Bière Brut

 THIS BEER'S FOR YOU IF YOU LIKE: DIAMONDS. POPPING CORKS. CHAMPAGNE BUCKETS. DRESSING UP FOR THE EVENING. ROMANCE. COMPLEXITY. BUBBLES. HIGH ALCOHOL. HERBACEOUS FLAVORS. SUBTLE FRUIT.

When you think of a truly celebratory and sexy beverage, chances are you aren't thinking about beer. You're probably thinking about the other amazing bubbly drink known as Champagne. Mmmm...Champagne. We love Champagne. Now before you call us traitors, let us remind you that a love of wine and a love of beer are not mutually exclusive. We think that beer is just as sexy as Champagne. And never do we get closer to a ménage à trois with beer and Champagne than the Bière de Champagne. This relatively new style of beer, also known as Bière Brut, embraces tradition while at the same time being totally innovative in its use of that tradition. If you still have a friend who says, "I'm not a beer drinker," this might be your ace in the hole. Even the pickiest palate can appreciate the rarity and complexity of these impressive beers.

Now, we all know of another "Champagne of Beer," but that's not at all what we're talking about here. Bière de Champagne is brewed (primarily in Belgium) and then undergoes the *methodé champenoise*, or the "traditional finishing method" that makes Champagne so special. Once the beer is brewed, it is fermented for the third time in the bottle and undergoes a months-long conditioning to mature and mellow. The beer then goes through the remuage (riddling) process by which, over many weeks, the beer bottles are racked with their necks pointed downward, turned slightly every day, and angled farther downward to allow the yeast sediment to drop out of the beer and release from the sides of the bottle. This process continues until the bottle is completely vertical and all of the yeast is collected in the neck. The final process of the method happens when the beer experiences dégorgement (disgorging). In this part of the process, the neck of the bottle is frozen, and the yeast is expunged by using the pressure contained in the bottle. What is left is a sparkling, clear, highly alcoholic, and conditioned beer. Some of these beers are actually shipped to the Champagne region of France for this special treatment.

These beers are delicate yet still rich and complex, spicy with a dusting of cardamom and coriander. This style is relatively aromatic, wonderfully effervescent, and, like Champagne, highly carbonated. Most of these beers are surprisingly high in alcohol, ranging from 10% to 14% ABV. However, the carbonation is so high and the bottle conditioning so refined that it's sometimes difficult to detect the ABV in these keenly balanced beers. Bière de Champagne usually comes in 750-milliliter Champagne bottles, complete with a fancy cork and cage enclosure (what do you think of beer now?). Like fine Champagne, these beers are a little pricier than other beers, sometimes running up near $50 a bottle in restaurants. But if you think about it, these beers are still cheaper than most of the great Champagnes of the world, and they're well worth it. Trust us. This beer style is especially good as an aperitif or as a tool of seduction.

Note: Be careful when you open these beers because they can overflow quite easily, just like real Champagne.

Here are some highly regarded Bières de Champagne:

○ **DEUS (BRUT DES FLANDRES):** Brouwerij Bosteels, Buggenhout, Belgium. Light straw colored with huge carbonation. Spicy and peppery with fruity notes of apricots, pears, and ginger. You'll definitely recognize the Belgian yeast qualities: a slight Orval-ian earthy funk. There's also some good lemon rind on the dry finish. In our opinion, an excellent beer. 11.5% ABV.

○ **MALHEUR BIÈRE BRUT (BRUT RESERVE):** Brouwerij de Landtsheer, Buggenhout, Belgium. Floral, with hints of citrus and vanilla. Try to find the Michael Jackson Commemorative Selection 2006. 11% ABV.

○ **MALHEUR BRUT NOIR:** Brouwerij de Landtsheer, Buggenhout, Belgium. A dark version of this great style. Black chocolate, malty sweet with dark Old World fruits: cherry, plum, and figs. 12% ABV.

○ **SCALDIS PRESTIGE (BUSH PRESTIGE):** Brasserie Dubuisson Frères, Pipaix, Belgium. Called Bush Prestige in Europe; matures for six months in oak barrels, creating woody tannins, honey, and malty whisky qualities. 13% ABV.

Mature Beer Fetish: Vintage and Barrel-Aged Beers

Barrel (or cask) aging is an old practice in beer. It harkens back to the days before stainless-steel and aluminum, before kegerators and top-of-the-line tap systems. In those days, wooden barrels were the only option, and brewers weren't always happy with the flavors an oak barrel would impart. The sour yeasts that would sometimes grow on the wood were an enemy to the ale and caused headaches for many a brewer. The unsanitary conditions of the time made barrel-aging a bit more difficult and risky. As the Lambic makers were loving the funk of the barrel in their beer, brewers of other styles were frustrated to find their brews turning sour and their precious ales dumped out into the street. Some

Be Proud of Your Cans

There's nothing better than cracking open a nice can of craft beer! Wait...did we just say "can" of beer? You bet your bubkes we did.

Though craft beer drinkers have been railing against the can as a symbol of icky beer for years, some craft brewers are now putting their beer in cans. But don't worry, these aren't the cans of old. New beer cans have a lining that prevents any kind of tinny, metallic flavor from getting into your favorite beverage. Also, remember that skunkiness in a beer comes from a chemical reaction that takes place when *light* strikes your beer. That's why most of the great beers in the world come in very dark bottles. Imagine how much more your beer is protected if it's in a can.

Most people are under the misconception that if you get your beer in a can you have to drink it from said can. But why is that the case? We wouldn't drink a Tripel Karmeliet out of the bottle just because it came in a bottle, so why would we drink a quality craft beer out of a can just because it arrived in one? Also, if you're concerned about the rising costs of craft beer, a brewery's use of cans is one way to keep the costs down because cans are lighter to carry, easier to ship, and virtually unbreakable. The environmental benefits are big because

even lined their wooden barrels with pitch (or resin), creating a seal that kept the beer from touching the wood and gaining any woody flavors.

One man's trash...Today craft beer has seen a huge resurgence of barrel-aged brews. The popularity of barrel-aging has been spearheaded by those brewers who are excited by the risks involved and seek the unique flavors wood can impart. They know it may take several batches before they figure out how best to age their beer. This often involves mixing different vintages of aging ale in the same way that Belgian brewers mix cans are easily recycled—and think about it, wouldn't it be great to have awesome craft beer on most major airlines or on the golf course, or any place else where glass is considered a weapon? Wouldn't that be delightful? Let's all embrace our cans. Here are some of our favorite canned beers:

- **MAUI COCONUT PORTER:** Maui Brewing Company, Lahaina, Hawaii. A unique Porter with a nice dose of coconut. Notes of chocolate and vanilla. Not too sweet but definitely not bitter; screams for surf and sand. 5.5% ABV.
- **GORDON:** Oskar Blues Grill & Brewery, Lyons, Colorado. An American Double IPA that packs a punch. Nice malty sweetness with notes of caramel and a big balance of bitter hops. 8.7% ABV.
- **FURIOUS:** Surly Brewing Company, Brooklyn Center, Minnesota. An American IPA with sweet toffee, citrus, and a balance of hops. Drinkable but big in flavor. 6.2% ABV.
- **ROYAL WEISSE ALE:** Sly Fox Brewing Company, Royersford, Pennyslvania. Sweet and tart with notes of citrus and spice, low in bitterness. 5.4% ABV.

different-aged Lambics to create the perfect Gueuze. Barrel-aging is a commitment; it takes space, money, patience (sometimes you have to dump your beer and start all over again), and a watchful eye.

So what happens to a beer aged in a barrel? The wood is porous (as is a cork in bottle-aging) and lets in a small amount of oxygen. This is possible because the alcohol (or sometimes just water in the beer) evaporates slightly. This evaporated part is poetically known as the "angels' share" (which, incidentally, is the name of a rare and beloved Belgian-style ale from the brewery Lost Abbey out of California). As this oxidation happens, chemicals are created that change the flavor of the beer. In beers that don't benefit from aging, like lighter low-alcohol beers, oxidation can create a wet-cardboard flavor. In bigger, high-alcohol beers, oxidation can bring about a sherry-like flavor or sometimes a metallic flavor. The sherry flavor can be a nice addition to certain beers but may not be great in others. It's a bit of a crapshoot sometimes. The sharp flavors of a hoppy or sour beer also tend to dull during this process, just as the sharp flavors of fruit or drying tannins can mellow out when bottle-aging wine.

Barrels used for aging beer tend to be oak and are often barrels that have been used to age bourbon or whisky, giving the beer flavors from these liquors and sometimes bumping up the alcohol percentage because of remnants of alcohol in the wood. Some daring breweries, like Russian River from California, make use of wine barrels that have been used for Chardonnay, Cabernet, or Pinot Noir, hoping to add a vinous complexity to their beer. Although other woods have been used, like cedar and chestnut, oak seems to be the easiest to work with and the most dominant in aging.

Barrel flavors are hard to control because one barrel may have different characteristics from the next. And if a barrel is used once to age a beer, then its second aging will often be dulled. For example, if the barrel had been used to age bourbon, then the second time it is used for beer aging it usually won't have the same amount of bourbon flavors to offer. So if consistency is desired, brewers must mix batches from various barrels or age in freshly used barrels every time. This can be costly and involves a lot of tasting and perfecting, which is often why barrel-aged beers fetch a higher price in liquor stores, craft beer bars, and restaurants. Most barrel-aged beers will say so on the label, as this is a point of pride for the brewer. Some will even tell you what kind of barrel was used and for how long; others will let you in on how many beers were blended together to create a big brew, such as a Barleywine. If you haven't had a barrel-aged beer, get on it; these are often remarkable beers that again expand your concept of what craft beer can offer.

Here are some of our favorite barrel-aged brews:

- **FIRESTONE XII:** Firestone Walker Brewing Company, Paso Robles, California. An American Strong Ale made from a blend of several different barrel-aged beers made by the brewery. Complex and bourbon-like, with smoke and earth and leather and chocolate— just about everything. 12% ABV.

- **PALO SANTO MARRON:** Dogfish Head Craft Brewery, Milton, Delaware. Famous for being aged in Palo Santo wood. An American Brown Ale with smoky notes and sweet nutty malt and hints of dark fruit. 12% ABV.

- **ALLAGASH CURIEUX:** Allagash Brewing Company, Portland, Maine. A Belgian-style Tripel aged in Jim Beam bourbon barrels; wood and vanilla, some fruit and spice. 11% ABV.

- **OAKED ARROGANT BASTARD:** Stone Brewing Company, Escondido, California. The oaked version of this classic American Strong Ale has a more nuanced, oaky flavor that adds a nice depth of character and tannic qualities. 7.2% ABV.

- **RUSSIAN RIVER CONSECRATION:** Russian River Brewing Company, Santa Rosa, California. A sour American Wild Ale aged for six months in Cabernet Sauvignon barrels; currants added to the brewing process. Earthy, funky, and sour; complex dark fruit profile. 10.5% ABV.

Once You Go Black

As we mentioned when talking about Porters and Stouts, dark beer suffers from a lot of stereotypes, and people new to beer seem to shy away from the darker brew. We've pointed out some dark beers that are much lighter in body and flavor than one would expect (see Chapters

4 and 5)—beers that aren't so high in alcohol and that are easy enough for a new craft beer drinker to get into. These are *not* those beers. Imperial Stouts and Smoked beers are definitely on the bigger side, not always because of alcohol content but because of a bold flavor profile. These are beers that benefit from having a bit of beer knowledge under your belt, simply so you can appreciate their complexity instead of being put off by their intensity. Graduating to a level in your Beer Journey where you can appreciate these beers is exciting, even titillating. These are beers that grab your attention and dominate your palate (if you're into that sort of thing).

Smoke Gets in Your Beer: Sexy Smoked Beers

THIS BEER'S FOR YOU IF YOU LIKE: BACON. BBQ. LAPSANG SOUCHONG TEA. WOOD FIRES. PEATY SCOTCH. BOLD FLAVOR. LOW HOPS.

On the more eccentric side of beer styles are smoked beers. They may even be the most fetishistic of this chapter due to their unusual flavor. These are beers made from malt that has been smoked over a flame (see, kinky!). Historically, in the absence of a kiln, malt was often dried in the sun, but aside from that, drying malt over an open flame was the only option. This of course produced smoke, which seeped into and flavored the malt. Smoked beers often have a sweetness underneath the smoke, which can be chocolaty and nutty, or a bit spicy. These beers tend to have a hop presence that dries out that sweetness, but the hops are not usually present as a strong flavor, and smoked beers are therefore typically low in bitterness.

The most famous smoked beer is the Rauchbier. Rauchbier (*rauch* means "smoke" in German) is a German style, primarily out of Bamberg, that is made from malt that has been smoked over an open flame using beechwood logs. (The malt is often actually dried in a kiln, but with the logs and flame underneath.) Rauchbiers range anywhere from 4% to 7% ABV and have such a pronounced smokiness that people often compare the taste to bacon or smoked meat. Rauchbiers are brewed in the sub-styles of Marzens (toasty seasonal lagers), Weizens (wheat beer), and Urbocks ("original Bock" beer), using the lager or ale process, depending on the style. Schlenkerla, one of the most famous breweries in Bamberg, even makes a Helles that has a touch of smoke due solely to its proximity to the smoking area during the brewing process. After the Rauchbiers at Schlenkerla are brewed, they are then matured in a 700-year-old cellar for six to eight weeks, allowing the smoke to mellow a touch. The beer is served at the brewery straight from oak barrels, keeping the history and tradition alive. Though people often taste a Rauchbier and exclaim, "It's good, but I couldn't drink a whole glass of it," Schlenkerla brewery advises drinking two or three, claiming that once the taste buds grow accustomed to the smoke, the beer gets exponentially yummier. (We can vouch for that!)

Besides Rauchbier, American brewers make their own smoked beers, using smoked malts for Porters, Stouts, Brown Ales, American Lagers, Scotch Ale, and so on. Experiments with smoke can be a thrilling process for craft brewers who want that little something special in their brew.

Beer with smoky flavors can be a challenge to the palate but, we think, a good challenge. After all, you're moving up in the beer world; time to face challenges head-on. A small percentage of people are predisposed to loving smoky flavors; others appreciate sitting round a campfire but don't like smoky flavors in their food and drink. So this style will shock the hell out of many of you, but keep an open mind; there is a time and place for every style of beer. The next time you serve BBQ or any smoked meat, try pairing it with some smoked beer, and dazzle your taste buds with these fine choices:

CRAFTSMAN SMOKED BLACK LAGER: Craftsman Brewery, Pasadena, California. Crisp, smoky, well-balanced, light body, roasted coffee, and ash. 5.2% ABV.

- **AECHT SCHLENKERLA RAUCHBIER URBOCK:** Brauerei Heller-Trum, Bamberg, Germany. Smells like a fireplace, huge smoke, touch of caramel, dry on the end. 6.6% ABV.

- **AECHT SCHLENKERLA RAUCHBIER MARZEN:** Brauerei Heller-Trum, Bamberg, Germany. Smells like smoked ham, bit of sweetness, touch of tangy hops, and huge smoke all around. 5.4% ABV.

- **ALASKAN SMOKED PORTER:** Alaskan Brewing Company, Juneau, Alaska. Smells like bacon, super smoky, sweet malt, best when aged awhile. 6.5% ABV.

Российский Императорский Стаут:
Russian Imperial Stout

THIS BEER'S FOR YOU IF YOU LIKE: RUSSIAN CZARS. BORSCHT. SHOTS OF ESPRESSO. 80% CACAO CHOCOLATE. HIGH ALCOHOL. BIG FURRY HATS. AN EXTRA-BITTER BITE. *DR. ZHIVAGO.*

The creation of the Russian Imperial Stout (RIS) is similar to that of the India Pale Ale. The main legend is that Peter the Great was a fan of the popular Porters (also called Stouts, see Chapter 4) he had tasted in England, but when he had them shipped to Russia, many had gone bad (embarrassing at any beer party!). The story goes that London's Barclay Brewery added hops to its Porter and upped the alcohol content to help it last the journey, et voilà—Russian Imperial Stout was born. The hops lent their preservative quality and added a higher bitterness to the dark Stout. The style supposedly became quite popular in the Russian court. Apparently, Catherine the Great became a devoted RIS drinker and shared pints with her court (this should shatter the myth that women don't like strong dark beers; if it's good enough for an empress, ladies...).

Russian Imperial Stouts have become a favorite style of the craft beer world. The high alcohol and hops support a variety of intense flavors and can be a great palate for brewers who want to get extreme. The flavors of an RIS often conjure up notes of bitter, strong espresso, and bitter, dark chocolate. More complex RISs can boast notes of dried fruit, ash, rum, vanilla, and Port. The Port or rum-like and vanilla qualities come out especially in RISs that are aged in barrels. The high alcohol makes these beers perfect for aging and especially for barrel-aging, which can also lend an oaky quality to the ale. Their alcohol can be anywhere from 7% to 14%, making them a great nightcap. Beer-geeks get all hot and heavy about extra-special RISs, especially those who seek out the biggest, boldest, most extreme beers.

There is nothing quite like a complex Russian Imperial. It really does upend any preconceived notions about beer's boundaries. Every sip can bring out a new level of depth. Barrel-aged RISs can be as fine as a great bourbon or Scotch and are fantastic with a cigar. And RISs can take on a whole new life on creamer faucets; the weight on the tongue goes perfectly with the deep bitter chocolate and coffee notes of a typical RIS, sometimes smoothing out a bit of the bitterness. At the end of the evening, sip on one of these and soak up the dark depths:

- **OLD RASPUTIN RUSSIAN IMPERIAL STOUT:** North Coast Brewing Company, Fort Bragg, California. One of our favorite brews; deep bitter espresso and dark, dark chocolate. A perfect nightcap, and great poured over vanilla bean gelato. 9% ABV.

- **THE ABYSS:** Deschutes Brewing Company, Bend, Oregon. A highly sought-after RIS, seasonal and rare. Aged in French oak bourbon barrels; notes of molasses, licorice, and dark fruit. 11% ABV.

- **ALESMITH SPEEDWAY STOUT:** AleSmith Brewing Company, San Diego, California. An intensely dark stout brewed with a ton of rich coffee. Dark chocolate notes with a rich toasted caramel. There is a barrel-aged version that is rare and adds notes of oak and bourbon. 12% ABV.

Imperial Everything! It's Good to Be King

The Russian Imperial Stout had such a fancy name, everyone wanted to get a piece of the crown. *Imperial* in the RIS came to refer not only to the court that loved to drink it but also to the higher bitterness and alcohol that defined and differentiated this Stout. Brewers today have stolen that word and applied its flavor associations to a variety of other styles, usually increasing the hops and alcohol and perhaps overall intensity of the beer. Imperial IPA, Imperial Porter, Imperial Pilsner, Imperial Oktoberfest, Imperial Pale Ale; these styles are popping up on labels at many craft breweries that want to get into the extreme beer world. Some breweries feel that they have to provide *at least one* extreme beer just to get themselves noticed in the craft beer world, and one way to do that is to take a popular Pilsner or Porter and make it a double, so to speak.

So if you see "Imperial" on the label, you can expect a beer that is more intense and higher in alcohol than the original style. It seems logical; after all, it was the kings and queens and emperors who loved excess. Double the diamonds, double the furs, double the feast, double the lovers, so why not double the beer and christen it Imperial?

THREE FLOYDS DARK LORD RUSSIAN IMPERIAL STOUT: Three Floyds Brewing Company, Munster, Indiana. Dark and oily, chocolate, vanilla and bourbon notes. Cherry and blackberry notes; alcohol is fairly well hidden. 13% ABV.

Does Size Matter? High-Alcohol-Content Big Beers

Yes. Yes, size matters. (Sorry, boys.)

It especially matters when you hit the Barleywine Festival a little too hard and do something that requires the walk of shame back to your apartment the next morning. Or when you don't know what the hell a Quadrupel is and down a whole 750-milliliter bottle at the pub, fueling your desire to stand on top of the bar and offer your best rendition of "Don't Get Around Much Anymore" to a room full of confused patrons. Barleywines are huge beers, usually with super-malty flavor profiles and sometimes sky-high alcohol contents. The following big beers must be consumed with caution and reverence. Sipping is key, not gulping. Even when you are careful, they can cause an embarrassing beer incident, but we know you can handle it...right?

Beer Goggles: Is It a Wine or a Beer?
Barleywine

THIS BEER'S FOR YOU IF YOU LIKE: OLD ENGLISH ALES. ANTIQUES. DRIED FRUIT. SIPPING. WINTER. HIGH ALCOHOL. PORT. WOODEN BARRELS. FESTIVALS.

There are some people who claim that Barleywine was named such because its ABV was so high that brewers felt that they should warn their customers. Other people say that the word *Barleywine* originated in the 18th and 19th centuries in England, apparently because England was so often at war with France that the consumption of French wine was considered unpatriotic in England (think "freedom fries"), so the upper classes called their strong ales Barleywines and drank them instead of the popular French Claret. Obviously Barleywines are not actually wine, because they are not made from fruit but from malted grains. This is why Americans call them Barleywine-style ales. A long name perhaps, but a bit more accurate. Barleywines are similar to what the British called Old Ale (Old Ale was not quite as high in alcohol as Barleywines and never had the hop bitterness that some Barleywines have). These ales have always been the strongest of the English ales and were often aged and saved for a special occasion or the holidays.

Barleywines are made with a high amount of malt, usually a pale malt, which is boiled for a long time, allowing it to reduce and caramelize and turn a deeper color. This high dose of malt leads to a high ABV, anywhere from 8% to 14%, and a rich sweet flavor. Because of this intensity, Barleywines are meant to be sipped slowly, like a liqueur. The typical Barleywine flavors are those of dried fruit or coffee and chocolate, with an intensely sticky mouthfeel and warm alcohol presence. They can be super hoppy or not hoppy at all; in England, the Barleywines tend to be less hoppy compared to the American beers, which typically tend to be well hopped. You may see some American-made Barleywines described as English-style, referring to the more traditional, lower hop presence.

Because of the high alcohol content and big flavor, Barleywines benefit from aging in barrels, and this common old English practice continues today. The aging can help mellow out the intensity and add dryness, which comes from the tannins in the wood barrels. If not aged in wood, simply the passage of time helps mellow these ales, just as it does for wine. Beer enthusiasts love to taste different vintages of Barleywine from the same producer, noting how the recipes for each year vary and how time can make one more nuanced than the other. These ales are released in the winter, which makes sense; nothing better than a rich Barleywine to warm you up in the cooler months. Here are some recent favorites:

- **BIG WOODY**: Glacier Brewhouse, Anchorage, Alaska. Intense English malt and fruit. Aged in Jim Beam and Napa Valley wine barrels for a year. 10.75% ABV.

- **ARCTIC DEVIL**: Midnight Sun Brewing, Anchorage, Alaska. English-style Barleywine aged in Port and whisky barrels; rich brown sugar, rum, oak, and fig. 13.2% ABV.

- **LOWER DA BOOM**: 21st Amendment Brewery, San Francisco, California. Sweet toffee, port, and caramel, with some bitter hops. 10.5% ABV.

- **SIERRA NEVADA BIGFOOT**: Sierra Nevada, Chico, California. An American-style Barleywine. Rich dark fruit and a huge bang of big, wet hops. 9.6% ABV.

Nice Quads: Quadrupels

THIS BEER'S FOR YOU IF YOU LIKE: LEG CURLS. HIGH ALCOHOL. BIG FLAVORS. STEROIDS. DEBATING. FORGETTING LAST NIGHT. VARIETY.

To us, a Quadrupel is sort of like a double-double Abbey Ale. It's a name sometimes given to super-strong Trappist, Abbey, and Abbey-style ales. They are the extreme beer of the Belgians, big and burly, fruity and full of spirit. Many beers are now calling themselves Quadrupel to make it known that they are brewed in the style of the Belgian Trappist beers, but bigger. There is much debate as to whether a Quadrupel is actually a true beer style. The Beer Judges Certification Program doesn't recognize the Quadrupel as a style, instead relegating many of these beers to a Belgian Strong Ale or Belgian Specialty Ale category. Official beer style or not, if you hear the word *quadrupel*, expect a super-malty and viscous sweet beer with notes of cherries, plums, figs, and sometimes chocolate, with lots of heat in the exhaust. The ABV on these Belgian bad boys usually *starts* at 10%, so strap yourself in and enjoy the ride. Check out these Quads:

- **PANNEPOT OLD FISHERMAN'S ALE:** De Struise Brouwers, De Panne, Belgium. Maple syrup, molasses, rum, toffee, and ginger highlight this extraordinary ale named after the fishing boats of De Panne. 10% ABV.

- **THREE PHILOSOPHERS BELGIAN STYLE BLEND:** Brewery Ommegang, Cooperstown, New York. Interesting, with warm dense chocolate notes. Made with tart and juicy cherry Lambic. 9.8% ABV.

- **KONINGSHOEVEN QUADRUPEL TRAPPIST ALE (ALSO BREWED AS LA TRAPPE QUADRUPEL):** Bierbrouwerij de Koningshoeven, Berkel-Enschot, The Netherlands. This is the beer that supposedly coined the Quadrupel name. Raisin, cranberry, and clove, with bananas on the nose and a shot of whisky at the finish. 10% ABV.

It Hurts So Good: Sour Beers

There comes a time in every beer drinker's life when you break through a beer barrier. A time when you drink a beer that your mother never would. A time when you try a beer that makes you stop after your first sip and go, "Whoa...is this good or bad? Is this the best beer I've had in my life or has something gone terribly wrong? Is this even beer?" Yes, we're talking about sour beers here, folks. Sour beers are at once complex and acerbic and wonderfully and painfully tart. It's the kind of pain that fulfills your desires and keeps you coming back for more. If a Pilsner is the nice comfortable down pillow of the beer world, sour beer is the leather whip. So coordinate your safe word with your respective craft beer drinking partner(s), and let's start experimenting with sour beers that hurt oh so good.

Ich Bin Ein Berliner Weisse

THIS BEER'S FOR YOU IF YOU LIKE: SHARP PINOT GRIGIO. RAINBOW SNOW CONES. FRUITY ESTERS. CHAMPAGNE. LOW ALCOHOL.

To ease you into sour beers, the first style we're going to talk about is the light and refreshing beer local to the city of Berlin called (what else?) Berliner Weisse. As the *Weisse* in the name suggests, the majority of this beer style's malt source comes from wheat, so this beer is technically classified as a wheat beer (see Chapter 3). However, because the flavor profile of this beer is so different from that of a typical wheat, we felt that it actually belonged in the sour beer section.

Berliner Weisse beers are known throughout Germany as summer refreshers and thirst quenchers. They are lemony and super light bodied, with an ABV usually around 3% or even less. However, in addition to using normal ale top fermentation, Berliner Weisse brewers also use a lactic bacterial fermentation called *Lactobacillus* (see Chapter 9), which gives this beer style a flavor punch with a sizzle of puckering sour lactic acidity, much like the zing found in wine from malic acid. In addition to the acidity, these beers are effervescent and super dry, and have virtually no hop bitterness.

Because these beers are distinctly sour, Berliner Weisse is usually served with one of two sweet syrups: Waldmeister or Himbeer. Waldmeister is made from an herb called woodruff (scientific name *Galium odoratum*), which is super grassy and lemony with notes of anise and vanilla. Himbeer is a raspberry syrup (the *beer* means "berry," not beer, in this instance). Sometimes other syrups, fruits, wines, and liqueurs will also be used to flavor Berliner Weisse, the most popular of these being Kümmel, which is a clear sweet-flavored liqueur made with cumin, caraway seed, and fennel.

But wait just a minute. Didn't we say earlier that the Germans have a purity law governing their beer that forbids brewers from adding any fruit or herbs to the brewing process? Well, it's true. Brewers can't add these syrups to Berliner Weisse, but bartenders, customers, and drinkers can. Another unusual aspect about this beer is how it's served in Germany. This beer is typically poured into a big bowl or saucer-like chalice and (get this) sucked through a straw.

Although we like the use of syrup, as it harkens back to the use of gruit in Witbiers (see Chapter 3), we also like to have a dry, clean Berliner Weisse without the syrup. In Germany, as a visitor, it's almost impossible to get this beer served without the syrup, and in America, it's almost impossible to find a Berlin-style wheat (Berliner Weisse made outside of Berlin) with syrup. Either way, it's a delicious step toward getting your feet wet in the world of sour beer. Here are some that we dig:

TELEGRAPH RESERVE WHEAT ALE: Telegraph Brewing Company, Santa Barbara, California. Uses *Lactobacillus* and *Brettanomyces*. Brewed with lemon verbena. 5% ABV.

1809 (BERLINER-STYLE WEISSE): Brauerei Weihenstephan, Freising, Germany. Lots of lemon, green apple, and grapefruit. A citrusy clean unfiltered wheat with a super-dry finish and Champagne-like carbonation. 5% ABV.

CRAFTSMAN BERLINER WEISSE: Craftsman Brewing Company, Pasadena, California. Light bodied, refreshing, crisp with bright lemon notes and just a touch of barny funk. But just a touch. 3.5% ABV.

I Feel Gueuze, I Knew That I Would

THIS BEER'S FOR YOU IF YOU LIKE: SOUR CANDY. GREEK YOGURT. FUNKY CHEESE. OLD WOODEN BARRELS. JAMES BROWN. A BLEND OF THE OLD AND NEW.

We're about to get a little James Brown funky all up in here. And we mean funky. Why? Because the next beer style we're offering you is just about the funkiest beer around. It's a little beer style called Gueuze. This super-sour style has been called "barnyard," which we like to call funky. Gueuze is a pale, dry, and obscenely complex beer, and it's not for the faint of heart. This beer is definitely an acquired taste and will make a decision maker out of you because it evokes either love or hate. We are big fans of this style. But we were also the kind of kids who started our own "Lemon Club" in grade school, whose initiation rite was to bite into a big wedge of lemon without making a face. But we digress.

Just like the Berliner Weisse is technically in the "wrong" style category in this book by virtue of it being a wheat beer, a Gueuze should actually be in the Lambic category because this style of beer is a blend of unfruited mature Lambic (usually one to three years old) and young Lambic (possibly as young as five months old). Gueuzes are bracingly tart, stunningly sour, acridly dry, and medium bodied, usually running between 4% and 6% ABV. They are citrusy, woody, herbal, earthy, moldy, and spicy like the best stinky cheese. And unlike any other style, these beers bring the farmhouse funk with a vengeance. This beer would have James Brown shouting, "Haaaaaaaaay!"

Note: There is a pronunciation debate regarding this beer. When we asked some French winemakers how to pronounce it, they said "GOOZE." However, we've also learned that the Dutch pronunciation of the word is something closer to "GER-ZER." Here are some Gueuzes you can drink to get your funk on:

- **LINDEMANS GUEUZE:** Brouwerij Lindemans, Vlezenbeek, Belgium. Known for making very sweet Lambics, this beer is a great starter Gueuze. Not too assaulting, super dry, like a tart Champagne with brief fruit and citrus notes. 4% ABV.

- **CANTILLON LOU PEPE GUEUZE:** Brasserie Cantillon, Brussels. A blend of one-, two-, and three-year-old Lambics. A copper orange Gueuze with grassy herbaceousness and an acidity more reminiscent of vinegar than Champagne. A more challenging Gueuze than the Lindemans. 5% ABV.

- **GIRARDIN 1882 BLACK LABEL:** Brouwerij Girardin, Sint Ulriks-Kapelle, Belgium. Our favorite Gueuze. A funk bomb on the nose with citrus, apricot, pear. Super barnyard sour with good acidity, with green grapes and apples in the finish. 5% ABV.

Sweet and Sour Sauced: Flanders Red Ale

THIS BEER'S FOR YOU IF YOU LIKE: WINES FROM TUSCANY. SOUR BLACK CHERRIES. WONTON DIPPING SAUCE. OAK BARRELS. BALSAMIC VINEGAR.

If you find you like the sour beers, it's time to try the Flanders Red Ale. Also called Belgian Red Ale, Flemish Red, or Old Red Ale, this style of ale hails from the western Flanders region of Belgium and uses the same kind of *Lactobacillus* that produces the sour flavors in some of the other sour beers. However, Flanders Red Ale distinguishes itself by using certain red, or Vienna, malts. The beer is matured, oftentimes for over a year, in large oak barrels, or tuns. It is this practice combined with the darker malts that creates the vinegar-like quality that gives Flanders Reds their exceptionally unique sweet-and-sour characteristics.

Because younger and older versions of Flanders Red are blended, similar to a Gueuze, and the permeating flavors are of dark fruits like cherries, prunes, and raisins, this beer style has prominent vinous or winey qualities, which has drawn comparisons to a Super Tuscan (a dense and tannic Italian red wine). Even though these Old Red Ales have a wide ABV range (4% to 8%) and can be anywhere from moderately to massively sour, you'll know a Flanders Red Ale when you see it and taste it. Try one of these great examples:

- **RODENBACH:** Brouwerij Rodenbach, Roeselare, Belgium. Brewed since 1836, this beer is a blend of 75% young beer and 25% aged beer. This deep, dark red-brown ale is fruity, slatey, and oaky, with a puckering tartness. 5% ABV.

- **DUCHESSE DE BOURGOGNE:** Brouwerij Verhaeghe, Vichte, Belgium. Known as the Burgundy of Belgium; sour cherry ale, deliciously layered. A blend of 8- and 18-month-old ales. 6.2% ABV.

- **LA FOLIE:** New Belgium Brewing Company, Fort Collins, Colorado. An American example, wood-aged and conditioned in French oak; earthy with sour apple acid and a dry finish. 6% ABV.

Born to Be Wild: American Wild Ale

THIS BEER'S FOR YOU IF YOU LIKE: RIDING AMERICAN HOGS ON THE OPEN HIGHWAY. INNOVATION. EXPERIMENTATION. A RENEGADE SPIRIT. RARE BEERS. LIMITED QUANTITIES AND NUMBERED BOTTLES.

Some innovative American brewers have headed out on the highway in pursuit of the American Wild Ale (AWA). These are American-made beer styles that might have used any kind of wild fermentation to achieve their flavor. They also sometimes use barrel-aging (see Chapter 6) and other advanced souring techniques (see Chapter 9). These beers are definitely influenced by Belgian ales and can be similar in style to any sour beer. But because sour beer styles like Lambics, Gueuze, and Berliner Weisse traditionally carry the style name that reflects their region of origin and specific ingredients, many American-made sour beers are grouped into a vaguely defined category called American Wild Ales.

So why, then, do we call La Folie (made in Colorado) a Belgian-style Flanders Red instead of an American Wild Ale? What's the difference? Well, from what we have gleaned in tasting these beers, what the beer is called and how it's classified into a style really comes down to the beer's trueness to a particular style. La Folie, for instance, is brewed as a very true Flanders Red style, with little variation from the traditional and quintessential style parameters. American Wild Ales, in contrast, have a tendency to be a bit more experimental and usually have more intense flavors and higher alcohol contents, ranging anywhere from 6% to 12% ABV.

American Wild Ales are an exciting trend in the American craft world. With this style, the artist that exists in every craft brewer can come out to play. Many of these experimental beers are released in limited amounts (sometimes just once a year) and, because of their deliciousness and their rarity, have developed a cult-like following. We know—we're cult members! Try some of our favorite AWAs that get our motors runnin':

- **LA ROJA:** Jolly Pumpkin Artisan Ales, Dexter, Michigan. Amber AWA, brewed in the Flanders tradition. Earthy and funky with notes of caramel. The barrel-aging brings out the sour fruit notes. Aged from 2 to 10 months. 7.2% ABV.

- **RUSSIAN RIVER CONSECRATION:** Russian River Brewing Company, Santa Rosa, California. This sour AWA is aged for six months in Cabernet Sauvignon barrels; currants added to the brewing process. Earthy, funky, sour, complex dark fruit profile. 10.5% ABV.

 PISSA MAUVAIS: Cambridge Brewing Company, Cambridge, Massachusetts. Named for the famed "wicked pissah" expletive uttered proudly by many a Bostonian. Medium bodied and tasty, with smoky, toasty, woody notes and a sour finish. 7% ABV.

Beers That Bite Back

You thought sour was serious? Well, get ready to rumble, because these bitter beers will teach your tongue a thing or two. If you are into hops in a big way, these will be your good friends on your Beer Journey. Careful about sharing these babies with neophytes, though; they might not be ready yet. An über-bitter beer can be a rude awakening to someone who is not well-adjusted to the hop experience. But if you feel it's time, and if you think you are ready, then go ahead and take the plunge into these frisky ales, and feel the wicked pleasure in the punch of hops.

A Hoppy Ending: American IPAs, Double IPAS, and American Strong Ales

THIS BEER'S FOR YOU IF YOU LIKE: BITTER DRINKS. BITTERNESS. BEING BITTER. HOPS. MORE HOPS. HOP-HEADS. HIGH ALCOHOL. THE RED, WHITE, AND BLUE. BOLD MOVES. AND DID WE MENTION BITTERNESS?

As we told you in Chapter 4, British IPAs and Bitters are not nearly as bitter as our American-style IPAs. American IPAs tend to boast a big hop profile. Perhaps this is because we Americans turn the rock 'n' roll way up; we add extra sauce to everything, we can throw a flashy half-time show like nobody else, and our fireworks are always bigger than theirs. Whatever the case, extreme craft beers seem to be much more popular in America than anywhere else, and hoppy beers are a huge part of that genre.

Once hop lovers developed a taste for big IPAs, they wanted more; enter the Double IPA (often called Imperial IPA; see page 148). An all-American invention, a Double IPA boasts nearly double the hops and alcohol of an IPA. These beers are also bigger and much more bitter, offering an intense experience all around. The hop flavor profile can vary depending on the hops: grapefruit, grass, apricot, marijuana, and so on. Some Double IPAs overdose on just a couple different kinds of hops, whereas others use three or more different varieties. The secondary flavor behind the hops in a Double IPA varies, from rich caramel to deep toffee to bold fruit. Though this can be considered a rather lopsided style, some Double IPAs are more balanced than others. Some flow seamlessly between bitterness and toffee sweetness or fruit; others can be all hops and no balance. The latter can make more than a sip unbearable (unless you're a hop-head).

Double IPAs are nothing to fear, and no one expects most newly baptized craft beer drinkers to make them a regular in the fridge. But they are great for those days when you just want something to shock the system. Those days when you want to erase the memories of work, of being stuck in traffic for three hours, or of a bounced check, take one sip of a super-hoppy Double IPA and everything else seems to disappear.

Beyond the IPA and Double IPA are other hoppy beers that don't necessarily fit a specific style. Beers like the (in)famous Arrogant Bastard, classified as an American Strong Ale, have a high hop profile and a nice dark-roasted malt presence. Many seasonal beers, often Christmas Ales, also have a big hop presence. This may be due to the seasonally appropriate pine-tree smell of northwest hops. Sierra Nevada's winter offering, Celebration, is considered an IPA with its intensely bitter, piney taste.

How to Tell If You're a Hop-Head

Do you ask for a bitter beer every time you go to the bar? Do you think American Pale Ales are watery? Do you think most IPAs are too sweet? Do you think all styles of beer are better when they're more bitter? Do you get all excited when you hear the phrases *dry-hopped* and *wet-hopped*? If you answered yes to any of these questions, you may consider yourself a hop-head. Hop-heads tend to be beer drinkers who can immediately acclimate to the bitterness of hops. These are people who have no problem with the intense flavors of any American-style IPA. These people often pooh-pooh more mild beers and seek out the extreme hop offerings from any craft brewery. They gravitate toward beers with *hop* written all over the label.

These beer lovers seem to dominate the craft beer websites; their addiction to hops drives them to rate hoppy beers the highest, which can sometimes skew the rating system. And indeed, we feel that the American beer rating system grades on a high-hop curve. This isn't necessarily bad, but it can be misleading for those who don't have such love for the super-bitter. We hear many a hop-head recommend bitter beers to unsuspecting new craft beer drinkers, which can lead to a bad beer incident, leaving new beer drinkers with the impression that

Here are a few of the best of the bitter:

○ **RACER 5 IPA:** Bear Republic Brewing Company, Healdsburg, California. Our favorite West Coast IPA. Well balanced, with juicy hops and a fruity background. Great with food and refreshing on a sunny California day. 8% ABV.

○ **MASALA MAMA IPA:** Minneapolis Town Hall Brewery, Minneapolis, Minnesota. The Midwest favorite; bitter with three different kinds of hops, caramel and citrus in the background. 5.9% ABV.

all craft beers are super-bitter. So while we appreciate the hop-heads as a strong force in beer—hell, we love a good Double IPA ourselves— we encourage the hop-heads out there to admit their addiction and respect differing palates.

Whether or not people are predisposed to liking hops, most craft beer drinkers go through a hop-head phase. After people get past the "I don't like bitter beers" phase, they start to crave that all-encompassing bitter mouthfeel. It's a fun phase, challenging fellow drinkers to find the hoppiest out there. This is definitely a milestone in your beer growth. Loving hops means you can handle pretty much any beer (the next milestone perhaps being the sour beer phase); however, most beer drinkers move past this point and learn to appreciate the dry, less bitter Belgian hops, seeking out a more nuanced, balanced beer, reserving Double IPAs for the rare occasion when their hop-lover past rears its ugly head. True hop-heads never move past the hoppy milestone; they have found happiness there and set up camp. We don't mean to say that they are immature in the beer world, just that they have found fulfillment in a certain style of beer and don't feel the need to look further.

○ **ARROGANT BASTARD ALE:** Stone Brewing Company, Escondido, California. As the name suggests, this beer is in your face, with a great bitter bite followed by a background of dark roasty malt. 7.2% ABV.

○ **BLIND PIG IPA:** Russian River Brewing Company, Santa Rosa, California. Award-winning IPA. Great big hop flavor with caramel, citrus, and tropical notes. Low ABV, making it an American version of a session beer. 6% ABV.

○ **PLINY THE ELDER DOUBLE IPA:** Russian River Brewing Company, Santa Rosa, California. Cult-favorite that is surprisingly well balanced between a large dose of hop and fruity malt. 9% ABV.

○ **MAHARAJA DOUBLE IPA:** Avery Brewing Company, Boulder, Colorado. Another hop favorite, big and bitter with grassy hops and notes of grapefruit. 10.5% ABV.

○ **HOUBLON CHOUFFE DOBBELEN IPA TRIPEL:** Brasserie d'Achouffe, Achouffe, Belgium. Citrusy and bready with a nice dose of Belgian hop bitterness. 9% ABV.

* * *

So turn the lights down low and the Barry White way up. Open a bottle of Bière de Champagne and light some candles. Go all the way, baby. It's time. You visited all the bases, time to round home plate. We know that when we pull out the big guns of beer, we can seduce pretty much anyone into drinking craft beer. And it's nice to know that beer has a dressier side: Saison is like classic white pearls, Barleywine is like a tux 'n' tails, Russian Imperial Stout is like the little black dress. Perhaps American IPA could then be the ass-kickin', handmade, real-leather cowboy boots, and the Double IPA is like those ass-less chaps. Use protection—know your ABVs—so that you don't have to suffer the walk of shame; we've all had a Double IPA night that got a little out of control. But if you take precautions, you can be relaxed and comfortable going all the way with the right beer.

SEVEN

Home Is Where the Beer Is

I would give all my fame for a pot of ale and safety.

—WILLIAM SHAKESPEARE. *KING HENRY V*

Fill Your Home with Beer

Being a beer lover means bringing that love into the home. You now have a long list of styles to choose from and an advanced palate to taste with. So why have a variety of wines and liquor on hand in your cabinet for every occasion and only one lonely six-pack of beer in the fridge? Now that you have embraced the breadth of the beer world, you'll want to have some choices when dining at home. Whether you plan a dinner party or have an unexpected soirée, or even a 3 a.m. booty call, pulling out a variety of special beers for your guests will leave a memorable mark on their minds and palates. In fact, having options for your guests is simply good manners for a beer lover. We tell you this from personal experience; we find that people remember the craft beers we served them as much as the good company when we throw parties. But beer in the home isn't just about the drink, it's about the whole aesthetic experience. In this chapter we'll tell you how to get the most out of your craft beer experience at home—How to serve it in the right glass, and what to keep around to have good beer feng shui.

You Know That Thing You Drink Beer From? Well, It's Important! Glassware

We're going to tell you something that wine enthusiasts have known for years: The glass matters! It *really* matters. Great glassware isn't just pretty; its function has a huge effect on a fine beverage. There's much more to glassware than a cheap pint glass or, even worse, the giant red plastic cup (The Horror!). Just like a white wine belongs in a different size and shape glass than red wine, different beer styles have their own glassware. Americans are finally catching on to the idea of using great glassware for beer, but this idea has been thriving for ages in Belgium and other beer-centric European countries. Thankfully, the resurgence in craft beer has brought back interest in using the proper glass. You may have even seen a few of these around town: the tulip-shaped glass, the chalice glass, or at least the tall Weizen glass. So how does the glass affect the beer?

The shape of the glass has great influence on the release of the carbonation in the beer. Think of a Champagne flute. It allows this bubbly elixir to retain its carbonation because of its narrow shape and small surface area at the opening. This is important for Champagne, which needs a nice dose of carbonation to balance out its sugary sweetness. Try putting Champagne into a big pint glass and see what happens. It will

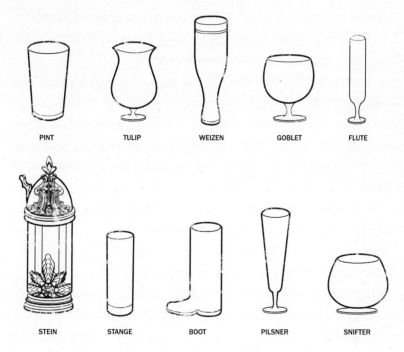

PINT TULIP WEIZEN GOBLET FLUTE

STEIN STANGE BOOT PILSNER SNIFTER

no doubt lose carbonation quickly and get syrupy sweet and cloying. Certain beers need the same attention to carbonation release. Lambics, for instance, benefit from a glass shaped like a Champagne flute so that they retain enough carbonation as you drink them to keep some balance and not be perceived as overly sweet or sour.

A glassware style known as the tulip also helps retain carbonation. The wide bottom and narrow middle decreases the surface area, creating a bottleneck, which keeps the CO_2 bubbles from releasing too quickly. The Belgian Golden Ale Duvel is traditionally served in this glassware. The head on a Duvel poured into this glass is huge, but that's no accident. The brewer wants a substantial head on that beer because the bubbles will lift the aromatics to your nose. Read the label on a Belgian bottle; it will likely indicate which type of glass best fits the beer. The Belgians make some of the best beer out there, and they have put a lot of thought into the best way to show off the beer and release its flavors. Orval, Tripel Karmeliet, Chimay, St. Bernardus, Saison DuPont—all of these beers have their own glassware, as do hundreds more.

But why are there *so many* different glass shapes and sizes for these different beers? These glassware creations are part marketing ingenuity (as the beer name is usually stamped across the glass) and part flavor enhancement. In fact, there is technically no right or wrong glass shape for a Belgian beer. The "correct" glassware for most of these Belgian beers is really determined only by what the *brewer* says. The brewer is the one who says, "Behold. I have created beer. This is how my beer should be served in order for it to taste how I intended." If the brewer thinks that the carbonation should release quickly to achieve the correct balance, he'll probably design a glass that is more goblet-like, with a wide surface area that provides unfettered CO_2 release—like the glasses for Chimay and Orval. If a brewer wants her beer to retain a lot of carbonation, she might decide that it be served in a flute, like Lambic, or a tulip glass, like Duvel. If the brewer thinks that the beer should be consumed at a warmer temperature, he will want his beer served in a big thin glass; this allows warm hands to help bring the beer to the right temperature. Inversely, if the brewer thinks the beer is better colder, he may have his beer served in a thick chalice. In all of these cases, the glass mirrors what the brewer says is the perfect way to enjoy his or her beer.

Some glassware, however, is determined by style. It's as simple as that. For instance, some beer styles are meant to be served in a good old pint-shaped glass known as a shaker. Porters, Stouts, and other English Ales can benefit from this glass, which allows for a quicker loss of carbonation. The reason for this is the same reason these ales hold up well on cask. With a lower carbonation, the roasted, toasted notes of these styles will show more on your palate when the carbonation has dissipated. Their style dictates that they should have a lower amount of carbonation so that none of the subtle malty flavors are hidden.

In addition to shape, the quality of the glass is truly important. Beer just tastes better out of good glasses. If you don't believe us, do a taste test. Pour a beer you like into both a cheap glass and a fine crystal wineglass. Taste the difference. See? Just as wine tastes different in various glassware, so does beer. We know that we're getting nitpicky here, but when you drink beer out of a fine glass, the entire experience is exponentially enhanced. If you are drinking a great beer out of a wisp of a glass with a beautiful curve that provides the correct carbonation release rate and temperature, you are treating craft beer and the artisans who make it with respect. And as craft beer continues to get the attention it deserves, people will see that great glassware is as essential to craft beer as the bottle opener.

Glass Houses

So you say you aren't going to stock 20 different kinds of glasses to appease us? Well, we don't blame you. We don't do that either, so don't worry about it. What we recommend when we consult for bars and restaurants that don't want to stock too many glasses is one simple kind of glass. Crazy, after what we just told you about all the varieties of glassware, we know, but if you just get one type of low-stemmed Burgundy-style glass (we like the Riedel Ouverture Magnum glasses), you should be set. This style, which is similar to a glass used by sommeliers for evaluating wine, is a great happy medium for all beers if you don't want to splurge on tons of different glassware. It's not technically *correct*, but it is minimalist chic. For a lot of our beer-pairing dinners, we serve beer in wineglasses, and we'll never turn away a craft beer served thus.

But if you feel like you're ready to commit to buying some good beer glasses, you might want to think about investing in a set. We like the German glassmaker Riedel. They make a nice overall beer glass, and Spiegelau (owned by Riedel) is our favorite. They make a great three-glass set that includes a tulip shape, a Pilsner style, and a taller classic wheat beer glass. These glasses are pretty accessible; you can even find them at Target. You can also try your local boutique wine and beer shop, or search online.

There is a certain satisfaction that comes from drinking a beer in its custom-engineered glassware in your own home. And yes, we each have a couple of specialty glasses with brewery names at home for our favorite beers. Unless you feel like bogarting these glasses from your local beer bar (which we *do not* recommend, by the way, unless you want to get 86'd for life), these glasses are pretty hard to come by. We've found a couple of websites where you can get them. They ain't cheap, but it's fun to experience the beer the way the brewer intended. Go online to the Global Beer Network (www.globalbeernetwork.com). You can also try the Beer Geek Shop (www.beergeekshop.com). Here are some examples of popular glass shapes and the beer styles that best fill them up:

- **PINT**: English Bitter, ESBs, Pale Ales, IPAs, Porters, Stouts, Irish Red, Amber Ales, California Common, American Lagers, Brown Ale. This ubiquitous glassware shape allows the beer to release carbonation at a constant rate and warm up in your hands.

- **FLUTE**: Bière de Champagne, Lambics, Gueuze, Faro. This narrow shape helps the beer maintain its balance by keeping the bubbles in and the sweetness or sourness of these beers in check.

- **TULIP**: Witbier, Saison, Scotch Ale, Bière de Garde, Belgian Strong Golden, Double or Imperial IPA, specialty herbed beer, Berliner Weisse. The wide bottom of this glass allows the beer to open up, but the bottleneck created by the narrowing toward the mouth traps a nice big head for aromatic enjoyment and carbonation retention, keeping a prickly bite that complements these styles.

- **CHALICE OR GOBLET**: Most Belgian beers, Belgian Pale Ale, Dubbels, Tripels, Flanders Red Ale. This class of glassware offers a stem so that the beer doesn't warm up too quickly, but the wide mouth allows for greater surface area and carbonation release. Beers served in this glassware benefit from opening up and often reveal layers of different flavors as they come to room temperature and lose some bubbles.

PILSNER: German and Czech Pilsners, Imperial Pilsners, Bocks, Dopplebocks, Schwarzbier. This slender style, sometimes shaped like an upside-down cone, usually holds 12 ounces and is ideal for head retention and showing off your pretty beers.

WEIZEN: Hefeweizen, American Wheat Beers, Dunkelweizen, Kristallklar, Weizenbock. This tall, thin glass allows for the huge head that can accompany the wheat styles that belong in them. It also helps focus the banana and clove esters that most wheat styles are known for.

STEIN OR MUG: German and Czech Pilsners, Maibock, Marzens. This sturdy-handled piece of glass or earthenware insulates a lot of beer...a *lot* of beer. Some even have a lid to keep the bugs out.

SNIFTER: Barleywine, Quadrupels, barrel-aged beers, Russian Imperial Stout, Eisbock, Winter Warmer. This glass functions much like a brandy snifter, concentrating aromatics and directing flavor. Because these bigger beers often have a high alcohol content, they benefit from swirling and warming up in your hands.

STANGE OR ROD: Altbier, Kölsch, Rauchbier. This smaller shape keeps some bubbles intact and the beer cold, allowing these beers to remain refreshing.

BOOT, HALF YARD, OR YARD: The lightest beer possible. This giant glass doesn't have much quality control. The first sip may be fine, but by the end, the beer will have lost too much carbonation and gained too much heat to be tasty. This goes for the pitcher scenario as well. But they sure are fun.

Stock the Fridge

Now that you have an array of empty glasses, you need a variety of beers to put in them (empty beer glasses are sooooo sad). You probably already have a small collection of spirits, a few bottles of quality

Grrrowlers!

 You've heard talk of them, they have that funny name, but WTF are growlers anyway? Tiny bears? Disgruntled pub-goers? In fact, no, growlers are just jugs o' craft beer. They are half-gallon jugs that people fill up from their local brewery or brewpub and take to go. They are usually made of glass and come in a variety of shapes. Growlers were supposedly named such because of the sound of the carbonation escaping as the top was opened. Some believe growlers gained popularity in areas where liquor was not available for purchase on Sundays, so people would stop by the brewery or pub to fill up a jug instead (you can close the liquor store, but we'll find a way!).

Growlers are a great way to take home some fresh beer. If sealed correctly, they can keep for over a week, but people usually get them for immediate consumption. Growlers are not sanitized, so they aren't meant for long-term storage because the beer could go bad. There's nothing better than showing up at a friend's BBQ with a growler of fresh beer from your local brewery. If you do that, be prepared to be loved.

red and white wine, but what about your beer selection? If you want to be a craft beer lover, you gotta keep some of these babies close. It can be frustrating to go to the fridge for a hoppy beer and find that all you have is milk and OJ. You don't want to boast the benefits of drinking craft beer and then not be able to deliver when a friend comes over. And you never know when a social evening will require a little impromptu beer lesson. You'll need to have a few good beers on hand to demonstrate.

It's good to make a grocery list of beers to have on hand for any occasion, if only for yourself and your many moods. Here are our recommendations for styles to have at the ready: Pilsner, Hefeweizen, Amber Ale, Pale Ale, IPA, Porter/Stout, Saison, Dubbel, and something for dessert (either a chocolaty Stout, a sweet Lambic, or a fruited ale). If you have a nice base of varied styles, you can then experiment with different beers the next time you hit the store.

Here is our advanced grocery list for beers that pair well with certain situations, be they good or bad:

- **AFTER-WORK BEER:** Racer 5 IPA—the hops cut through all the bullshit your boss spewed at you all day.

- **PRE-PARTY BEER:** Sierra Nevada Pale Ale—a nice crisp start to an evening that won't mess up your palate or get you too drunk before the fun begins.

- **LIQUID COURAGE BEER:** Arrogant Bastard Ale—the name makes you feel strong, and the ABV is a nice 7.2%. The bold hops will make you ready to face any frightening future event.

- **THE IN-LAWS ARE COMING OVER BEER:** Duvel—a strong beer that you can drink fairly quickly. It looks light in the glass, so if they show up before you're done drinking, you can pass it off as a Pilsner and no one's the wiser.

- **JUST GOT FIRED BEER:** North Coast Russian Imperial Stout— dark, bitter, lots of alcohol.

- **YOU JUST LOOKED AT YOUR CREDIT CARD BILL BEER:** PBR—'cause you're poor.

- **BEAUTIFUL SUMMER DAY IN THE BACKYARD BEER:** Kölsch— light and lovely.

- **GONNA GET LAID BEER:** DeuS—subtle herbaceous quality and fruit give you something to talk about, high alcohol greases the wheels, cork and high carbonation make for lovely romance and ritual.

- **DINNER WITH FRIENDS BEER:** Saison DuPont or Saison Foret—to impress your friends because of the big bottle and cork finish. The dryness of the Saison style will go with most meals.

LIFE SUCKS!! BEER: No beer.

HAVING A BBQ BEER: Rauchbier—to bring out the smoke in the meat. Or try a Dales Pale Ale served in a can—to remind you and your friends of the BBQs you had in college when you couldn't cook to save your life.

LATE-NIGHT BEER: Allagash Curieux—aged in Jim Beam barrels. This complex Belgian-style ale has a bourbon whisky flavor that is perfect for those used to a brandy snifter and cigar after dinner.

DEUS EX MACHINA BEER: Quelque Chose—actually made for heating up for that unexpected surprise! Serve it for dessert with a scoop of cinnamon gelato; no matter what happens at dinner, this will be the memory people will retain.

Beer Tools and Craft Beer Needs

Beyond the beer and the glasses, there are a few beer tools that will make your home happy and fulfill your desire for cool beer gear. The only absolute necessity in the list is the bottle opener, for obvious reasons, but the rest will enhance your beer drinking at home and impress your guests.

BOTTLE OPENER: Sounds obvious, but you should make sure you have something to open a specialty cork-finished bottle. Also, it's nice to have a cool-looking opener, 'cause then you look cool.

ICE BUCKET: This is important for serving beer at the table. Not every beer should be kept ice cold, but for those that need to keep cool, you should have a good-looking ice bucket. These also work well as dump buckets for beer tasting parties.

WINE/BEER FRIDGE: You'll need a wine fridge (refrigerated cellar) for storing your fine beer, as we'll discuss in a moment—something that allows you to be specific about the temperature, which should roughly be between 50°F and 60°F. You can end up

spending anywhere between $300 and $2,000 on these, so start
wherever your budget allows.

○ **KEGERATOR:** This is not a necessity but is a wonderful thing to
have for a beer lover. A kegerator is essentially a tiny home version
of a draught system. It consists of a small refrigerated unit big
enough for a small keg. It will also come with its own CO_2 system,
beer line, coupler, regulator tap, faucet and handle, and drip tray.
These tend to start at $500 and run up to a couple thousand,
which is a big investment. But having a home tap system is a way
to make your beer parties that much better.

○ **HOMEBREW KIT:** If you want to brew, you'll need this, of course
(see Chapter 9).

○ **EMPTY BOTTLES:** Don't throw these away! You can disinfect
them and use them to bottle your homebrew when it's ready. If you
are planning to brew, you'll need these babies, so keep them in a
box somewhere till you're ready.

Lay Down a Cellar, Lay Down Some Beer: Aging Beer

When you are truly ready to commit to beer, it's time to move
a few things around and make space for your beer cellar. We
recommend a small beer/wine fridge. Now this isn't the same thing as
those crappy little fridges that people throw out; we mean a good-looking
one with a glass front that allows you to get nice and specific about the
temperature. They can run anywhere from $300 to $2,000, depending
on your pocket and preference. Beers should be aged between 50°F and
60°F. It's hard to keep this consistency without a dedicated fridge. Maybe
if you live in a cool climate with an actual cellar, you could forgo the
refrigerator; just make sure the beer doesn't get too warm or cold. If the
temperature changes too dramatically, the living yeast that is still working in certain beers may die, hampering any hope of additional bottle

conditioning and perhaps even creating off-flavors. Keeping the beer out of sunlight is important as well. Sunlight can kill a beer as it does wine, especially if it interacts with the hops, which can cause off-flavors in the brew.

When starting your cellar, think about what you want to accomplish. Do you want beers that would fetch a high price from other beer lovers? Are you focused on the dollar value of your beer cellar? Or do you want to age beers that are your favorites, just to compare with newer vintages? Or perhaps you just want to experiment with aging, just to see how it treats a variety of beers. And how long are you willing to wait? Are you willing to wait a year or two? Or are you looking to drink your stock in the next month?

If you want to focus on monetary value, research the highest-rated beers on beer websites and look up the beers being auctioned on eBay. Find varieties in craft beer bars and stores that fetch the highest price. Check out our list of Beers to Drink Before You Die (page 132). For a more personal take, pick the big beers that you love the most and lay a few down. It's great to see how your favorite Gueuze or Porter can change. Tasting the older vintage against the new is a great beer party pastime. If you want to experiment, be aware that some of your aging may not turn out so well. Some beers are not perfectly suited to aging, just as some wines don't age as well as one hopes. There's a risk in aging beer. First of all, know that lighter beers don't tend to handle oxidation well; they can end up tasting off, creating some wet-cardboard flavors. And some lighter beers can't handle the funkier flavors that may come from aging. Note that pasteurized and filtered beers do not benefit from aging. They have had everything living killed, and so no change will happen, except that the beer will most likely go bad.

It's best to cellar higher-alcohol beers that are not filtered or pasteurized. Beers that age well tend to be over 7.5% alcohol. Alcohol is, after all, a preservative and keeps the beer from spoiling. Beers that have both huge flavors and complex flavors tend to age well. Highly hopped beers can benefit from aging because the hops also act as preservatives, and their bitterness is allowed to mellow out over time. This reduced bitterness means some of the other fruit, spice, and nutty malt flavors can come through. Sour beers like Lambic and Gueuze can get a lot funkier and lose some of the harsh tartness of the style. Belgian brewers of these styles have practiced aging them for years. Here are a few styles that generally benefit from aging:

- Abbey Ale
- American Strong Ale
- Barleywine
- Belgian Strong Ales
- Gueuze (these can age well even if they are below 7%)
- Imperial IPA/Double IPA (though you may not want to mellow out the hops)
- Imperial Pilsner
- Imperial Porter
- Lambic (these can age well even if they are below 7%)
- Old Ale
- Porter (over 7% is best)
- Quadrupels
- Rauchbier
- Russian Imperial Stout
- Smoked beers
- Sour beers
- Stout (over 7% is best)
- Trappist Ales

Just be aware that aging beer is never a sure thing. And the amount of time a beer can age is a guess; it can be anywhere from 1 year to 30 years. It's hard to know if a beer has reached its peak, meaning that it should be drunk after a certain amount of aging but not beyond that. If you are concerned with the risk, then try to age beers that are not that expensive and buy several of the same beer, tasting them at different increments of aging to determine the best amount of aging for that style.

Here are a few more tips for quickly building a valuable beer cellar:

- Find the highest-rated high-ABV beers on beer websites and in beer magazines; buy the newly produced bottles and age them.

- Go to local, regional, and national beer festivals and find a few of your favorites as well as the winners; try to get ahold of some bottles for aging.

- Get on a mailing list at a fine beer store and try to buy a few of your favorite rare ageable beers when they first come in. Drink one now and take notes, then age one and compare the flavors when you drink it.

- Get seasonal beers and hold on to them. Christmas in summertime is a great theme for a beer dinner party, and many holiday ales are high in alcohol and boast big holiday spices or hops that benefit from mellowing. Also, giving a fellow beer-lover a vintage holiday ale is a fantastic and economical gift.

- Make sure to label your beers when you lay them down. You can tack a note on the neck of the bottle, use a piece of tape, or just keep a ledger. Write down the year the beer was made (its vintage), the date you bought the beer, the date it went into the cellar, and other info about the unique qualities of the beer. It's also nice to write down any personal stories surrounding it. Was it a gift? Did you have to wait in line for it? Did you buy it on holiday? The more detail, the more to reminisce about when you finally open it.

*　*　*

You should feel better about your home now that beer is a part of it. You'll never again be caught without craft beer in your fridge. You've got your glassware ready and some beers to grow old with. Hang the hops over the hearth and welcome your beer-loving friends into your new and improved happier home.

EIGHT

The Beer Lover's Kitchen

It was as natural as eating and, to me, as
necessary. I would not have thought of eating
a meal without drinking a beer.

—ERNEST HEMINGWAY

Now You're Cookin' with Beer

U p until this point, we've just talked about beer alone. And
while beer can be great and completely satisfying on its

own, beer and food are perfect partners. But if the extent of your

beer pairing is a can o' light lager with a hot dog, it's time to wake up

and smell the mussels and Witbier. And if your only idea of cooking

with beer encompasses a recipe called Beer Can Chicken, you've

been missing out. We admit that a nice light lager can go well with some spicy chicken wings or some fish and chips. There *is* something to be said for old-school thoughts on beer, and there's definitely a pleasant sense-memory response to a foot-long and a plastic cup of beer at the ballpark. We're not saying these old ideas are ill-conceived notions. We're not trying to rob you of your favorite memories with your father. But what if instead of a lager with the fish and chips, you were to pick a wheat beer brewed with lemongrass? Your flavor experience would be an amazing cacophony of citrus and coriander, beer flavors that enhance the fish and chips rather than merely acting as a thirst quencher. And imagine the chicken wings paired with a slightly sweet and smoky Porter, flavors that help balance the hotness of the wings while adding another dimension to the barbecue sauce. It's just better.

Some innovative chefs are already pairing their beloved creations with craft beer and creatively using beer in their recipes. And forward-thinking restaurant owners are offering well-thought-out beer lists in addition to the requisite wine lists. In general, the food industry is just on the cusp of welcoming beer into the fine-dining world. It's an exciting time for craft beer, but there's still a long way to go. Unfortunately, just as beer drinkers align themselves with their mass-produced brand, some people are still under the impression that they like *one* beer, and that *one* beer should go with all food, period. They don't even consider that there might be a better beer style for the dish in front of them. This narrow approach is unfair to the breadth of the craft beer world and to the creativity of the culinary world. Why would you paint with just one color? Yes, beer belongs at the backyard BBQ, but it also belongs on the white-clothed tables of Le Bernardin.

We're here to help beer claim its rightful place at the table. We offer you some beer and food pairings and recipes featuring beer that will get your creative juices flowing. If you already consider yourself a chef or a foodie, this part of the Beer Journey may be your favorite. We'll talk about what makes a great food and beer pairing and how professional chefs use beer to enhance flavors in food. You can combine your kitchen know-how with your newly gained beer knowledge. This is your chance to get creative and to let craft beer breathe new life into your culinary experience.

A Perfect Match: Artisanal Beer and Food, Together at Last

Some people have found their way to pairing a Pale Ale with a burger. But has the cheese on the burger been considered? And how hoppy is that Pale Ale? Is the beer interfering with the flavors in the burger or is it complementing it? Would the aged Gruyère on that burger be better paired with a Belgian Dubbel? We're going to show you how to get specific about pairings in the same way that you've gotten specific with beer flavor profiles.

Not only is beer as great as wine with certain foods, but it sometimes makes an even *better* pairing than wine. The effervescence of beer can cut through heavy foods in a way that wine cannot. Fermented grape juice is not always the best complement to a dish. (We know some wine enthusiasts are fainting right now.) Certain foods that are historically hard to pair with wine, like asparagus, artichokes, eggplant, and some spicy foods, harmonize wonderfully with certain beers.

Unlike wine, there are no hard-and-fast rules that govern beer pairing (which is good because we both have issues with authority). But it does behoove us to follow some well-established food-pairing guidelines as a base for choosing a beer. Here are the things that we take into consideration when we're deciding which beer to serve:

BALANCE IS EVERYTHING. We'll say it again. Just as we discussed in Chapter 2, the key to all food and beer pairings is balance. Take strawberries, for instance. The best strawberries are the ones that are both sweet and tart. If the strawberry is picked too early, the sugars won't have had time to develop, leaving the fruit too sour. If the strawberry has become overripe, the flavor is too sweet. The strawberry is considered at its best when both the sweetness and the tartness balance each other. The same applies to beer. The sweetness of the malt in beer needs the dry and bitter balance of the added hops. If the beer didn't have this sweet-bitter balance, the beer could end up tasting like syrup—overly sweet and cloying, without much complexity or nuance. Think about contrasting flavors or mouthfeel. In addition to considering how the beer and food will complement each other, think of pairings in terms of what is missing from one that the other might fulfill and therefore provide balance. For instance, roasted pork is traditionally served with sweet baked apples. Why not pair that roasted pork with a beer like Unibroue Ephémère Pomme, made with green apples? Or what about pairing a hot, spicy curry with a refreshing and cooling Witbier?

LET THE FOOD AND BEER ENHANCE EACH OTHER. Some pairings are awesome when the food and the beer share similarities. Perhaps it's the spice profile or the aromatics or the mouthfeel. Think of how a toasty Porter would work with a nutty Parmigiano Reggiano cheese, or how a Chocolate Stout would pair with a double chocolate cake, or how an earthy, pungent Orval Trappist Ale would go with a mustard sauce.

THINK ABOUT YOUR ENVIRONMENT. Just like you think of white wine in the hot summer months and associate red wine with getting cozy in the winter beside a roaring fire, you need to take your environment into consideration when you're pairing food and beer. A big, heavy Russian Imperial Stout with a braised roast, or turkey and stuffing paired with Tripel White Sage Ale, is probably not something you're going to be down with in 90°F weather. But in the chill of winter, these pairings could be perfect.

MATCH INTENSITY LEVELS. You don't want your beer to overpower your food. It's no good if your beer has taken your palate hostage. You also don't want the beer to disappear in the pairing. It's important to think about the intensity levels of both the food and the beer. A big hoppy Double IPA would kill all the flavor in kampachi sashimi, and a soft Kölsch would taste like water after an intense concentrated demi-glace sauce.

GO CRAZY WITH UNPREDICTABLE PAIRINGS. Mismatches sometimes make the greatest pairings. We're talking Bogie and Bacall here, not Minnelli and Gest. Sometimes the beers and foods that you thought wouldn't go together in a million years end up making the most amazing flavor combinations. Think salty, briny oysters and a dry Stout, or smoky Rauchbier and vanilla ice cream!

As we said before, there aren't any hard-and-fast rules when it comes to beer pairing. The best and only way to really learn how to pair beer with food is by experimenting. You can start slow with familiar beers and small bites or cheeses (see page 184), or you can dive right in. Go to a restaurant that has a reputation for serving excellent food and great beer. Knowing what you now know about the general flavor profiles of different beer styles, take a stab at ordering a beer based on what food you'll be getting. You're not always going to get it right (we are still smarting from the chili beer–red curry incident of 1999). But we can assure you that if you put some thought into your pairings and use the techniques we've discussed, you'll make many more good pairings than bad. Economist Irving Fisher said, "Risk varies inversely with knowledge." If you've read this book, you've probably got more knowledge than your waiter. Your risk is mitigated. Listen to Fisher, even though he was a Prohibitionist.

The chart at right gives a few of our favorite pairings and why we think they are so damn good.

FOOD	PAIRED WITH	WHY IT ROCKED
Seared diver scallops with lemon sherry vinaigrette, wild arugula, and fried capers	The grassy, sour, and peppery Glazen Toren Saison D'Erpe-Mere	This was an amazing pairing that worked on many levels. The citrus in the beer enhanced the vinaigrette, the tartness in the beer worked perfectly with the fried capers, the spicy peppery notes in the Saison harmonized brilliantly with the arugula, and the dryness from the hops of the beer provided a nice contrast with the fattiness of the scallops.
Fuyu persimmon, fig, and fennel salad with shaved beets and Hachiya persimmon vinaigrette	The sweet, hoppy, and citrusy Tripel Karmeliet (Browerij Bosteels)	The richness of the nonastringent Fuyu persimmon and the sweetness of the figs were enhanced, crossed, and brought to life with the acid-like citrus quality in the beer. The anise from the fennel and the rustic beets matched the secondary herbaceous and earthy notes in the Karmeliet. The big tannins in the astringent Hachiya persimmon cleaned up the big malts in the beer. So cooperative.
Pumpkin mezzaluna with brown butter and sage	The earthy, roasty, and dry Green Flash Nut Brown Ale	Sweet and savory delectable pumpkin stuffed half-moon pasta in a roasted brown butter sauce with crispy sage basically made out with the toasty, nutty, herbaceous, and dry ale. That's how great this pairing was.
Mascarpone cheesecake	The fruity, dry, and tart Lindeman's Pêche Lambic Ale	This beer is a little too sweet for us on its own. But matched with this tart, melt-in-your-mouth cheesecake, the beer worked miracles, cutting through the creaminess and acting as the delicious sweet fruity sauce for this simply delicious dessert.

CHEESE LOVES BEER AND
BEER LOVES CHEESE

Beer Pairing Philosophy from Cheesemonger
Andrew Steiner

 Every major beer expert has had their own favorite special moment with beer and cheese. Ours was with a Mothais goat cheese, which was aged in 100% humidity, and a funky Cantillon Iris Gueuze. To get the skinny, we talked with Andrew Steiner, one of Los Angeles's most notable cheese authorities. Andrew was maitre d'fromage at the world-famous Patina before opening his own store, Andrew's Cheese Shop, in Santa Monica. Here's what he had to say:

I think that pairing cheese with beer is like cheating. Fermented products tend to have many flavor similarities. This is why cheese, wine, bread, and beer all work together on some level. Classically, wine and cheese is the go-to pairing, but you have to be careful because many flavor clashes lurk out there. It is also not uncommon for the power or texture of a cheese to overpower those same attributes in a wine (or vice versa). This is rarely the case with beer. The main reason for this is the bubbles.

The two major ingredients of cheese are salt and fat. Sorry to be the one to break it to you, but that's the way it is. This also happens to be why cheese is so delicious. The bubbles from beer cut into the fat for contrast, and salt does the same little dance on your palate as the bubbles. I think far too many people are terrified of getting their pairings wrong. Some of the most inspired pairings I have experienced came from the most unexpected risks. Remember, we're talking about beer and cheese here. We've got alcohol, fat, and salt. If you screw up the pairing, what's the worst thing that will happen? The truth is, I have learned so much more from getting it wrong than getting it right.

The most important factor to consider when pairing cheese and beer is weight. Low-alcohol beers, like wheat beers or blondes, tend to work better with milder and gentler cheeses, like fresh young goat's milk cheeses or triple-crèmes (a little hint, triple-crèmes work with everything). Call me a traditionalist (you'd be the first), but I love Belgian and Belgian-style ales with Trappist style cheeses. (Many Trappist breweries also make cheese.) These are probably the most natural pairings due to their similar origins. I have a picture in my mind of lots of happy monks somewhere in Belgium drinking lots of beer with some nice, smelly cheese. One of my favorite pairings is always sheep's milk with a nice, hoppy IPA. Sheep's milk cheeses usually have a touch of bitterness on the finish, and the hops really work to enhance this flavor. My final beer/cheese marriage is always the last one in my Grilled Cheese and Beer events. We pair blue cheese with something big and chocolaty like a Stout, London Porter, or Chocolate Bock. You get those nice, big roasty-sweet flavors to offset and match the power of the blue.

If you are interested in nibbling at Andrew's Cheese Shop or his Grilled Cheese and Beer events, go to www.andrewscheese.com for information, shopping, Cheese 101, and to join his Cheeses of the Month Club.

HEY, THERE'S FOOD IN MY BEER!

We can't talk about using beer in food without talking about the beer that was made *with* food: Oyster Stout! Originally named thus because of the popularity and ubiquity of both oysters and Stouts in the pubs and taverns of the United Kingdom, these beers were meant to be consumed with and to complement oysters. But the New Zealand brewer Young and Son Portsmouth took the idea a bit further in 1929 and made a Stout using actual oysters *in the boil*.

It's a bit counterintuitive to imagine how oysters and Stout taste together, but along with Barleywine and blue cheese, this match is one of the great traditional food pairings of the beer world. The toasty, roasty, and dry finish of the Stout contrasts with the salty, briny, sweet flavor of the oyster and provides a lovely taste treat.

Nowadays, finding this style of beer is rather challenging. Most Oyster Stouts are not made with oysters, but some bold microbreweries still add a dozen or so oysters, or ground oyster shells, to the brew, which can balance any sour flavors. The resultant beer rarely tastes at all fishy, and oyster flavors are very difficult to detect in the finished beer.

Some pubs offer Oyster Shooters. These aren't the vodka- or hot-sauce-inspired shooters that you'll find in trendy restaurants. This is a glass of Stout (we also like Porter) with a nice plump raw oyster in the bottom. This is obviously not for the weak of heart, but if you like oysters, you will definitely want to try this exotic treat. We've done a couple variations of this idea that we loved, using the Deschutes Black Butte Porter with Malpeque oysters and the Rogue Morimoto Black Obi Soba Ale with Kumamoto oysters. Forget about it.

The First Ingredient Is Beer: Cooking with Beer

As with much of the ritual that surrounds beer, the history of cooking with beer is long. The oldest beer was probably thick, bread- or porridge-like, almost a meal in itself. Beer was refined over the years and often stepped in to flavor meat or help create tenderness in dishes. Beer can be used in many recipes that call for a liquid, like wine. Think of cooking with beer whenever you might use a reduction, sauce, marinade, or dressing. Try it in soups and stews, where wine is often used; the right beer may just improve the dish. British-style onion and cheese soup benefits from a nice bottle of Bitter dumped into the pot. Mussels cooked in Witbier is a classic dish from Belgium. And if you've never had ice cream made from a chocolaty Stout, you don't know what you're missing.

We've been lucky enough to taste some inspiring beer recipes from our own culinary culture in Los Angeles, and we've asked some of our favorite chefs to provide us, and you, with some of their most beloved beer recipes.

JENN GARBEE, *SECRET SUPPERS* AND *SISTERS OF THE SUDS*

J enn Garbee is a regular contributor to the *Los Angeles Times* Food
section and *LA Weekly*'s SquidInk food blog, and is the beverage col-
umnist for Tribune Media's national newspaper wire. The former pastry chef is the author of several books, including *Secret Suppers: Rogue
Chefs and Underground Restaurants in Warehouses, Townhouses, Open
Fields, and Everywhere in Between,* an insider's look at the underground
restaurant movement. We met her when she interviewed us for a story in
the *Times* about women and beer, and we immediately became friends
and beer-drinking buddies. Jenn got so bitten by the beer bug that she
is currently working on a book called *Sisters of the Suds*, which explores
the history of female brewers. She is also a contributing editor for *EAT
Los Angeles* and an amazing baker. You'll know it once you've tried this
herbed beer bread.

Rosemary-Thyme Beer Bread

Jenn says: Beer. Breads. Fresh herbs. What could be better? A beer to go with it. You may substitute all thyme for a milder flavor. A Pilsner or other Pale Lager is best here—avoid Stouts or other full-bodied beers because they will lend bitterness to this savory bread.

2½ cups flour

½ cup cornmeal

1 tablespoon baking powder

1 teaspoon salt

1 tablespoon sugar

One 12-ounce bottle of Moonlight Brewing Company's Reality Czeck, room temperature

3 tablespoons butter, melted

1 teaspoon minced fresh rosemary

1 teaspoon minced fresh thyme

Preheat the oven to 350°F. Grease a 9×5 inch loaf pan with butter or cooking spray (pay close attention to the corners, as this bread tends to stick).

In a large bowl, combine the flour, cornmeal, baking powder, salt, and sugar.

In a medium bowl, combine the beer, butter, and herbs. Stir into the dry ingredients until just combined, being careful not to overmix.

Pour into the prepared pan, and bake until golden and a knife inserted in the center comes out clean, about 45 minutes. Remove from the oven, cool for 10 minutes, then run a knife around the edges to loosen and turn onto a rack to cool.

Serve warm with butter.

Makes 1 loaf

Lucy Saunders, *Cooking with Beer* and *The Best of American Beer and Food*

A prolific beer expert, writer, teacher, author, and cook, Lucy Saunders (aka the Beer Cook) has been changing the way we appreciate and include beer in our dining world for over 20 years. Not only has Lucy forged a path for women in beer (for which we are mighty grateful) but she also walks the walk, having published her first highly informative book, *Cooking with Beer*, as well as another of our favorites, *Grilling with Beer*. She also published *The Best of American Beer and Food: Pairing and Cooking with Craft Beer*. Lucy is a fount of information, and she travels the country leading beer events and dinners, bringing cuisine a la bière to the forefront of the modern dinner table. With her most recent project, Lucy is one of three female beer writers who contributed an essay to the book *Beer Hunter, Whisky Chaser*. The book is a tribute to the late great beer writer and legend Michael Jackson.

The circle of women in beer is a pretty small one, so we are lucky enough to have been in touch with Lucy for years. After reading all her books and trying her recipes, we knew that we had to have one in this book. Lucy just understands how beer works with food in an unpretentious yet delicious and very forward-thinking way. We're so happy to be featuring this grilled fennel and orange salad because it illustrates wonderfully that beer can be used in cooking in so many innovative ways!

Grilled Fennel and Orange Salad

Lucy says: This is made with a Strong Golden Ale and may be paired with the same ale or with a Dunkelweizen. Because I live in Milwaukee, Wisconsin, I used the locally brewed Sprecher Abbey Tripel Ale to make the marinade. The result: a refreshing side salad to serve with grilled chicken.

FOR THE MARINADE

½ cup olive oil

⅓ cup Strong Golden Ale

1 tablespoon minced garlic

1 teaspoon dried thyme

¼ teaspoon ground coriander

¼ teaspoon red pepper flakes, or to taste

Sea salt to taste

FOR THE SALAD

Two 10-ounce fennel bulbs, cut in quarters

2 bell peppers, assorted colors, cut into large slices

1 medium sweet onion, cut into quarters

2 large oranges, sectioned, membrane and seeds removed

Salt and freshly ground black pepper to taste

Balsamic vinegar to taste

8 large Romaine lettuce leaves

Preheat a grill to medium-high.

In a large bowl, whisk together the marinade ingredients until emulsified. Add the fennel, bell peppers, and onion, and toss to coat. Set the vegetables aside to marinate for 30 minutes. Use a slotted spoon to lift the vegetables from the marinade; reserve the remaining marinade, and set aside.

Place the vegetables in a grill basket or on a fine mesh grill grate. Grill until tender and slightly caramelized, 10 to 12 minutes, turning often and covering the grill to capture the steam. Remove the vegetables from the grill, and let cool until warm enough to handle.

While the vegetables cool, chop the oranges and add the fruit and collected juice to the large bowl; toss with the reserved marinade. When vegetables are cool enough to handle, chop into bite-size chunks, removing any tough end pieces, and add to the oranges, mixing to combine. Taste and adjust seasoning with salt and pepper. Add a bit of balsamic vinegar if you wish. Serve on top of Romaine lettuce leaves on a large platter.

Serves 6 to 8

Matt Accarrino, Chef de Cuisine, Craft and Craftbar

C hef Matt Accarrino has come a long way from his humble beginnings washing dishes in New Jersey. He's studied abroad in Labico, Italy, working at the Michelin Guide–rated Antonello Colonna restaurant. While in Italy, he visited farms and "foraged for the restaurant's ingredients" on a daily basis. He was opening sous chef at Thomas Keller's Per Se in New York City, which received the near impossible four-star rating from the *New York Times* and three stars from the Michelin Guide. He's cooked for Charlie Palmer in New York City and Todd English at Olive's at the W in Union Square. Matt developed quite the following as the chef de cuisine of Tom Colicchio's Craft and Craftbar in Los Angeles.

Matt has been featured in *Wine Spectator*, *Food and Wine*, *Food Arts*, *Los Angeles Times*, and *Los Angeles Confidential*. Oh, and he teamed with us at Craft L.A. to cook at one of the most mind-blowing and innovative beer-pairing dinners of all time! We are thrilled to share one of the dishes from that dinner with you.

Australian Suzuki with Beer-Braised Mussels, Leeks, Trumpet Royale Mushrooms, and Chorizo

Matt says: Mussels and chorizo are a classic pairing in Spanish cooking and a perfect way to highlight the buttery suzuki. Instead of using wine, I used Saison DuPont, which provided tart citrus notes that worked with the seafood and peppery notes that packed a subtle punch.

FOR THE MUSSELS

> 2 shallots, thinly sliced
>
> 1 small garlic clove, thinly sliced
>
> 6 tablespoons olive oil
>
> Salt to taste
>
> 24 Bouchot mussels, washed and debearded
>
> One 375-ml bottle Saison DuPont Ale
>
> 5 sprigs flat-leaf parsley, stems and leaves reserved separately
>
> 1 cup reduced unsalted chicken broth
>
> Sugar to taste
>
> 2 tablespoons unsalted butter
>
> ½ leek, white part only, cut into small dice
>
> 3 trumpet royale mushrooms, halved lengthwise, scored, and cut crosswise
>
> 3 ounces dry-cured chorizo, diced

FOR THE SUZUKI

> Four 5-ounce portions suzuki (Japanese seabass), skin on
>
> Salt and freshly ground black pepper to taste
>
> 3 tablespoons olive oil
>
> 2 tablespoons unsalted butter
>
> 2 sprigs thyme

THE MUSSELS

On medium heat, sweat half the shallots and half the garlic in about 2 tablespoons of olive oil in a 5- to 6-quart heavy pot until soft, seasoning lightly with salt. Add the mussels, and increase the heat to high. Pour in the beer, and add the parsley stems. Cover and steam until the mussels open. Strain the mussels, reserving both the broth and the mussels. Pick the mussels from their shells, reserving both the meat and the liquid. Discard the vegetables and shells.

Place the reserved liquid from the mussels back into the pot, and add the chicken broth. Season with salt and sugar to balance out the natural bitterness of the beer. Using an immersion blender, incorporate 2 tablespoons of the olive oil and the butter into the reserved liquid. Set this broth aside.

Preheat the oven to 375°F.

In the remaining 2 tablespoons of olive oil, sweat the remaining shallots and garlic and leeks. Add the mushrooms and chorizo. Cook until the vegetables are tender without coloring; set aside.

THE SUZUKI

Season the suzuki with salt and pepper. Sear the pieces skin side down over medium-high heat in the olive oil in a medium sauté pan with a metal handle. Transfer the fish to the oven, and roast for about 5 minutes, or until it flakes easily with a fork.

Return the pan to the stovetop over medium heat. Add the butter to the pan and flip the fish over, skin side up. Add the thyme, and baste the fish with the pan juices. Allow the fish to finish cooking for 1 or 2 minutes. Remove the fish and blot on paper towels.

Add the mussels to the chorizo mixture and warm through on medium-high heat for 1 to 3 minutes. Stir in the parsley leaves, and allow to wilt slightly. Divide the vegetable-mussel mixture among four large bowls. Froth the reserved broth with an immersion blender and spoon several tablespoons of the liquid over the vegetables. Finally, place the fish atop the broth and vegetables in the bowls and serve.

Serves 4

EVAN FUNKE, EXECUTIVE CHEF, RUSTIC CANYON WINE BAR AND SEASONAL KITCHEN

Before Evan Funke was a James Beard semifinalist in 2009 for Rising Star Chef of the Year, he was mastering his technique in one of L.A.'s toughest kitchens, Spago Beverly Hills. Evan has worked with some of the world's greatest chefs, including Alain Ducasse, Thomas Keller, Eric Ripert, Mario Batali, Charlie Trotter, Nobu Matsuhisa, and Wolfgang Puck. Evan left Spago in 2006 to teach at Le Cordon Bleu in Pasadena, and in 2007 he took a life-changing three-month apprenticeship under master pasta maker Alessandra Spisni in Bologna, Italy. At La Vecchia Scuola Bolognese, Evan mastered the techniques of pasta *fatto a mano* (handmade pasta), and upon returning from Italy, he started as executive chef at the market-fresh Santa Monica restaurant Rustic Canyon Wine Bar and Seasonal Kitchen.

It was at Rustic Canyon that we met Evan and were happy to learn that one of his many talents was his taste for great beer! We quickly planned several beer dinners, pairing Evan's wonderfully thoughtful food with delicious beers from around the world. When we introduced Evan to the Reissdorf Kölsch, he was hooked. Not only did his family have roots in Cologne, Germany (where the beer style originated), but he was inspired to make an amazing and delicate *fatto a mano* rabbit dish. Enjoy.

Kölsch-Braised Rabbit with Wild Ramps and Roasted Porcini

Evan says: I love Kölsch beer; it's bright, well rounded, and pairs perfectly with rabbit. The earth of the porcini does well with the restraint of this beer, and the spicy wild ramps in this dish set off all the beer's wonderful apricot, grainy accents. You can have your butcher break the rabbit down into smaller pieces, but this dish does so well with a braised whole rabbit for large hungry groups who love beer and love to eat with their hands. This is a springtime dish, a primal offering, so don't think too much. Can't find ramps? Use spring onions. Can't find porcini? Use some other wild mushrooms. It's that simple.

4 or 5 button porcini mushrooms

Three 500-ml bottles Reissdorf Kölsch beer

1 spring rabbit or hare*

Salt and freshly ground black pepper to taste

All-purpose flour, for dredging

6 tablespoons butter or olive oil

2 leeks, sliced

2 large carrots, cut into medium dice

2 large shallots, cut into medium dice

1 brown onion, cut into medium dice

1 bulb fennel, cut into medium dice

3 stalks celery, cut into medium dice

2 quarts chicken stock

1 bunch marjoram

1 bunch wild ramps, sliced

Clean the mushrooms with a damp towel, wiping any dirt off of the cap. With a paring knife, carefully scrape the shaft of the mushrooms to clean them of any dirt or blemishes. Cut in half and set aside.

*If desired, substitute free-range, organic skinless chicken thighs.

Open the beer (no one will mind if you take a swig).

Season the rabbit with salt and pepper and dredge lightly in flour on all sides.

In a large heavy-bottom pot, melt 4 tablespoons of butter over medium heat. Once the butter is lightly browned, add the rabbit and cook on each side for 2 to 3 minutes, until golden-brown delicious. Remove the rabbit and set aside. Discard the fat.

Melt 2 tablespoons of butter in the same pot. Add the leeks, carrots, shallots, onion, fennel, and celery, and allow to caramelize lightly over medium heat, 5 to 7 minutes. When the vegetables have some color, add the beer (saving one last splash) and the chicken stock. Add the marjoram, and adjust the seasoning of the broth with salt and pepper to taste. Return the rabbit to the pot. Cover, reduce the heat to very low, and cook for about 2 hours, or until the meat is very tender to the touch.

When the rabbit is tender, remove the meat and set aside on a serving platter; cover with foil to keep warm. Add the mushrooms and ramps to the pot along with the last splash of fresh beer. Simmer for 15 minutes, until the liquid is reduced and ramps are tender. Then spoon over rabbit and serve.

Serves 4

SAMIR MOHAJER, CHEF/OWNER, THE CABBAGE PATCH

The farmers' market rocks!" is Samir Mohajer's credo. The tattooed, Iranian-born chef grew up in Santa Monica around some of the best farmers' markets in the country. At an early age, he gained an appreciation for fresh, locally grown, seasonal food from shopping with his grandfather, and the cooking bug bit. In 1999, Samir graduated from Le Cordon Bleu and started pursuing his dream with a stint at the salad station at the locally renowned Axe restaurant in Venice, California. There he quickly worked his way up to chef de cuisine before heading on to the Little Door in Hollywood, making a name for himself as sous chef. In 2007, he became the executive chef at Rustic Canyon in Santa Monica, opening the restaurant to stellar reviews.

Samir is now the chef/owner of the Cabbage Patch in Beverly Hills. He concentrates on natural beef, wild-caught fish, sustainable methods, and locally grown organic produce—purchased straight from the farmers' market, of course. One of the first beer dinners we hosted featured this amazing recipe for beer-braised short ribs with mushrooms and polenta. It's a fantastic recipe that will stir your taste buds and melt in your mouth.

Belgian Beer–Braised Short Ribs with Wild Mushrooms and Soft Polenta

Samir says: Beer-braised ribs are a classic dish. Westmalle has a sweet maltiness that seeps into the meat and a subtle spice profile that complements the other spices in this recipe. The earthiness of the mushrooms is enhanced by the herbaceousness of the beer.

FOR THE SHORT RIBS

Four 1 ½- to 2-inch cut short ribs, bone on

Salt and freshly ground black pepper to taste

3 tablespoons olive oil

2 large carrots, cut into large dice

2 ribs celery, cut into large dice

2 large onions, cut into large dice

6 garlic cloves, smashed

Sachet: ½ bunch fresh thyme, ½ bunch Italian parsley, 4 bay leaves, and 1 teaspoon whole black peppercorns, tied together in cheesecloth

2 tablespoons tomato paste

3 cups Westmalle Dubbel, or another Abbey or Belgian-style Dubbel

Chicken stock to cover

FOR THE POLENTA

1 cup whole milk

1 cup water

2 ounces butter

Salt and freshly ground black pepper to taste

¾ cup medium-ground polenta

FOR THE MUSHROOMS

Butter, as needed

Olive oil, as needed

2 tablespoons finely chopped shallots

1 garlic clove, minced

1 pound assorted wild mushrooms (chanterelle, shitake, oyster, black trumpet), cut into medium dice

Salt and freshly ground black pepper to taste

1 tablespoon roughly chopped Italian parsley

4 sprigs thyme, optional

Freshly shaved Parmesan cheese to taste, optional

THE SHORT RIBS

Preheat oven to 350°F. Season the short ribs liberally with salt and pepper. In a large braising pan, bring olive oil to the smoking point on high heat, and sear the short ribs on all sides until browned. Remove the ribs, and add the carrots, celery, onions, and garlic with the sachet of herbs. Sweat over medium heat until slightly caramelized. Add the tomato paste, and sauté for 3 to 4 minutes. Deglaze the pan with the beer, and return the ribs to the pan. Allow the beer to reduce by half over medium-high heat (15 to 20 minutes). Cover the ribs with chicken stock, and bring to a boil. Cover the pan, and place in the oven to braise for about 3 hours, until the meat begins to fall off the bone and the broth is reduced.

THE POLENTA

In a small stock pot, bring the milk, water, and butter to a boil. Season with salt and pepper. Reduce the heat to a simmer, and rain in the polenta while whisking rapidly for 2 to 3 minutes. Turn down heat to avoid burning, and cook, stirring occasionally, until the grit is cooked out and the polenta is creamy.

THE MUSHROOMS

In a sauté pan over medium-high heat, melt equal parts butter and olive oil to cover the bottom of the pan. Add the shallots and garlic, and sweat until translucent. Add the mushrooms, and season with salt and pepper. Sauté until slightly caramelized.

Add the parsley, and remove from heat.

To serve, divide the polenta among four plates, then place the short ribs on top, cover with the broth, and top with the mushrooms. Garnish with a sprig of thyme and a bit of shaved parmesan, if you like.

Serves 4

Govind Armstrong, Executive Chef, and Jacob Wildman, Chef de Cuisine, Table 8 and 8 oz. Burger Bar

Now the executive chef and owner of Table 8 and 8 oz. Burger Bar, with restaurants in Los Angeles, Miami, and New York City, Govind Armstrong knew what he wanted to do from an early age. Govind was raised in Costa Rica and in Los Angeles, and at age 13 he was already earning his chops working for the famed Wolfgang Puck at the original Spago. He has trained under the likes of Nancy Silverton at Campanile, Mary Sue Milliken and Susan Feniger (of Ciudad and Border Grill fame) at City Restaurant, and Joachim Splichal at Patina and Pinot Hollywood before finally opening up his own highly successful restaurants.

Influenced by his travels around the world, Govind has developed a unique style, becoming one of the country's brightest culinary stars and a purist in California cuisine. Featured as one of *People* magazine's 50 Most Beautiful People in 2004, Govind's widespread media credits include *Bon Appetit*, *Food and Wine*, *Gourmet*, *Wine Spectator*, *O: The Oprah Magazine*, *Iron Chef America*, *The Today Show*, *Top Chef*, and *Fine Living*. Govind's first cookbook was titled *Small Bites, Big Nights*, which Tyler Florence called "everything you're looking for in a cookbook."

We saw Govind's commitment to quality as well as his sense of good simple understated food when Christina helped develop the beer list for the new 8 oz. Burger Bar on Melrose Avenue in Hollywood. One of the things that we love about Govind is his relaxed spirit and his willingness to bring some fun into the dining experience. He turns classics on their heads and seems to have a reverence for things old school, serving beers like Schlitz and Olympia in the can at his gastropub 8 oz. He and his chef de cuisine, Jacob Wildman, came up with this down-to-earth in style but lofty in flavor beer-can chili.

Two-Can Chili: Heirloom Bean and Beer Short Rib Chili

Govind says: There's nothing better than a one-pot meal. This recipe is easy to make and can easily be adjusted for all tastes and preferences.

1 pound boneless short ribs, diced*

Salt and freshly ground black pepper to taste

All-purpose flour, for dredging, plus a little extra for thickening

2 tablespoons olive oil

2 white onions, diced

2 tablespoons chopped garlic

5 tablespoons chili powder

4 tablespoons paprika

3 tablespoons ground cumin

2 tablespoons dried oregano

1 teaspoon cayenne

2 cans Olympia beer

4 cups canned diced tomatoes with liquid

8 cups cooked heirloom beans**

Chicken stock, as needed

Season the meat with salt and pepper, and toss it in the flour. Dust off the excess flour, and brown the meat in the olive oil in a large stock pot over medium-high heat.

Add the onions and garlic, and cook until translucent.

Add all of the herbs and spices and 2 tablespoons flour; stir until well incorporated, about 1 minute.

Add the beer, bring to a boil, and immediately reduce the heat to a simmer.

*Skirt steak and flank steak make great substitutes.
**Try cranberry beans, pinquito beans, vaquero beans, midnight black beans, or red appaloosa beans.

Add the tomatoes and beans, and simmer for 2 hours, incorporating some chicken stock along the way, a couple of cups at a time, until the chili reaches your desired consistency.

Serves 8 to 10

Zoe Nathan, Chef/Co-Owner, Huckleberry Café and Bakery

Zoe Nathan is the chef/co-owner of Huckleberry Café and Bakery in Santa Monica. Huckleberry features hand-crafted breads, breakfast pastry, and dessert, as well as savory sandwiches, salads, rotisserie chicken, and deck-oven pizzas. Zoe is also co-owner of Rustic Canyon Wine Bar and Seasonal Kitchen, where she has been the pastry chef since August 2007. Zoe thinks of herself as more of a baker than a pastry chef; her desserts are rustic in style, with a focus on seasonal ingredients and traditional French technique. She was named one of the top 10 Best Food Related Things of 2008 by S. Irene Virbila in the *Los Angeles Times*, was a James Beard semifinalist in 2009 for Outstanding Pastry Chef, and has been featured in *Food and Wine* and numerous other publications. Zoe honed her craft at Tartine in San Francisco and as the opening baker at BLD in Los Angeles. She has also worked in the kitchens of such notable establishments as Joe's in Los Angeles and Lupa in New York City.

Zoe has been a beer fan for years and is hooked on beer's wide variety. She has created many beer-infused desserts, like Stout gelatos and sweet beer reduction drizzles. When she tasted the Allagash Curieux, a complex beer aged in Kentucky bourbon barrels, she amended her famous flourless chocolate cake recipe, which normally uses rum, to incorporate a reduction made from the beer. People line up around the block to get a taste of Zoe's baking. Now you can make this at home and see what all the fuss is about.

Flourless Chocolate Cake with Allagash Curieux

Zoe says: I used to make this cake with rum, but when I tasted Allagash Curieux, I knew it would be an awesome addition. The Curieux has that wonderful bourbon flavor because of its barrel aging, and it goes so exquisitely with Valrhona chocolate. This combo proves that beer is just as elegant as any liquor in the culinary world.

1 cup Allagash Curieux

½ cup toasted walnut pieces

1 tablespoon Valrhona cocoa powder

5 tablespoons granulated sugar, plus more for topping

6 ounces butter

8 ounces Valrhona chocolate, 66% cocoa

6 egg yolks

¾ cup brown sugar

½ teaspoon plus a hearty pinch salt

6 egg whites

BEER REDUCTION

Bring the Curieux to a boil in a small saucepan, reduce the heat, and simmer until the beer is reduced by half, about 20 minutes. Set aside 2 tablespoons of the reduction to use in the cake, and reserve the rest for a topping.

CAKE

Preheat the oven to 325°F. Grease a 10-inch round cake pan (the height doesn't matter) with melted butter, and line the bottom with parchment paper.

Grind walnuts, cocoa powder, and 1 tablespoon of the granulated sugar in a food processor. Melt the butter, and pour it over the Valrhona chocolate to melt it. Set aside to cool.

Beat the egg yolks and brown sugar in a mixer on high for a full 3 minutes. Add 2 tablespoons of the beer reduction and ½ teaspoon of salt, and mix well.

Fold together the egg yolk mixture, the melted chocolate and butter, and the walnut mixture. Set aside.

In clean mixer bowl, whip the egg whites with a hearty pinch of salt. Slowly add the remaining 4 tablespoons of sugar. Whip to stiff peaks. Fold the egg whites into the batter; *do not mix completely*. Pour into the prepared pan. Top with plenty of granulated sugar to form a crust (about 3 tablespoons). Bake for about 55 minutes. When the top of the cake cracks along the entire surface, bake for 5 more minutes and remove from oven. Cool completely on a wire cake rack.

To serve, drizzle each slice with some of the reserved beer reduction.

Serves 8

ANN KIRK, PASTRY CHEF, LITTLE DOM'S AND DOMINICK'S

Ann Kirk's fascination and passion for pastry began at an early age when she used to assist her mom in the kitchen, licking spatulas and otherwise getting in the way. She began her illustrious career as a lowly pastry cook under pastry chefs Kimberly Sklar and Roxana Jullapat at Suzanne Goin's award-winning Lucques restaurant in Los Angeles. In 2004, Ann went on as a pastry chef in her own right to the well-known La Terza restaurant in Los Angeles. Like many good chefs, Ann then took a sabbatical to Italy, studying every pastry along the way before returning to L.A. and working as the pastry chef in Chris Kidder's Literati 2 kitchen. In 2007, Ann was offered the position of executive pastry chef for Little Dom's (which was named one of the 10 best new restaurants in Los Angeles by *Los Angeles* magazine), Dominick's, and the 101 Coffee Shop in Los Angeles.

It's always good to have pastry chef friends. But it's even better to have a pastry chef friend who is a beer aficionado. We've spent many a night with Ann discussing the nuance of beer X and how it would work so well with dessert Y and getting excited about how beer often really does pair better with chocolate than wine does. What's more, Ann has a reputation among her coworkers for creating boozy desserts! Here's one of our favorite boozy-beery desserts from her.

Oatmeal Stout Panna Cotta

Ann says: As a pastry chef with a sweet tooth, I've always been a big fan of every type of Stout, from vanilla to chocolate to oatmeal; and panna cotta is one of my favorite traditional Italian desserts. Together, they seem like a match made in heaven. Samuel Smith's Oatmeal Stout has a toasty flavor with notes of cocoa and coffee, which complements the panna cotta perfectly.

1 ½ teaspoons powdered gelatin

2 tablespoons cold water

1 ¼ cups Samuel Smith's Oatmeal Stout

¾ cup whole milk

¾ cup heavy whipping cream

1 vanilla bean, cut lengthwise and pulp scraped

⅔ cup sugar

⅔ cup plus 2 tablespoons crème fraîche

1 cup heavy whipping cream

Dash of cinnamon

In a small stainless-steel or other heat-proof bowl, combine the gelatin and cold water, and set aside to soften.

Over medium heat, bring the Stout to a boil in a medium saucepan, and reduce the beer to ¾ cup. Keep an eye on the Stout because it will reduce quickly. Set aside.

In a medium pot, combine the milk, ¾ cup heavy whipping cream, vanilla bean pulp and pod, and sugar. Bring to a boil.

Meanwhile, fill a small pot of water one-third full, and bring to a boil. Set the heat-proof bowl on top of the pot, and stir the gelatin until dissolved.

Note: This is a soft panna cotta, and unmolding is not recommended unless ½ teaspoon more gelatin is added.

Remove from the heat and whisk into hot cream mixture. Next, whisk in the Stout reduction, and then ⅔ cup crème fraîche.

Strain the panna cotta mixture into a pitcher, and pour into 6 serving glasses. Cover the tops with plastic wrap to avoid forming a skin. Chill until set, at least 6 hours.

In a clean bowl, whip together 1 cup heavy whipping cream and the remaining 2 tablespoons of crème fraîche. Whip to soft peaks.

When ready to serve, top each dessert with a dollop of the whipped cream and a dash of cinnamon. This is excellent served with a butter cookie or chocolate wafer.

Makes six ½-cup servings

*   *   *

So now you're pairing beer with food on your own, elevating your dining experience, and creating new bold flavors and combinations. You are on the cutting edge of the beer world. How does it feel? You are on par with pioneer restaurant owners and chefs from all over the country. Isn't dining more interesting? A whole new world, *n'est pas*? Take your pairing power to the people; next time you go out with friends, order a 750-milliliter bottle of beer for the table and give them something to talk about.

Brewing at Home

It is my design to die in the brew-house; let
ale be placed to my mouth when I am expiring,
that when the choirs of angels come, they may
say, "Be God propitious to this drinker."

—SAINT COLUMBANUS

Be the Beer

Homebrewing is not a new phenomenon. George Washington famously made note of his homebrew recipe. And both he and Thomas Jefferson had brewing operations under their roofs. Families have been homebrewing as far back as the dawn of beer itself. Women and men routinely made beer as part of their daily regimen. However, as taverns and commercial breweries took hold, beer was readily available at every pub, and homebrewing was not always necessary. In 1920 in America, the Eighteenth Amendment put the kibosh on breweries. Many had to shut their doors, and the variety of styles dwindled as the economy of brewing was siphoned. When Prohibition was repealed in 1933 (thank God!), breweries could reopen, but there were far fewer than before, and they had to rebuild a business that was hurt by the dry period. Sadly, when they repealed Prohibition, they forgot to legalize homebrewing. It was okay to make your own wine, but someone forgot to mention the word *beer* (George Washington must have rolled over in his grave a couple of times!). Enter Jimmy Carter. On October 14, 1979, he finally legalized homebrewing (it took only *46 years!*) and became the favorite president of many a beer lover (October 14 is a holiday for most beer-geeks). Of course, people had been brewing tasty beer in secret up until that point, as a rebellion against the light lagers that dominated the beer scene. In the 1980s, they were finally able to brew without risk.

It is now legal to brew beer at home (except in Alabama—what's up with that?), as long as you are 21 and don't brew more than 100 gallons a year. It is illegal to sell your homebrew, so don't go setting up shop unless you want to go through the official procedures it takes to become a legal brewery.

Brewing is the logical next step for you, the beer lover. Nothing will bring you closer to beer than becoming its creator. You will understand the ingredients and flavor profiles in a profoundly new way once you're following brewing recipes and adding your own imagination to the pot. For many beer connoisseurs, this is the most rewarding part of the Beer Journey: being able to concoct a beer and share their homebrew with friends and family. And this will make you even more comfortable in conversations with brewmasters on brewery visits and in quality brewpubs. But don't worry, brewing isn't as complicated as it may seem.

If you break down the basics of homebrew—boiling, cooling, mixing, and storing—it's basically cooking. It is done in a pot, uses ingredients, and is served to guests. The only difference, of course, is that it is alcohol (bonus!). Though it may seem overwhelming the first time you look at a homebrew recipe and get ready to brew, don't fret. Remember the days when you would look at a food recipe and fear the seven steps and different measurements? You eventually found that it was easier to do than it looked. It's the same with homebrewing; daunting at first, but with practice it does get easier and more fun. And at the end of it, you have beer!

So, first things first, you need to have a homebrew equipment kit. As with any kit, you can buy the necessities separately or conveniently prepackaged together, depending on your preference. A basic homebrew equipment kit will cost you anywhere from $70 to $200, depending on how geared up you want to be. We paid about $120 for our equipment. Once you have made this initial investment, homebrew gets a lot more economical. Ingredients will cost you on average about $30 per five gallons of beer. That ends up being about 60¢ for a 12-ounce bottle, a damn good deal.

The next section is a list of things you will need to have to get to brewin'.

Tools

- **BREWPOT:** Yes, it looks like a silver pot with a lid. But it needs to be big, at least 20 quarts, and stainless steel is best. This is where you'll cook the malt and add some hops and, well, make the beer.

- **BUCKET:** You've seen these: a big cylindrical plastic thing, which often has a handle. You'll need a large vessel, seven to eight gallons, with a good, secure, tight lid. The lid does need to have a hole in it that fits an airlock perfectly. This will be your primary fermenter, the vessel in which you will put the yeast and let your beer begin the fermentation process. The plastic needs to be food-grade, so double-check the quality of the bucket. Alternatively, you can use a glass carboy—a big glass thing that looks like those vessels people put in the watercoolers at the office. You'd need one that holds about five gallons. Unlike the

Clockwise from left: brewpot, glass carboy with fermentation airlock and stopper, bottling bucket and hose, bottling cane and hose, capper, beer bottle, thermometer, yeast, bottle brush, siphoning cane and hose, and wort chiller.

plastic bucket, the carboy allows you to see the fermentation happening, and the glass seems nicer than the plastic. Note, though, that the carboy is harder to clean and easier to break.

○ **FERMENTATION AIRLOCK AND STOPPER:** This is a plastic device that is wedged into the top of the fermentation vessel (your bucket lid or carboy opening) and allows for CO_2 to release during fermentation but prevents outside air from entering, which could spoil the beer.

○ **STRAINING BAG:** This is similar to a teabag or cheesecloth. You can use this to strain the mash. You will scoop all of the mash from the boil into this bag and then squeeze out as much liquid as possible. You don't want to lose any of the sugar from the malt, so the squeezing is necessary. This can also be used to strain out hops at different increments during the brewing process.

○ **WORT CHILLER:** This is a device used to cool down the wort, enough so that you can add the yeast. If the wort is too hot, the yeast will die or act weird, and there will be no good beer (sad face).

○ **SIPHON CANE AND HOSE:** This is the vehicle the newly made beer will travel through to get to a secondary fermenter. Be sure you use food-grade plastic.

○ **BOTTLE FILLER:** This device looks like a little wand with a ball valve at the end that allows you to stop the flow of beer to keep the beer from overflowing your bottles.

○ **EMPTY BEER BOTTLES AND CAPS:** Remember when we told you to hold on to your empty bottles? This is why: You are probably going to want to bottle your beer. This is where your beer will undergo a secondary fermentation. Most homebrewers save bottles and then sterilize them. If you are making a five-gallon batch of beer, you will end up with 40 to 50 bottles. You can keg your beer, but beginners usually start off bottling, which makes it easier to keep and transport, and give as gifts to your lucky friends. Unfortunately bottle caps cannot be reused, but you can buy them along with new beer bottles (if you didn't save yours) at a local homebrew supply store.

○ **BOTTLE BRUSH:** A long brush used to make sure the bottles are clean and properly sanitized.

○ **BOTTLING BUCKET:** After primary fermentation, you will transfer your beer into this bucket, which has a spigot on the bottom, and then transfer the beer into bottles.

○ **SANITIZER:** This is extremely important! Sanitizing is perhaps the most annoying part of homebrewing (who likes to clean, really?), but it is crucial to the health of your beer. You don't want certain bacteria to get into your beer and make it taste bad. Get a commercial beer sanitizer; these usually have iodine, chlorine, or bleach. We suggest BTF Iodophor Sanitizer.

○ **FLOATING THERMOMETER:** Because you need to do certain steps at certain temperature points, you need a good thermometer—unless you can measure liquid temperature with your eyes.

○ **HYDROMETER:** This measures the density of a liquid against the density of water. You will need to take an initial measurement of the density of the beer before and after fermentation. This will help you figure out your beer's ABV.

○ **CAPPER:** This little handy dandy device puts those flat caps onto your bottle. Wow, magic.

Brewing Vocabulary

Before you can start to brew, you will need to know what the hell people are talking about in those recipes for homebrewing. There are a few words that pop up a lot in this world, some of which you may already know, but it's good to have a refresher. The definitions are in the order in which you may encounter them when brewing. Take note of these essentials (no, there will not be a quiz):

○ **MASH:** The process in which the crushed grains are mixed into hot water, and enzymes change the starch into fermentable (sometimes unfermentable) sugars for the yeast to eat.

○ **PARTIAL MASH:** Brewing using a wort made partially from grain and partially from malt extract.

○ **ALL GRAIN OR FULL MASH:** A brew made using grains—raw malted barley—instead of malt extracts. This requires space and time and is quite advanced in the brewing world. This is often the practice of professional brewers.

○ **MASH TUN:** The name of the vessel that contains the mash during all-grain brewing.

○ **BASE MALT:** The malt used as the main source of sugar for fermentation.

○ **MALT EXTRACT:** A concentrated liquid formed from wort that contains the sugars needed for brewing. This is what most homebrewers use instead of all-grain brewing.

○ **SPECIALTY MALTS:** Smaller amounts of malt used for flavoring and nuance. These can be steeped like tea instead of turned into a mash.

○ **SPECIALTY GRAIN BILL:** This is a list of specialty grains, typically malt, in a beer recipe to be used in addition to the malt extract. These are grains that will be crushed in the grist process and then usually steeped like tea during the boil.

○ **STEEPING GRAINS:** These are used to add flavor, nuance, or color for brewers using a malt extract. These do not need to be converted to sugar and can also be steeped like tea.

○ **SPARGING:** This comes after the mash, when grains are removed and the liquid is separated, becoming the wort.

○ **GRIST:** A mixture of grains that is crushed in a mill and prepared for mashing.

○ **WORT:** The name for the liquid that is extracted from the mash. It is pronounced WERT.

○ **ADJUNCT:** A starch used in brewing other than malted barley, sometimes used for flavor and sometimes for mouthfeel. It is sometimes used instead of an amount of malt, making the beer cheaper to make.

○ **HOP PELLETS:** Little things that look like gross vitamins. These are used by most homebrewers in lieu of a bunch of dried or fresh hops.

○ **BITTERING HOPS:** Hops used early in the boil to bitter the beer, not to add aroma.

○ **FLAVOR HOPS:** Hops used later in the boil to add some aroma and flavor.

○ **AROMA HOPS:** Hops added last to the boil, meant to add hop aromas, not bitterness or flavor.

○ **ATTENUATION:** The term used to describe the amount of fermentation that happened (meaning how much sugar the yeast ate) and how much the original gravity decreased. Refers to the final ABV.

○ **RACK:** The process of moving the beer at different stages of homebrewing.

○ **PITCH:** The term for adding the yeast to the cooled wort, as in "time to pitch the yeast!"

○ **PRIMING:** The addition of sugar (priming sugar) to beer that has already fermented. This occurs as the beer is being bottled or kegged to promote more flavor nuances, more alcohol and carbonation, or all three.

○ **ORIGINAL GRAVITY:** The measurement of the density of the liquid wort before fermentation; important for later ABV determination.

○ **FINAL GRAVITY:** The final measurement of the density of the wort after fermentation; using the original gravity and final gravity, you can calculate the ABV.

How to Brew

The basic brewing process consists of these steps: making the wort, fermenting, conditioning, bottling, and drinking. It's really that simple. The complexity depends on the recipe, the ingredients, your equipment, your patience, and proper sanitation. There are a ton of great resources out there with extensive details that will help you learn how to brew well. We offer a quick, basic step-by-step here but encourage you to pick up some of the books mentioned at the end of this chapter, and visit the many homebrew websites on the Internet.

First, gather your equipment and your ingredients based on a recipe. Start with something simple; nothing with fancy yeast or spices or fruit. Some styles are easier for homebrew, like a Pale Ale or a Porter, but don't assume that darker brews are harder to brew. Everything is hard to perfect or do as well as a professional brewer, but some beers are good starter styles. An ale is easier for a beginner than a lager because, as you know, a lager needs to ferment at a steady low temperature for a long time. This requires some sort of large refrigerator for your homebrew, which most people don't have. Ales can ferment at a high room temperature, and they take a shorter amount of time. We suggest brewing small batches; five gallons is standard for a homebrew and still makes a lot of beer.

The following steps are for brewing with malt extract instead of malted grains because extract is the best jumping-off point for beginners. Consult more advanced homebrew books if you feel you are advanced enough to graduate to all-grain brewing.

STEP ONE

Sanitize your equipment. Again, we know how annoying this may seem, but you *must* do it. Bacteria can ruin your brew, and it's a shame to go through the process and wait for your beer to be ready only to find it tastes off because of bacteria. You need to soak *all* of the equipment you are going to use in a sanitizer/water mix (1 ounce per 5 gallons of water). This means you need a soaking tub or big sink. Soak for about 15 minutes, then rinse everything thoroughly so that the sanitizer doesn't end up in your brew.

STEP TWO

Get the water boiling. Fill up your brewpot, leaving some room (about 6 inches) at the top. When you add the ingredients, the water level will rise, and you don't want the dreaded boilover. You will eventually add the boiled liquid, or wort, to more water after the boil, but try to boil as much of the water as you can, for sterilization reasons.

STEP THREE

Add your malt extract. Remove the water from the heat first so that you don't get boilover when you add the malt. You will most likely be dumping this syrupy substance (taste it, it's yummy!) from a plastic container. Use some of the boiling water to rinse the container and get all of the extract out. Stir this mix and bring back to a boil. Don't leave it alone because you don't want the extract to burn on the bottom of the pot. Let the mixture boil for 15 minutes. You will add hops (probably hop pellets, but possibly whole hops) at certain increments based on the recipe you're following. This will vary. After the hop additions, you will boil for a while, stirring occasionally.

STEP FOUR

Cool down the mixture, also known as the wort. There are several ways to do this, none of which is particularly simple, but you *must* cool it down before you transfer the liquid to your fermentation vessel (the plastic bucket or carboy). This goes for both ales and lagers; both must be cooled down before you add the yeast. You can put the pot into a sink or tub full of ice, or you can use a wort chiller, which is a spiral copper tube that you will have sanitized and can put into the wort. You then run cold water through the tube; the water travels through the copper and cools the wort before coming out the other end. The good thing about this is that it is fast; the slower you cool the wort, the longer you leave it open to contamination. We recommend catching the water at the end of the wort chiller and using it to water your yard.

STEP FIVE

Get ready to pitch your yeast. If you have liquid yeast from a vial, just shake it up and wait for the wort to reach the correct temperature. This temperature should be around 78°F. The temperature has to be cool enough to keep the yeast alive; high temperatures will kill the yeast, and you will have no beer. If you are using a dehydrated yeast, you'll have to rehydrate it, using boiled water for sanitation purposes.

STEP SIX

Before you pitch the yeast, move the wort to the fermentation vessel (either a bucket or a carboy). Be careful and get help so that you don't spill too much. If you want to filter out some of the stuff left in the wort, like the hops you may have added, use a funnel with a mesh bag, or hop bag, in it. Make sure everything has been sanitized! Most recipes require filtration because hops and malt can go bad if left in the beer. You can also use a siphon tube called a racking siphon. This will transfer your wort to the carboy quite well.

STEP SEVEN

Pitch that yeast! Go ahead, you've earned it! But wait! Use your thermometer to make sure the wort is at 78°F or below. Be patient and wait for the mixture to cool down to this temperature. If the temperature is above this, the yeast may produce off-flavors or die.

STEP EIGHT

Put in your airlock, which allows the CO_2 to get out without letting air with bacteria in. These thingies have a little tube you need to fill up with vodka (you can use another type of alcohol, but vodka is the best because it lacks taste, so if some of it gets into the beer, it won't alter the flavor). The alcohol helps keep any bacteria from getting in.

STEP NINE

Let the beer be. Ales are happiest fermenting between 60°F and 70°F, so find a cool dark spot. Lagers need to be fermenting between 45°F and 55°F, so you'll need a refrigerated spot. If you are using the glass carboy, keep it away from sunlight because this may ruin the beer. After a bit, the airlock will start to bubble, and you'll know that fermentation is happening. Let this sit for 10 to 14 days. You'll know the fermentation is done if the bubbling in the airlock has decreased to about one bubble a minute.

STEP TEN

Bottle your beer. You need to sanitize the bottles and caps. You can soak the bottles in sanitizer, or run them through the dishwasher alone, or be super thorough and use the bottle brush to be sure they're clean. The bottle caps need to be sanitized, too, but make sure you don't ruin the seal by overheating them in any way. This could affect the seal on the bottle and in turn ruin your beer. Before bottling, transfer the beer via a siphon hose to your bottling bucket and add dissolved priming sugar, which will get the yeast eating again and create a secondary fermentation in the bottle (good for flavor, CO_2, and a higher ABV). Again, via siphon, you will send the beer to the bottles and then cap them. Leave 1 to 1.5 inches below the cap.

STEP ELEVEN

You wait. An ale will take about a week until it's ready, a lager about two weeks. You can always test this by opening a bottle and tasting. Put your beer somewhere cool and out of direct light. Many people use a closet, but beware, beers have been known to explode if the fermentation in the bottle gets out of hand. This is rare, but it happens, so don't put it with your clothes or anything you don't want beer on.

If you want to put labels on your beers, which is fun and makes the beer a great gift, try www.worldlabel.com/Pages/bottle-labels.htm, which offers printable bottle labels and a downloadable bottle label template. Now you get to name your beer and put whatever image on it you want (we hope you don't use a huge picture of your face, 'cause that's, well, lame).

Don't get discouraged if your beer comes out subpar. It's going to take a few batches before you start to understand how best to brew. Try to wait before making beers with fancy ingredients until you have perfected a simpler recipe. Once you graduate to another level, however, you can get creative, adding various spices, yeasts, and fruit. This is where the chef in you can express his or her artistry. Most breweries started out with a determined homebrewer trying different recipes and finding a true passion for the beverage. You never know, this hobby may become your new profession.

Advanced Brewing Techniques: Beer 401

If you have conquered some of the easier brewing recipes, you may be ready to get all crazy and create your own funky beer. You can do this by using advanced yeast strains, adding unique flavorings, changing up the hop varieties, and so on. Or perhaps you are ready to make your first lager and ferment at low temperatures. Once you delve into the more creative world of brewing, you will definitely end up with some pretty gross mistakes, and you have to accept that as part of experimentation and learning. But you may also end up with a truly unique brew that will give you a sense of satisfaction you hadn't yet felt in the world of beer—the satisfaction of being a beer artist.

The following sections discuss a few advanced aspects of brewing that you may want to experiment with.

Yeast Is Complicated: *Brettanomyces*

Yeast is a bit hard to control, as it has a mind of its own, and using more advanced yeast is tricky. The sour yeasts can invade everything if not properly cared for, and sometimes the flavors they impart will be unbearable at first, but after some aging, they can become wonderful. There are more strains of yeast than we can count, and some breweries create their own "scientific" mix and keep vials safely stored away. Each beer style has anywhere from 20 to 40 yeast strains for you to choose from. Most recipes will ask for a specific traditional yeast strain that isn't too complex, and these have all kinds of different names, like American Ale Yeast and Muntons Premium Gold. The more advanced recipes, however, will require some complex yeasts that can get a little funky. If you are into this and want to start experimenting, get to know this word: *Brettanomyces*.

Brettanomyces is the most famous of the funky ale yeasts and is affectionately called Brett for short. This is a determined and invasive little fungus that will eat pretty much any sugar, whether it be in the beer or the barrel or the floor. It's famous for the complex flavors it imparts, which tend to conjure up these words: sour, funky, smoky, earthy, horse blanket, barnyard, dirty socks, sweaty saddle, and old cheese. Though this may sound really disgusting, trust us, it can be the perfect flavor addition to many different beers. We love earthy, funky, sour beers, and we count ourselves among those who desperately seek out Brett. Brett is notoriously hard to control, and some homebrewers will have entirely separate equipment for their Brett brews. If Brett gets loose, it could get into all of your present and future brews.

Brett beers are also a bit advanced because they require some aging. The funk of Brett can taste quite harsh if the beer isn't allowed to mellow out and develop more complexity. Your Brett beer may need six months to a year before the sour earthy flavors become a good thing. Brett is often used as an additional yeast, something you add at the end after the original yeast is pitched. This will create a complex fermentation process that can go a bit wild, and it will no doubt take some practice for you to befriend Brett, but if you love the sour funky flavor like we do, the practice is well worth it.

Partial Mash and All Grain: Not for Kids

If you are wondering what lies beyond the world of malt extract, then get to know these terms: *partial mash* and *all grain*. As you know, using malt extract is the quick way to create your wort. Someone else has gone through all the trouble of turning grain into malt and has reduced it to a nice sweet syrup or powder you can easily dump into the boil. But if you want to get more involved with your malt, you can begin by making partial-mash homebrews. This means that you will use some of the malt extract and some dry malt, which you will grind in a grist and steep yourself (almost like tea). There are many recipes that offer this combo brew, and it's a great way to begin to understand the complexities of all-grain or full-mash brewing, the process that most professional brewers go through. The great thing about using some quality grains in your brew is that you can add some layers of flavor that you can't get with a tub of malt extract. You can do a mix of a pale and chocolate malt that will bring out a complexity to your Brown Ale you hadn't had before. The quality of beer will improve greatly as you move to more and more grain. If you feel ready, and have the room to make an all-grain or full-mash beer, be prepared for a bit of a mess. This is not a popular choice for most homebrewers because it involves a lot of space for the boil. See the recommended brew books at the end of this chapter for more info on partial-mash and all-grain brewing.

Just Throw in the Spice Rack: Flavorings and Adjuncts

If you want to get super crazy with your brewing, try adding some adjuncts and flavorings. As in cooking, fruit, spices, and herbs are a huge part of brewing beer. Also like cooking, these ingredients may not turn out the way you expected them to once you taste the final product. So start out simply. We recommend using a beer you feel you've mastered, perhaps a Porter of some sort, then add a flavoring that isn't too complicated and would obviously go well with the flavors of that Porter, perhaps chocolate or vanilla. It's tempting to throw in a bunch of crazy things, but try to build up to flavorings like chai, which uses a collection of spices. After you perfect the vanilla or chocolate or cinnamon Porter, you can add nutmeg the next time and cardamom the next, to keep building complexity. Use some recipes that do a few adjuncts or flavorings and note how much the brewer recommends adding and when. Just to get your creative juices flowing, we've made a suggestion list of adjuncts (unmalted grains added as a supplement to malted barley for brewing) and flavorings (extras added to some beers solely for flavor) we've seen used in craft brewing:

ADJUNCTS

Candi sugar	Rice
Corn	Rye
Oats	Wheat

FLAVORINGS

Agave	Basil	Chili
Allspice	Brown sugar	Chipotle pepper
Anise	Cacao nibs	Chocolate
Apples	Chamomile	Cinnamon
Banana	Cherry	Citrus peels

Clover	Licorice	Raspberry
Coconut	Maple syrup	Rosemary
Coffee	Mint	Sage
Coriander	Molasses	Seaweed
Ginger	Mugwort	Spearmint
Heather	Nutmeg	Star anise
Honey	Oak chips	Tea
Jalapeño pepper	Orange	Thyme
Juniper	Oysters	Vanilla
Lavender	Peach	Watermelon
Lemon	Pine needles	Yams
Lemongrass	Pumpkin	Yarrow

Advanced Hops

When you get into brewing and drinking hoppy beers, you will, no doubt, come across these two suggestive phrases: wet-hopped and dry-hopped. They're not as dirty as they sound. Dry-hopping is the process in brewing when dried hops are added to the wort after the boil or to the fermenter. This would be after you've made other hop additions during the boil. Dry-hopping is not meant to add bitterness and dryness but to enhance aroma and flavor. Wet-hopping (get your giggles out now), on the other hand, uses freshly picked hops that have not been dried or put onto pellet form. This process is said to impart a green flavor to your beer, a grassier, earthier taste. Wet- and dry-hopping are often used to make seasonal specialty beers seen around the holidays, as hops are harvested in September.

Here is one wet- and one dry-hopped beer to try:

SIERRA NEVADA HARVEST ALE: Sierra Nevada Brewing Company, Chico, California. This wet-hopped American IPA has the fresh grassy notes that are typical of wet-hopping. Notes of caramel, citrus, and pine; nice oily bitterness. 6.7% ABV.

○ **OLD GUARDIAN BARLEY WINE DOUBLE DRY HOPPED:** Stone Brewing Company, Escondido, California. A dry-hopped Barleywine with notes of spice and dried fruit, and an aromatic hop bitterness. 11.3% ABV.

Hops come in many different varieties, and all of the varieties impart different aromas, flavors, and general effects on beer. You will want to gain a general idea of the flavors of different hops and experiment with them as you get into brewing. Here's a short list of some hops that you might wanna get to know:

○ **AMARILLO:** American hop widely used.

○ **CASCADE:** Created in Oregon from a combo of Russian and Fuggle hops; extremely popular in America and made famous by the flavors it imparts to Sierra Nevada Pale Ale. Named for the mountain range. Has a lot of citrus and grapefruit to it.

○ **CENTENNIAL:** Derived from a few English hops, this is a popular American hop. Bitter and floral.

○ **CHINOOK:** American hop derived from Golding. Big piney flavor and nice spice.

○ **COLUMBUS:** American hop, high acid and bitter flavor.

○ **FUGGLE:** English hop variety widely used in the United Kingdom. Not as sweet as Golding.

○ **GOLDING:** Same as Kent Golding, but not grown in Kent.

○ **HALLERTAU:** Named after the Hallertau area in Germany, a huge producer of hops. Spicy and drying.

○ **KENT GOLDING:** English hops grown in Kent and used in most English ales. Flavorful and mild.

○ **MOUNT HOOD:** Derived from Hallertau. Spicy and clean.

- **SAAZ:** Classic Czech hops used in Pilsners. Spicy but mild.

- **STERLING:** Floral American hop derived from several others.

- **TETTNANG:** From Tettnang in southern Germany. Used in lighter beers. Also grown in the United States, but has stronger flavors.

- **WILLAMETTE:** American hop known for its spicy woody aroma.

There are many more varieties of hops out there, and knowing their different flavors is essential to becoming a quality brewer. You need to know which are primarily used for bittering purposes, for aroma, and for flavor. A hop mistake can definitely make a brew unpalatable. If you can master your hops, your homebrews have great potential. See the brewing references at the end of the chapter for more information on hops.

Recipes

As you move ahead as a homebrewer, you will begin to truly appreciate the skill of the master brewers. There's nothing like doing something yourself to appreciate others who do it every day. You will taste beer in a different way, wondering about the grains, the hopping process, the strain of yeast used. You will fall in love with beer all over again, with a deeper understanding of how a beer is born.

We asked some of our favorite brewers to supply a few of their homebrew recipes. These are people who really know what they're doing and have been brewing for years and years, working hard to make the greatest brews. Before you try them out, you might want to brush up on your homebrew techniques with online tutorials (for example, www .beertools.com/html/tutorial/index.shtml) or the homebrew books mentioned later in this book.

Woman's Work: Female Brewers

You may think brewing beer is a man's job, and some women may feel that stirring the pot of mash is foreign to their sex, but oh how wrong you are! Women have always been stars of the kitchen, so it shouldn't surprise anyone that they brew up some of the best. In fact, women were brewing beer as far back as ancient Babylon, where female brewers were considered high priestesses. Discovery of early Peruvian remains has lead archaeologists to confirm that women of that society were master brewers as well. And these female brewers were not slaves or servants but highly regarded women of the society. In medieval times, it was not unusual for the women to be the primary brewers of the household and town. Female brewers in early England and Scotland were generally known as brewsters (though this may not have been the case in certain parts of Europe, where *brewster* also referred to male brewers) and added beer to their list of items to make during the day. At that time, women often sat among male brewers, entrenched in the business of beer. Sometimes women inherited a brewery when they became widows. As the official Brewers Guild gained power after the 1300s, however, women were rarely allowed to be certified brewers. Men wanted this business for themselves, and this eventually took women out of the running to be professional and successful brewers.

It's taken a while for female brewers to take their power back, and perhaps this is because beer is not marketed to the modern woman. The craft brewery world often seems to be dominated by men, but this is not true. As we write this, there are many women brewing beer in their own breweries and at home. And we're thrilled to see women's brewing clubs popping up all around the country. Women are embracing their history as brewsters and beer lovers, and we're all the better for it.

To see a list of bona fide female brewers, check out the Pink Boots Society (www.pinkbootssociety.com), a group of women active in the business of beer.

Culver City Home Brewing Supply

Culver City Home Brewing Supply (CCHBS) is our go-to for any of our homebrewing needs. Founded in 1994 and now owned by Kevin Koenig, Greg Beron, Craig Corley, and Tim Bardet, this store and homebrewing hub has been an invaluable resource for not only supplies but also advice, knowledge, and recipes. This store also happens to be the home and headquarters of our homebrewers club, Pacific Gravity (www.pacificgravity.com). CCHBS now stocks over 60 different brewing grains, along with more than 20 varieties of hops.

Most of the store's recipes have names reflecting movie titles, which is appropriate because Culver City is a center of film production. Greg and Kevin have amazing know-how and are determined to teach Angelenos how to brew. We bought our first brew kit from Greg, and he showed us the ropes. The following four recipes are great for those new to homebrewing. Find a store like his in your neck of the woods and bring your recipe in. Someone there will help you get the right equipment, pick out the right ingredients, and even measure out the smallest ounce amount for you. Your local homebrew store might even teach classes and have group brewing sessions like CCHBS. Happy brewing.

Little Mac Scottish Light -/60

Little Mac Scottish Light -/60 is a malty, flavorful beer that's also low in alcohol. The -/60 stands for 60 shillings, which was the cost for a barrel of ingredients when the style was created.

SPECIALTY GRAIN BILL

> 6 ounces British Crystal 37L*
> 6 ounces British Crystal 77L
> 2 ounces CaraMunich
> 1 ounce roasted barley

MALT SOURCES

> 3 pounds Munich extract
> 1 pound light dried malt extract

HOPPING SCHEDULE

> 0.7 ounce Challenger (7.6%) hops, boil 60 minutes

YEAST

> Wyeast 1728 Scottish Ale or White Labs WLP028 Edinburgh

FERMENTATION TEMPERATURE

> 65–75°F

PRIMING SUGAR

> 0.5 pound corn sugar dissolved in 1 cup boiling water and cooled to room temperature

In a small pot, heat 3 or 4 quarts of water to around 150°F (bubbles start to form on the bottom). Remove from the heat, and stir in the specialty grains. Cover and steep for 20 to 30 minutes.

---

*This number stands for the degrees Lovibond, which refers to the degree of darkness of the malt. The higher the number, the darker the malt. The unit is named after Joseph Lovibond, who developed this measurement in the 1860s.

Meanwhile, fill a large brewpot half full with water, and bring to a boil. When bubbles start to rise from the pot, turn off the heat and stir in both types of malt extract.

After the grains have steeped, pour the liquid and grains through a strainer directly into the main brewpot. Add some hot water to the small pot, and rinse the grains in the strainer in the hot water to extract as much flavor and sugar as you can from the grains. This is the sparging process. Add this liquid to the main pot.

Bring what is now called wort to a full, rolling boil. Watch for boilovers! Once the foaming stops, add the contents of the hop package. Maintain the boil for 60 minutes.

Meanwhile, sanitize your fermenter, strainer, airlock, and stopper.

When the boil is done, cool the pot in a sink until the sides are cool to the touch.

Pour the wort into the sanitized fermenter, add prechilled water to bring it up to 5 gallons at about 75°F, and pitch the yeast.

Ferment in the recommended temperature range for 7 to 10 days or until bubbling in the airlock has decreased to about one bubble a minute.

Bottle with dissolved priming sugar when fermentation is complete. (See Step Ten and Step Eleven on page 224.)

Yellow Brick Road Wheat Beer

This Hefeweizen, American Wheat, Fruity Wheat Beer is an easy recipe for beginners but still satisfying for experienced brewers. By varying the yeast used, it can have the qualities of either a German Hefeweizen or an American Wheat Beer, and with the addition of a fruit extract, it makes a tasty Fruity Wheat Beer, too.

MALT SOURCES

6 pounds wheat extract

HOPPING SCHEDULE

0.45 ounce Perle (8.3%) hops, boil 60 minutes

YEAST

For American Wheat Beer: Wyeast 1010 American Wheat or White Labs WLP320 American Hefeweizen

For German-style Hefeweizen: White Labs WLP300 Hefeweizen Ale or Wyeast 3333 German Wheat

OTHER INGREDIENTS

For Fruity Wheat Beer: 4 ounces fruit flavoring (apricot, blackberry, cranberry, lemon, mango, raspberry); add either to secondary fermentation or at bottling

FERMENTATION TEMPERATURE

65–75°F

PRIMING SUGAR

0.5 pound corn sugar dissolved in 1 cup boiling water and cooled to room temperature

Fill a large brewpot half full with water, and heat until bubbles start to rise. Turn off the heat, and stir in the malt extract.

Add water to bring the total volume up to 3.5 to 4 gallons. This is now called wort. Bring it to a full, rolling boil. Watch for boilovers! Once the foaming stops, add the contents of the hop package. Maintain the boil for 60 minutes.

Meanwhile, sanitize your fermenter, strainer, airlock, and stopper.

When the boil is done, cool the pot in a sink until the sides are cool to the touch.

Pour the wort into the sanitized fermenter, add prechilled water to bring it up to 5 gallons at about 75°F, and pitch the yeast.

Ferment in the recommended temperature range for 7 to 10 days or until bubbling in the airlock has decreased to about one bubble a minute.

Bottle with dissolved priming sugar when fermentation is complete. (See Step Ten and Step Eleven on page 224.)

Evil Monk Belgian Pale Ale

Evil Monk Belgian Pale Ale is best described as an entry-level Belgian beer. It's low in alcohol for a Belgian, and is less challenging to ferment than stronger examples.

SPECIALTY GRAIN BILL

> 4 ounces Caravienne malt
>
> 4 ounces Carafoam malt
>
> 4 ounces aromatic malt
>
> 4 ounces biscuit malt

MALT SOURCES

> 6 pounds Pale Malt extract

HOPPING SCHEDULE

> 1. 0.6 ounce Perle (8.3%) hops, boil 60 minutes
>
> 2. 0.4 ounce Saaz hops, add after 45 minutes
>
> 3. 0.2 ounce Saaz hops, add at 60 minutes

YEAST

> Wyeast 3522 Belgian Ardennes or White Labs WLP550 Belgian Ale or Wyeast 3942 Belgian Wheat or other Belgian

FERMENTATION TEMPERATURE

> 65–80°F

PRIMING SUGAR

> 0.5 pound corn sugar dissolved in 1 cup boiling water and cooled to room temperature

In a small pot, heat 3 or 4 quarts of water to around 150°F (bubbles start to form on the bottom). Remove from the heat, and stir in the specialty grains. Cover and steep for 20 to 30 minutes.

Meanwhile, fill a large brewpot half full with water, and heat until bubbles start to rise from the pot. Turn off the heat, and stir in the malt extract.

After the grains have steeped, pour the liquid and grains through a strainer directly into the main brewpot. Add some hot water to the small pot, and rinse the grains in the strainer in the hot water to extract as much flavor and sugar as you can from the grains. This is the sparging process. Add this liquid to the main pot.

Bring what is now called wort to a full, rolling boil. Watch for boilovers! Once the foaming stops, add the contents of the first hop package, and set the timer for 45 minutes.

Meanwhile, sanitize your fermenter, strainer, airlock, and stopper.

When the timer sounds, add the second addition of hops, and set the timer for 15 minutes. When the timer sounds, add the last hop addition and turn off the heat.

When the boil is done, cool the pot in a sink until the sides are cool to the touch.

Pour the wort into the sanitized fermenter, add prechilled water to bring it up to 5 gallons at about 75°F, and pitch the yeast.

Ferment in the recommended temperature range for 7 to 10 days or until bubbling in the airlock has decreased to about one bubble a minute.

Bottle with dissolved priming sugar when fermentation is complete. (See Step Ten and Step Eleven on page 224.)

Sunset Boulevard Amber Ale: American Amber Ale

This is Culver City Home Brewing's version of the style that's a staple of brewpubs and microbrews around the country. The use of Munich malt extract lends it a malty flavor, which is nicely balanced by a restrained hoppiness.

SPECIALTY GRAIN BILL

>2 ounces chocolate malt
>
>12 ounces British Crystal 77
>
>4 ounces Crystal 40

MALT SOURCE

>6 pounds Munich malt extract

HOPPING SCHEDULE

>1. 0.35 ounce Summit (16.7%) hops, boil 60 minutes
>
>2. 0.4 ounce Willamette hops, add after 45 minutes
>
>3. 0.6 ounce Crystal hops, add at 60 minutes

YEAST

>White Labs WLP051 California V/Wyeast 1272 American Ale II or Wyeast 1056 American Ale/White Labs WLP001 California Ale

FERMENTATION TEMPERATURE

>65–75°F

PRIMING SUGAR

>0.5 pound corn sugar dissolved in 1 cup boiling water and cooled to room temperature

In a small pot, heat 3 or 4 quarts of water to around 150°F (bubbles start to form on the bottom). Remove from the heat, and stir in the specialty grains. Cover and steep for 20 to 30 minutes.

Meanwhile, fill a large brewpot half full with water, and bring to a boil.

When bubbles start to rise from the pot, turn off the heat and stir in the malt extract.

After the grains have steeped, pour the liquid and grains through a strainer directly into the main brewpot. Add some hot water to the small pot, and rinse the grains in the strainer in the hot water to extract as much flavor and sugar as you can from the grains. This is the sparging process. Add this liquid to the main pot.

Bring what is now called wort to a full, rolling boil. Watch for boilovers! Once the foaming stops, add the contents of the first hop package, and set the timer for 45 minutes.

Meanwhile, sanitize your fermenter, strainer, airlock, and stopper.

When the timer sounds, add the second addition of hops, and set the timer for 15 minutes. When the timer sounds, add the last hop addition and turn off the heat.

When the boil is done, cool the pot in a sink until the sides are cool to the touch.

Pour the wort into the sanitized fermenter, add prechilled water to bring it up to 5 gallons at about 75°F, and pitch the yeast.

Ferment in the recommended temperature range for 7 to 10 days.

When the bubbling in the airlock is down to less than twice a minute, move the beer to a secondary fermenter. This can be another bucket or glass carboy. This allows the beer more time to ferment and adds another layer of complexity to the flavor profile before bottling.

Bottle with dissolved priming sugar when the fermentation is complete.

ROB TOD, FOUNDER/BREWER, ALLAGASH
BREWING COMPANY

We are big fans of Allagash brews, and have been fortunate enough to share pints with Rob and pick his brain on beer-related subjects. His interest in brewing began in the early 1990s when he worked for Otter Creek Brewery in Vermont. Through Rob's travels, he had sampled many styles of beer and was struck by the inventiveness and depth of Belgian beers. Though Belgian styles were scarcely heard of in the United States at the time, Rob saw this as an open niche in the microbrewery market. In 1995, Rob founded Allagash Brewing Company and began his venture with the release of his award-winning flagship, Allagash White. Since then, Allagash has added a number of beers to its portfolio, including a barrel-aged series, a series of philanthropic beers, and a series that uses Allagash's own proprietary *Brettanomyces* yeast strain.

Tripel

Rob says: This is a Belgian-style Tripel that usually ends up at 9% ABV. This Tripel can push the traditional style guidelines a little bit, depending on the yeast selection.

The yeast strain a brewer chooses is critical to the overall character of the beer, especially with Belgian-style beers! The simple malt and hop components of this recipe allow the yeast to express itself; we use this same concept at Allagash for our Tripel.

The sugar addition raises the specific gravity of the beer (and the alcohol content) without adding sweetness. It is essentially 99% fermentable by the yeast, so no residual sweetness or body remains from the sugar after fermentation. Use a Belgian candi sugar, a readily available cane sugar, or rock candy (all are sucrose).

It is important to use a Belgian yeast strain for this recipe. The traditional yeast would be an Abbey strain. Most homebrew shops will have one of these strains. You can also push the style guidelines of this beer by fermenting it with a Belgian Strong Golden Ale yeast, or even a Belgian Wit yeast. Try brewing this recipe with different strains of yeast, and you will end up with beers that have markedly different character.

MALT EXTRACT

9 pounds Light/Pilsen malt extract

HOPPING SCHEDULE

1. 1.5 ounces Hallertauer hops (bittering), boil 60 minutes
2. 0.25 ounce Saaz hops (taste), add after 60 minutes
3. 0.25 ounce Saaz hops (aroma), add at 75 minutes

YEAST

Wyeast 1214 Belgian Abbey or Wyeast 1388 Belgian Strong or Wyeast 3944 Belgian Wit

FERMENTATION TEMPERATURE

65–75°F

> 1.25 pounds sugar dissolved in 1½ cups boiling water and cooled to room temperature

In a brew kettle, heat 6 gallons of water to a boil. Remove from the heat, and add the malt extract. Return to a boil.

After 15 minutes, add the Hallertauer hops, and boil 60 minutes. Add the first Saaz hops, and boil 15 minutes. Remove from the heat, add the remaining Saaz hops, swirl the contents of the kettle to create a whirlpool, and allow to rest for 15 minutes.

Cool the wort and rack (move) to your fermenter, leaving as much of the solids behind in the kettle as possible. Use a strainer if you can.

Once the wort is at 75°F or below, pitch the yeast, and ferment at the recommended temperature.

Add your dissolved priming sugar dose, and bottle when fermentation is complete.

Patrick Rue, Founder/Brewer, The Bruery

Patrick Rue is one of the brewers and owners of the Bruery in Orange County, Californina, who found his true calling in making beer rather than being a lawyer. The Bruery is spelled so because of Patrick's last name and because it is a family-run business. The Bruery specializes in Belgian-style ales crafted with a distinctive twist. All of its beers are 100% bottle-conditioned, meaning the beers undergo fermentation in the bottle, which allows a complexity of flavor to arise. We are inspired by Patrick's use of interesting flavorings, like Thai basil and lavender. His creations step outside the norm and give our palates something to ponder.

One of our favorite Bruery beers is Black Orchard, which is a traditional Belgian Wit made untraditionally with chocolate malt. That combination is quite a unique experience. For the following recipe, Patrick turns the tables on a traditional Saison by using a darker malt, like those used for Dunkel styles. The ABV should end up at around 7.8%.

Saison Noir

Enjoy this dry, fruity, complex ale!

SPECIALTY GRAIN BILL

> 1 pound Weyermann Dehusked Carafa III

MALT SOURCE

> 7 pounds light dried malt extract

HOPPING SCHEDULE

> 0.5 ounce German Hallertauer Magnum Pellet (11%) hops, boil 60 minutes

OTHER INGREDIENTS

> 1 pound Buckwheat honey
>
> 0.25 ounce dried spearmint (bagged), add at end of boil
>
> 0.25 ounce dried chamomile (bagged), add at end of boil

YEAST

> White Labs WLP565 Belgian Saison I Ale
>
> Wyeast 5112 *Brettanomyces bruxellensis*

PRIMING SUGAR

> 4 ounces cane sugar dissolved in ½ cup boiling water and cooled to room temperature

Add the grain to a steeping bag, and steep cold in a kettle or pot with 5.5 gallons of water for 20 minutes.

Remove the grain. Bring the water to a boil, and remove from the heat. Add the malt extract, and stir well until dissolved. Add the hops.

Bring to a boil, and boil 60 minutes. Remove from the heat, and add the honey. Mix well. Add the spearmint and chamomile, and let sit 5 minutes.

Chill the wort as cold as possible, preferably to 50°F. Pitch the Belgian Saison yeast.

Let the fermentation temperature naturally rise as high as possible, preferably to 90°F to 95°F. This temperature will be reached after about 2 days of fermentation. If the beer doesn't get warm enough, wrap the fermenter with a towel to try to retain heat.

When fermentation starts to slow down (the bubbles in airlock slow to at least twice a minute), transfer to a secondary fermenter, leaving most of the yeast behind.

Pitch the *Brettanomyces bruxellensis*, which will add carbonation and some rustic, funky notes. Make sure the yeast is well mixed, then bottle immediately.

BOTTLING

It is recommended that you bottle and condition this beer in Belgian-style bottles (corked and caged) or Champagne bottles (capped, or corked and caged).

Boil the cane sugar in 4 ounces of water, cool, and add to the fermenter, gently stirring into the solution. Transfer to bottles, and let condition for 2 months. This beer will become more rustic and funky with age but should have a noticeable *Brettanomyces* character within 2 months.

Chris McCombs, New Belgium Brewing Company

New Belgium Brewery in Fort Collins, Colorado, was founded by Jeff and Kim Jordan. It has become one of the most popular microbreweries in the world. This environmentally friendly brewery (almost entirely wind powered) is famous for its Fat Tire Amber Ale and for a multitude of Belgian-style ales. We love the green focus of this brewery, and follow closely its specialty series Lips of Faith, which offers cult beers like La Folie, La Fleur, and Dark Kriek. The brewery refers to this series as its playground series, emphasizing the boundary-free imagination that gives birth to unique beers. This recipe is from Chris McCombs, the plant engineer, who first brewed it at the Salt Lake City 2002 Winter Olympics.

Bière de Garde

This Belgian-style ale has a nice complex fruit and spice profile that makes for a fun brewing process. The nuttiness of the malt will be balanced by the hop additions.

SPECIALTY GRAIN BILL

>1.25 pounds C-40 crystal malt
>
>1.25 pounds flaked oats, unmilled
>
>0.5 pound Carapils malt

MALT SOURCE

>6.6 pounds Pale malt extract
>
>1.1 pounds wheat malt extract

HOPPING SCHEDULE

>1. 0.625 ounce Tettnang hop pellets, add at 15 minutes
>
>2. 0.5 ounce Cascade hop, add at 75 minutes

FIRST SPICE ADDITION (ADD AT 30 MINUTES)

>1 ounce organic Turkish apricots, chopped
>
>0.1 ounce fresh ginger, chopped
>
>0.125 ounce coriander, ground fresh

SECOND SPICE ADDITION (ADD AT 60 MINUTES)

>0.94 ounce coriander, ground fresh
>
>0.94 ounce fresh ginger, chopped

YEAST

>Wyeast 1056 American Ale combined with Wyeast 5112 *Brettanomyces bruxellensis*

FERMENTATION TEMPERATURE

>About 74°F

> 0.5 pound corn sugar dissolved in 1 cup boiling water and cooled to room temperature

Fill a large brew kettle with about 4 gallons of water, and steep specialty grains in a game bag (which is similar to a large teabag made of cheesecloth) in the brewing water while heating up the water to boiling. Remove the bag before water temperature reaches 175°F. Continue bringing the liquid to a boil.

Remove kettle from the heat, and add the malt extracts, stirring to dissolve. Return the kettle to the heat, bring back to a boil, and set the timer for 15 minutes.

After 15 minutes, add the first hops addition, and set the timer for 15 minutes. Place the ingredients for the first spice addition in a game bag, and add when the timer sounds. Set the timer for 30 minutes.

Place the ingredients for the second spice addition in a game bag, and add to the kettle when the timer sounds. Set the timer for 15 minutes. When the timer sounds, add the second hop addition, remove the brew kettle from the heat, and let rest for 15 minutes.

Cool the wort to about 75°F, and pitch the yeasts.

Ferment at the recommended temperature for 7 to 10 days.

We recommend a secondary fermentation. Transfer the beer to another bucket or carboy for 2 to 4 days more before bottling.

Add the dissolved priming sugar and bottle. We recommend letting the bottles sit for a couple of months for conditioning (so the yeast continues to work, adding a depth of flavor to the beer) before serving.

BRIAN THOMPSON, TELEGRAPH
BREWING COMPANY

Brian Thompson started Telegraph brewery with a focus on hand-crafted unique American ales that embrace the heritage of California's early brewing pioneers. The brewery uses as many locally grown ingredients as it can, and its award-winning beers embody the philosophy that a local brewery should reflect the traditions of its region. We love the local focus of Telegraph's beers, and you can find its California Ale and Stock Porter on tap all over Los Angeles.

We first met Brian in August 2007, when he was kind enough to attend one of our beer dinners at which we were featuring a couple of his delicious beers.

West Coast Belgian Ale

This beer is reminiscent of the kinds of beers that were being brewed on the West Coast during the gold-rush era of the 19th century, when American beers were spicy and earthy and represented local ingredients.

SPECIALTY GRAIN BILL

1 pound 40 Lovibond caramel malt

MALT SOURCE

8.25 pounds Pale liquid malt extract

HOPPING SCHEDULE

1. 2.0 ounces Cascade pellets, boil 60 minutes
2. 2.0 ounces Cascade pellets

SPECIAL INGREDIENTS

4 ounces orange peel

2 chamomile teabags

YEAST

Wyeast 1214 Belgian Ale or White Labs WLP530 Abbey Ale

FERMENTATION TEMPERATURE

70–75°F

PRIMING SUGAR

0.5 pound corn sugar dissolved in 1 cup boiling water and cooled to room temperature

In a small pot, heat 3 or 4 quarts of water to around 150°F (bubbles start to form on the bottom). Remove from the heat, and stir in the specialty grain. Cover and steep for 20 to 30 minutes.

Meanwhile, fill a large brewpot half full with water, and bring to boil. When bubbles start to rise from the pot, turn off the heat and stir in the malt extract.

After the grains have steeped, pour the liquid and grains through a strainer directly into the main brewpot.

Add some hot water to the small pot, and rinse the grains with the strainer in the water to sparge. Add this liquid to the main brewpot.

Bring what is now called wort to a full, rolling boil. Watch for boilovers! Once the foaming stops, add the first hops addition and set the timer for 60 minutes.

Meanwhile, sanitize your fermenter, strainer, airlock, and stopper.

When the timer sounds, add the second hops addition and the special ingredients. Immediately remove from the heat, and let rest for 15 minutes.

Cool the pot in a sink until the sides are cool to the touch.

Pour the wort into the sanitized fermenter, add prechilled water to bring it up to 5 gallons at about 75°F, and pitch the yeast and ferment between 70°F and 75°F.

Bottle with dissolved priming sugar when fermentation is complete. (See Step Ten and Step Eleven on page 224.)

LARRY CALDWELL, HOMEBREWER AND GENERAL MANAGER, FATHER'S OFFICE

Not only is Larry Caldwell the current general manager and beer buyer at the famed Father's Office in Santa Monica, California, but he also knows more about beer than almost anyone we've ever met. His passion and enthusiasm are contagious. He is an avid collector and an award-winning homebrewer. He has introduced us to many great beers, but one of the best ones was a stunning sweet and tart Pomegranate Ale. When we asked him who the brewer was, he said, "I am!" We were astounded and impressed and begged him for the recipe.

Pomegranate Tart

Larry says: This beer is based loosely on one of our favorite beers, New Glarus Brewing Company's Wisconsin Belgian Red (see page 81), as well as its Raspberry Tart. Both are beers that feature the fruit strongly to the point of being something between a beer and a cider-style drink. This is a great dessert beer on its own, but also a great pairing with desserts like chocolate truffles and cheesecake.

SPECIALTY GRAIN BILL

12 ounces 60 Lovibond Belgian Caramunich

0.5 ounce Carafa III (huskless debittered black malt)

MALT SOURCE

2 pounds dry light extract

2 pounds dry wheat extract

HOPPING SCHEDULE

0.5 ounce Saaz Hops, boil 60 minutes

SPECIAL INGREDIENTS

1 tablet Whirlfloc (a clarifier)

1 pound pomegranate molasses*

1 gallon pomegranate juice**

YEAST

1 tube White Labs WLP400 Belgian Wit***

PRIMING SUGAR

4 ounces corn sugar dissolved in ½ cup boiling water and cooled to room temperature

FERMENTATION TEMPERATURE

68–70°F

*This specialty molasses can be found in most gourmet or Indian food stores. It's simply pomegranate juice reduced to a syrup. Regular molasses *cannot* be used as a substitute.
**Pure juice, not concentrate, and with *no* preservatives.
***Larry says that any American, English, or Belgian yeast would work fine, but he likes the spicy, tart qualities of this specific yeast.

Heat 2 gallons of water in a steeping pot to 170°F to 172°F. Remove from the heat. Place the grains in a grain bag and add to the pot. The water temperature should drop to 153°F to 155°F once grain is added. The higher mash temperature will leave a fuller-bodied beer. Cover and steep (mash) for 30 minutes.

Bring 4.75 gallons of water to a boil in a large stockpot, and cool to 170°F.

After the grains have steeped, pull the bag out of the steeping pot and dip it in the stockpot (water temperature around 170°F).

Add the water from the steeping pot to the large stockpot, and return to a boil. Allow the grain bag to drain dry in the steeping pot. You can add the reserve liquid to the main boil later.

Just before the liquid in the stockpot comes to a boil, add the malt extracts. Be sure to stir thoroughly so that the extracts don't clump up and are well integrated into the wort.

Bring the wort to a steady, rolling boil. Immediately add the hops. After 45 minutes, add the Whirlfloc tablet. After 15 minutes more, remove the stockpot from the heat and add the pomegranate molasses, stirring thoroughly to dissolve.

Cool the beer to 65°F to 68°F. Transfer the liquid from the stockpot to a food-grade plastic fermenter. Pitch the yeast. Close the lid, add the airlock, and shake vigorously for 1 to 2 minutes to aerate.

Ferment at the recommended temperature.

Once the fermentation is complete (7 to 10 days, when airlock is no longer bubbling), add the pomegranate juice. This will bring the beer up to 5 gallons. Because the juice is full of sugar, this will kick off another fermentation.

Once the second fermentation is complete (let the beer rest for 7 days to ensure all fermentation has subsided), transfer the beer to a bottling bucket, and add the corn sugar dissolved in ½ cup of water. Stir thoroughly, and bottle the beer.

The beer should be carbonated in about 2 weeks.

Note: The beauty of this recipe is that you can do this with any fruit you want. Cherry (sweet or tart), blueberry, and peach work well. Just make sure the juice you use isn't full of preservatives and is 100% juice because you don't want extra additives and flavorings. You can also substitute whole fruit for the juice. It's a little messier and harder to handle, but it's how the best breweries get their fruit flavors. A good rule of thumb is 2 pounds of fruit for every gallon of beer. I prefer using frozen fruit because it's been cleaned and is rid of any wild yeasts that could affect the beer. Just thaw the fruit, and add it to the beer after the first fermentation is complete. Let it re-ferment and age for a short time, then filter out the fruit and bottle.

STONE BREWING COMPANY

The brainchild of cofounders Greg Koch and Steve Wagner, the Stone Brewing Company in Escondido, California, is at the forefront of the West Coast extreme beer movement. We describe undesirable beers as "fizzy yellow water" because Greg coined the phrase. In addition to its amazing array of beers, like Arrogant Bastard Ale and Stone Ruination IPA, Stone has built the Stone Brewing World Bistro & Gardens, where they take food pairing and beer education to new heights.

Stone Vertical Epic '08

Greg donated the recipe for Stone's piney, resinous, and fruity beer Vertical Epic, which is a bottle-conditioned specialty beer that is brewed just once each year—one year, one month, and one day from the previous year's edition. Greg gave us the all-grain recipe for the 2008 version, which was brewed on 08-08-08. Larry Caldwell, who donated the Pomegranate Tart recipe (page 255), was nice enough to render his extract interpretation of this special beer. To see the original all-grain recipe for all the Vertical Epic Ales, go to www.stonebrew.com/epic.

SPECIALTY GRAIN BILL

> 2 pounds Belgian Pils malt
>
> 1 pound flaked oats

MALT SOURCES

> 6 pounds dry malt extract*

HOPPING SCHEDULE

> 1. 0.5 ounce Warrior hops, boil 60 minutes
>
> 2. 0.5 ounce Simcoe hops and 0.5 ounce Amarillo hops, boil 15 minutes
>
> 3. 1 ounce Athanum hops, added at end of boil

ADDITIONAL INGREDIENTS

> 1 tablet Whirlfloc (a clarifier)
>
> 1 pound white table sugar

YEAST

> 2 tubes of White Labs WLP570 Belgian Golden Ale

FERMENTATION TEMPERATURE

> 68–70°F

DRY-HOPPING

> 0.5 ounce Simcoe hops and 0.5 ounce Amarillo hops

---

*Use the lightest you can find, preferably a Pilsner malt extract such as the one Briess makes.

4 ounces corn sugar dissolved in ½ cup boiling water and cooled to room temperature

Heat 1 gallon of water in a steeping pot to approximately 165°F. Remove the pot from the heat, and add the specialty grains to a grain bag. Add the bag to the pot; the water temperature should drop to 148°F to 150°F once the grain is added. Cover and steep the grains for 30 minutes.

Bring 5.5 gallons of water to a boil in a large stockpot. Let it cool to 170°F.

After the specialty grains have steeped, remove the grain bag and dip it in the stockpot to help rinse any extra sugars off of the grains.

Add the water from the steeping pot to the stockpot, and allow the grain bag to drain dry in the steeping pot. You can add the reserve liquid to the main boil later.

Return the stockpot to a boil. Just before the liquid boils, add the malt extract. Stir thoroughly so that the extract doesn't clump and is well integrated into the wort.

Bring what is now wort to a steady, rolling boil. Immediately add the first hops addition. Set the timer for 45 minutes. When the timer sounds, add the second hops addition and set the timer for 15 minutes.

When you add the second hops addition, add the tablet of Whirlfloc, if desired. It will help clarify the beer during fermentation.

Turn off the boil and add the final hops addition.

Once the boil is done, add the table sugar. Stir thoroughly to dissolve. At this point the beer should have reduced to about 5 gallons.

Cool beer to 65°F to 68°F. Transfer the liquid from the stockpot to a food-grade plastic fermenter, and pitch the yeast. Close the lid, add the airlock, and shake vigorously for 1 to 2 minutes to aerate.

Ferment at the recommended temperature.

Once the fermentation is complete, add the dry-hopping addition. This imparts a strong aroma of hops to the finished beer. Let beer dry-hop for 7 days.

Transfer the beer to a bottling bucket, and add the corn sugar dissolved in ½ cup of water to the bucket. Stir thoroughly, and bottle the beer.

The beer should be carbonated in about 2 weeks.

Brewing Resources

You'll need to read more about homebrew as you get into advanced brewing. Sometimes a handy guide can offer tips for troubleshooting. Maybe you want to geek out about the history of brewing. Or perhaps you are getting too good, and you want more information about opening a brewery of your own. Whatever your homebrew needs, here are some invaluable resources on the subject.

Books

Bennet, Judith M. *Ale, Beer, and Brewsters in England: Women's Work in a Changing World.* New York: Oxford University Press, 1996. An insightful look into the history of brewing and the female role in the world of beer.

Calagione, Sam. *Brewing Up a Business: Adventures in Entrepreneurship from the Founder of Dogfish Head Craft Brewery.* Hoboken, NJ: John Wiley & Sons, 2005. A popular brewer's story about his experience starting up his brewery. Lots of great business advice mixed in with humorous personal trials and tribulations. A must-read for anyone who wants to start up a brewery.

Hieronymus, Stan. *Brew Like a Monk: Trappist, Abbey, and Strong Belgian Ales and How to Brew Them.* Boulder, CO: Brewers Publications, 2005. For advanced brewers who want to perfect Belgian styles, this is an in-depth journey into the hearts and minds—and recipes—of the best Belgian brewers out there.

Mosher, Randy. *Radical Brewing: Recipes, Tales and World-Altering Meditations in a Glass.* Boulder, CO: Brewers Publications, 2004. A creative look at brewing, with loads of history and a description of truly unique ales. Mosher offers an approach to brewing that encourages the rebel brewer in all of us.

Nachel, Marty. *Homebrewing for Dummies.* Hoboken, NJ: Wiley Publishing, 2008. It's what you think it is: some info for those of us who need to take it slow and simple.

Papazian, Charles. *The Complete Joy of Homebrewing.* New York: HarperCollins, 2003. President of the American Homebrewers Association and the Association of Brewers, this author offers everything you need to begin to brew. Recipes, charts, and guidelines for all styles are found within these pages.

Snyder, Stephen. *The Brewmaster's Bible: The Gold Standard for Home Brewers.* New York: HarperCollins, 1997. This is for the beginner and more advanced brewer. The book has loads of recipes; style definitions; and detailed analyses of yeast, water, grains, adjuncts, and more.

Magazines

Brew Your Own (www.byo.com). The leading magazine for people who want to brew their own beer at home. It covers the entire hobby, from simple how-to tips to more advanced technical articles on brewing fine beer. Regular columns include "Tips from the Pros," "Style of the Month," "Recipe Exchange," and "Help Me, Mr. Wizard."

Zymurgy (www.beertown.org). Published by the American Homebrewers Association (AHA), a division of the Brewers Association, this bimonthly is for the brewer who has a few beers under his or her belt. Topical and timely, it stays on top of the trends, provides good recipe development suggestions, and publishes a timeline of beer competitions for when you're a good enough homebrewer to say, "Hey, my beer rocks. Somebody should give me an award for this." Free with membership to the AHA (www.beertown.org/homebrewing/member ship.html).

Websites

Beer Tools (www.beertools.com). Great resources for brewers, including a recipe generator, a recipe calculator, and online brewing tutorials.

BX Beer Depot (www.bxbeerdepot.com). Offers everything from kits to ingredients to equipment. Great pictures!

Homebrewers Outpost (www.homebrewers.com). Brew and winemaking supplies.

More Beer (www.morebeer.com). Absolutely everything for beer making.

White Labs Pure Brewers Yeast (www.whitelabs.com). Where the real brewers go to get their yeast.

*   *   *

Now you're really living it! You've fully incorporated beer into your life. If we knew you, we would be friends. In fact, do share your brews with us if you can. Trading homebrews with the neighbors is a bit better than sharing sugar. There is no better way to know beer than by creating it. You'll learn more from your homebrew batch than from a million books, so get your tools ready and begin the exercise. We dub you "homebrewer."

Entertaining with Beer

Fill with mingled cream and amber,
I will drain that glass again.
Such hilarious visions clamber
Through the chambers of my brain.
Quaintest thoughts—queerest fancies
Come to life and fade away;
What care I how time advances?
I am drinking ale today.

—EDGAR ALLAN POE

Nobody Puts Beer in a Corner

Now it's time to share the love! The craft beer movement is thriving because of a kind of grassroots movement. It's simple economics. The more people know about craft beer, the more they will demand it in fine restaurants, bars, and gastropubs, and thus the more it will be supplied by distributors and importers alike!

It's time for you to become an active participant in this grassroots movement, a beer activist if you will. Invite your friends and colleagues into your newly adjusted craft beer friendly home and blow their minds. Use the beer recipes, brew up some beer, get the cheese pairings together, open up the beer cellar, and share your beer knowledge wealth with some of your favorite people.

Spread the Word: Hosting a Beer-Tasting Party

Beer tastings have been going on in the craft beer world for years, but they had little impact on the outside world until very recently. Craft beer is finally catching on in hipster circles and is becoming the latest greatest tipple in the fast and furious foodie world. Specialty and gourmet foods have become more available and popular with the rise of the celebrity chef and the advent of the Food Network and shows like *Top Chef* and *Hell's Kitchen*. On the coattails of this foodie revolution rides craft beer. Now people young and old are seeking out great craft beer to entertain with, and this outside-the-box thinking is leading to altogether new and creative ways of entertaining. People are starting to throw beer-tasting parties the same way that they were hosting wine tastings 10 years ago.

We know this because people are hiring us to help them host these parties. We're not here to write ourselves out of a job, but we are here to tell you that you can do it on your own! Have no fear, we'll show you how to do it from start to finish. Instead of having to hire us, you can cut out the middleman and have a truly unique party for your friends. Just follow a few simple steps.

Research, Research, Research: Start with the Beer

Entertaining with craft beer can be challenging because of its lack of availability. So we suggest that before you decide on a theme for your tasting or food to cook or pairings to make, you actually see what beers are available to you. Although there is a smattering of specialty beer shops popping up here and there, the best place to find rare artisanal and craft beer is at boutique wine shops. These shop owners have been on the cutting edge of craft beer since the revolution began and often know as much about the beer as they do wine. Some are even employing beer experts and buyers (love that). As a matter of fact, our local Whole Foods Market has created a beer specialist position and has an amazing selection of craft and artisanal beers.

Craft beer bars are also a great resource. Not only are the beers available at local craft beer bars a good representation of what you'll be able to get in the area but, we hope, the bartenders and managers are knowledgeable enough and friendly enough to give you good information about what beers are coming soon, what beers are going away, what beers are rare in the area, what beers were a once off (a one-time sale), what beers are seasonal, and so on. If for some bizarre reason the staff isn't in the know or isn't friendly (they bloody well should be, but if they aren't), craft beer bars are also a Mecca for beer-geeks who *love* to talk about the latest and greatest secrets in craft beer (and from whom we've received many great tips). So sit down at the bar, see what's in stock, have some beers, and talk to the people there. Sounds like some grueling research, no?

Practice, Practice, Practice: Picking the Beers

Now that you've researched and evaluated the available beers, you can start thinking about a tasting. Use the criteria you now know and start thinking about how the beers could work in a lineup. Think about which beers are very different from each other and which beers are similar. Think about which ones are true to style and which ones taste much different from what you had expected based on the name, style, or color. Sometimes we pick beers based on a theme of a special event or the time of year, but we always try to pick a wide variety of different beer flavors.

You won't be able to please everybody all the time. But if you have a nice selection that covers many different flavor profiles, you will be able to suit many different palates.

Here are some examples of themes that we've done for beer tastings:

- **GEOGRAPHIC REGIONS:** Travel around the world through your taste buds. Concentrate on different beer styles or different labels from one country. Do a north meets south tasting of Germany, or taste the beers of northern France.

- **A TRAPPIST TASTING:** Always a crowd pleaser; to be able to compare and contrast some of the rarest, greatest, and most definitive beers in the world is truly a treat.

- **AN EXTREME BEER TASTING:** Taste a super-hoppy beer, a mega ABV beer, the funniest name, the rarest, the most expensive— whatever you decide—just make sure the beer pushes the limit.

- **ALL ONE STYLE:** This tasting is really a great way to understand and experience the diversity that exists even in just one style of beer. Buy only Wheat Beers, Stouts, Belgian Doubles, or Lambics.

- **A SINGLE BREWERY TASTING:** Taste many beers from only one brewery. It's a fun way to explore a brewery's entire repertoire, and it's also an interesting study to see how the brewer works with ingredients—how the beers are similar and how they are different when they all come from the same room.

- **ON-DRAUGHT-ONLY TASTING:** If you are feeling super-motivated, this is a fun tasting to do. Go around to your local breweries and see if they'll sell you growlers of their draft beer. It's great to do a tasting of beers you can only get at craft bars or on tap at your house.

When we do beer tastings, we usually pick 8 to 10 different kinds that will challenge our guests' perceptions of beer. The order in which these beers are tasted is of the utmost importance. It's essential that the beers be tasted from least intense to most intense. The last thing you want to do to your guests when you want them to experience every nuance of the beer is to kill their delicate palates. When you taste a subtle beer after a super-hoppy beer, you can barely taste it. For instance, if you were to taste the Anderson Valley Hop Ottin' IPA and then a light-bodied Reissdorf Kölsch directly afterward, the Kölsch would taste like Pellegrino (The Horror!).

Once you've made a list of the beers that you want for the tasting, it's time to go and get them. Even though we've gone through this process many times, there has never been a single time that we've been able to get every beer on our researched list. It's frustrating to be sure, but that's where the surprises and the fun come in. Say there was an article written in *USA Today* about Unibroue's Blanche de Chambly Witbier, and now you can't find it anywhere. Try picking out a different label of the same style; no big whoop. Remember that this is craft beer. It's coveted and it's rare, and sometimes it's a "you snooze, you lose" world. Just stay fluid and you'll be okay. Your beer-tasting party won't suffer one iota.

You also might be wondering how much beer to buy. Really it all depends on what you're trying to achieve. A beer-*drinking* party and a beer-*tasting* party are two different animals. Obviously, if you are planning a beer-drinking blowout, get as much as you think you need (be careful with the ABV). But if you are hosting a beer-tasting party, conservatively you will need to buy no more than four ounces per person, per beer. Actually, we will pour only two to three ounces of each beer, but we buy enough to accommodate four ounces to mitigate any agitation, carbonation, or foaming issues.

Set It Up

Make sure that your guests have everything they need. Each person should have a good, clean glass so he or she can swirl and aerate the beer and enhance the aromatics. If you don't have specific beer glassware, that's fine. Burgundy or Pinot Noir wineglasses work great for beer tastings (see Chapter 7). Make sure that you have a water pitcher set out. This water isn't just for staying hydrated. When a beer is particularly strong or unique, you will need to rinse out the glassware to avoid corrupting the next beer.

It's vital that you have something to nosh on during the tasting. The last thing you want is to have your guests tasting beer on an empty stomach. You will also need a dump bucket. This is usually a Champagne chiller or something equivalent that your guests can dump their beer into after they've tasted it if they have anything left, are being formal and spitting, or simply don't like the beer.

Before you start your tasting, make sure you've given yourself enough time to chill the beer. If you are using bottles, most styles need about two hours in the refrigerator or about an hour on ice. Make sure you take the beer out of the refrigerator or off the ice for a couple of minutes before you serve it, so the beer flavors are not inhibited by the cold. Again, most beers should be consumed at around 51°F. Also, make sure that you have an opener with you that has a corkscrew as well as a bottle cap opener. You will be embarrassed if you pry off that bottle cap on a highly anticipated Lambic only to see a cork in the neck of the bottle with no way of getting it out, and 20 people are staring at you, salivating. No bueno.

Go Time: Hosting the Party

Now is where you get to show off a bit. The first beer that we like to pour at the beginning of any beer tasting is a bit of the mass-produced industrialized fizzy yellow water that has been passing for beer in our country for almost 100 years. Have your guests go through the whole tasting process with it. Show them how to evaluate beer. Teach them to look at the beer and see what the color might say (or not say) about that beer.

Tell them how to appreciate the aromatics of their beer and to get their noses way down in the glass and take a big whiff, exploring primary and secondary impressions. Let them swirl the glass and inhale the aromas (or lack of aromas). This is a great frame of reference for any tasting, and a good way to teach them how to taste properly.

As you move along with tasting each beer (from least intense to most intense), make sure to give a little explanation of each beer. Let your guests know the style of the beer, the brewer, where it's from, and the ABV. During wine tastings, it's considered bad form to say aloud what flavors you are picking up because flavor and aroma perception is so susceptible to suggestion. But we've found that most people are unaccustomed to evaluating beer in the way they evaluate wine, so it's actually good to go ahead and help novices overcome their shyness by getting the ball rolling, using terms like smoky, buttery, asphalt, leather, and tobacco. Your guests will start chiming in, and eventually you won't have to lead them at all. Of course, let more advanced tasters come up with their own flavors. Encourage questions. If you can't answer them all, that's fine. Have this book at your side for a quick reference; this will be a chance for you to learn as well.

At the end of a successful tasting, guests are happy and astounded. We hope you've given them something they've never had before and shown them how to appreciate beer. If you want to go that extra mile, you can send your guests home with a little gift. We like to get a couple extra six-packs (or as many bottles as are needed) of one of the beers from our tasting and give one to each guest as a party favor. We also like sending our guests away with a little knowledge. We will type up and print out the beers listed in order of the tasting, with a couple of tasting notes and information on where they can buy the beer. This, of course, is going above and beyond, but once you've turned people on to beer, they have a tendency to become pretty enthusiastic about it. So if you don't feel like getting 13 phone calls the next day asking you the name of "that fantastic beer" from the party, you might consider a handout.

Here's a checklist for everything you'll need:

- ○ **Beer—duh**
- ○ **Glassware—duh (see Chapter 7)**
- ○ **Bottle opener with corkscrew**
- ○ **Dump bucket**
- ○ **Ice for chilling**
- ○ **Pitcher for water**
- ○ **Lots of water**
- ○ **Something to nosh on**
- ○ **Tasting sheets for note taking (see page 299)**
- ○ **List of beer descriptions and a buying guide**

Use Protection: The Safety of Your Guests

When hosting a beer tasting or beer dinner, you should take on some responsibility for your guests' safety. They are your friends, and you don't want to send them home destined for a DUI. We're used to cutting people off from working at bars and restaurants where this is no joke. The law puts responsibility of inebriation on the establishment and imposes huge fines. This becomes even more important when it involves people you know, though it's sometimes harder because you don't want to offend them. You won't be fined, but you will be horribly worried if you let a guest drive home drunk as a skunk. This can happen at beer dinners and tastings, where people are unfamiliar with the variety of ABVs. People may know when to say when if the drink is wine or a cocktail, but when it comes to beer, they may not realize that the American Wild Ale they've been drinking is 10% alcohol. You have to help them along the way.

First, make sure you have food readily available at a tasting. And have something substantial, not just fruit and veggies; some sort of bread, like a baguette, is good for soaking up alcohol. Second, be sure to have loads of water around, and put it out on the table, right next to the beer. People will get a bit parched when drinking alcohol, but if water isn't in front of them, they may forget to drink it. Do some sparkling water if you want to keep it classy. If you are doing a beer dinner, have a separate glass for water and several bottles of sparkling on the table, or a pitcher of regular water. And if no one fills their water glasses, do it yourself after the first few courses. You don't have to be a mom about it, just think of it as being a gracious host.

When hosting a beer tasting, be sure to tell people to treat it as a wine tasting, spitting out or dumping beers after they've tasted. This is tough to enforce, but keep the dump buckets out there, and do it yourself to get the ball rolling. Usually people will find one or two beers that they will drink in their entirety, which is great—they've found their new favorite—but not every beer will be, so encourage the dump. The best way to make sure no one goes overboard is to pour the correct amount for a tasting or beer dinner: a three- to four-ounce pour. This may seem skimpy to some of your more lushy guests, but assure them that there is plenty of beer coming, and that you don't want drunkenness to dull their senses. This should get them excited and encourage restraint.

Some signs of drunkenness we've learned to look for from years in the restaurant biz are the following: slurred speech, red eyes, inability to focus, swaying, dropping drinks, and taking off one's shirt and singing George Michael's "Freedom! '90" If you've done all you can, and everyone still hit the sauce a little too hard, take their keys, call them a cab, offer them the couch, or give them a ride if you are sober. As embarrassing as this may be for you and your guest, it's actually brave, noble, and far better than the alternatives.

Beyond the Kegger: Throw the Coolest Dinner Party on the Block

So remember what a huge hit your beer-tasting party was? Well, your beer-pairing dinner is about to blow it out of the water. It's true that beer dinners are significantly more work, but they are oh so worth it. As we mentioned in Chapter 8, pairing beer with food can be a truly rewarding experience. In the greatest pairings, not only does the beer enhance the food but the food enhances the beer. A beer dinner is the time for these pairings to shine. It's a sort of seduction into craft beer, and if done well, your guests will be true beer lovers after the first course.

Think outside the box. Many beer-pairing dinners get trapped in a category, like German beers paired with German food or Belgian beers paired with Belgian food. While that's all fine and dandy, pairing beer, with all of its varieties and complexities, begs the act of rebellion. As we said, there are no real rules. Cook an Italian or French meal and instead of the wine, pair each course with a beer. Heresy! Experiment with Asian dishes and Belgian-style beers. Shocking! Go nuts and serve some courses that are cooked with beer as an ingredient (see Chapter 8), and then pair them with a different beer! What? That's crazy! The beer-pairing world is yours to explore.

Like the beer-tasting party, make sure that you have clean glassware, that you serve your beer at the right temperature, and that you have dump buckets readily available. Also, make sure not to "soak" your guests. It's a good idea to stick to six or fewer food courses, serving your guests no more than four ounces of beer for each course, and again, keep water on the table. Different, though, from the beer-tasting party, the dinner is more of a sensory experience and less of a classroom. It's good to be armed with knowledge about the beer pairings, and it's still a great idea to print out the menu and information about the beers for guests to take home. But this is not teaching time; this is close your eyes and appreciate time. This is the time to step onto the starship *Sensory Voyager*.

Here is a menu from a beer dinner we hosted. We encourage you to be inventive.

National Beer Wholesalers Association's "Real Women Drink Beer" Dinner

CRAFT LOS ANGELES

October 20, 2008

Chef de cuisine Matthew Accarrino and pastry chef Catherine Schimenti developed this amazing menu, and Christina picked the beers used for cooking and pairing and led guests through the dinner held at *Top Chef* head judge Tom Colicchio's renowned restaurant, Craft Los Angeles. The dinner was sponsored by the National Beer Wholesalers Association. Take note of the way the beers are paired with the food in sometimes contrasting, sometimes complementary, and sometimes surprising ways—but always tasty. In our experience, even seasoned foodies are usually blown away by a thoughtful beer pairing. Attendees at beer-pairing dinners are almost always amazed at the variety that encompasses beer as well as how wonderfully beer pairs with more refined food.

FIRST COURSE

Chimay Cinq Cent and Guinea Hen Consommé with Hop Foam
Paired with good old Sierra Nevada Pale Ale

This lemony and herbaceous Trappist beer was a perfect accompaniment to the golden consommé, which, topped with the white hop foam, looked exactly like a mini pint of beer.

SECOND COURSE

Kampachi, Hitachino White Ale Gelée, Crispy Hen of the Woods Mushrooms, Heirloom Apple, and Sorrel
Paired with Unibroue Blanche de Chambly

Chef Accarrino made a gelée out of the Hitachino Witbier, creating a concentrated solid beer cube, which was somehow still effervescent. The concentrated flavors of apricot and other stone fruits married wonderfully with the raw kampachi and the heirloom apples in the sauce.

THIRD COURSE

Beer-Braised Pekin Duck Pyramid Pasta and Spiced Pine Nuts
Paired with Deschutes Black Butte Porter

This pairing was sick! The earthiness of the duck stuffed in succulent pyramid pockets with roasted, spicy, and grassy pine nuts harmonized perfectly with this delicate smoky and toasty Porter.

FOURTH COURSE

Roasted Suzuki, Saison DuPont–Braised Mussels, Japanese Leeks, and Dry Cured Chorizo
Paired with Saison DuPont

See page 194 for the chef's notes on why this is an amazing pairing.

CHEESE COURSE

Mothais Goat Cheese, Quince Crepe, Lambic Gastrique, and Frisée
Paired with Cantillon Iris Gueuze

This may have been the best pairing of the evening. This special cheese was aged in 100% humidity, making for one funky dairy product. Paired with the barnyard, earthy, immensely sour, and bone-dry unblended Lambic Ale—forget about it. This was a truly inspired combination.

DESSERTS

Young's Double Chocolate Stout Beer Cake
Salted Corn Nuts and Reissdorf Kölsch Ale Sorbet
Samuel Smith Nut Brown Ale Chocolates
Blackberry and Peach Lambic Jell-O Shots
Old Rasputin Russian Imperial Stout Float

We love beer and dessert pairings. This one knocked it out of the park and really showed how beer could be used in massively creative ways.

James Beard Award nominee pastry chef Catherine Schimenti made a cake, sorbet, chocolates, Jell-O shots, and an ice cream float, all using beer and all delicious.

BhD: Get Your Doctorate in Beer, Become a Beer Sommelier

Do you want to be known as Dr. Beer? Sir Brews-a-lot? The Honorable Master of Ale? Queen of the Malt? Well, that's never going to happen. We aren't quite saving people's lives here (though we are vastly improving them) or curing diseases, so don't expect to be knighted because of your beer knowledge (unless you live in Belgium, where they do that for real). You may be asked to preside as a beer judge at a beer festival, but don't show up in robes with a gavel. Look, we chose the terms *beer expert* and *beer sommelier* because when we started, there wasn't really a word for what we do. There is no all-encompassing term for someone who can guide you on a quality Beer Journey, create inspiring beer pairings, or professionally host a beer dinner, so we just chose what we thought made sense. So if you're looking for a beer sommelier box on job surveys, don't hold your breath. And there are many respectable beer writers, experts, lovers, and brewers who have never been certified, so don't think that this is something you have to do to be a valued member of the craft beer world.

There is a way to get some respect in the upper echelons of the beer world, however, but they involve a dreaded four-letter word: *test*. So if you want to prove to the world that you know enough about beer to school anyone, crack the books and brew the coffee—it's time to cram. You can take a beer equivalent of the famous master wine sommelier test, and there are a few choices.

CICERONE: Pronounced SIS-UH-ROHN, this is a special title for a beer expert who has passed a trademarked beer test. Run by Ray Daniels—beer judge, beer author, and the president of the Craft Beer Institute—this is a serious program that is highly regarded as the sommelier test of the beer world. Cicerone is an English word referring to, as quoted from the website (www .cicerone.org): "one who conducts visitors and sightseers to museums and explains matters of archaeological, antiquarian, historic or artistic interest." Sounds a bit complicated, eh? This website offers an intensive test for those who want to be taken seriously as beer experts.

○ **BEER JUDGE CERTIFICATION PROGRAM:** Affectionately called the BJCP (www.bjcp.org), this program offers a test that certifies one to be, you guessed it, a beer judge. Now anyone may consider themselves a good judge of beer, but this program gets specific with its test and is the go-to in the craft beer world for specific style guidelines and rules about brewing those styles.

○ **AMERICAN BREWERS GUILD:** If you want to become a brewer, you can take courses with the ABG, based in Vermont, and learn it all. They have a program titled the CraftBrewers Apprenticeship (CBA), in which you learn everything in a 28-week program, including an apprenticeship at a working brewery. Visit www .abgbrew.com for more information.

○ **GREATBREWERS.COM:** This website was created by beer educators Eric McKay of L. Knife and Son, a giant in beer distribution, and Sam Merritt, formerly of the Brooklyn Brewery and currently of Civilization of Beer, which offers beer knowledge and tutorials through the website www.civilizationofbeer.com. GreatBrewers is run by a passionate group of beer wholesalers and offers users the Great Beer Test (GBT), which is a 20-question quiz about the history of beer, brewing process, styles, and more. The questions for each quiz are randomly drawn from a bank of continually changing questions. They also offer a 100-question test for the brave. Go through their education process, and you can be dubbed Beer Authority. Their passion here is education of the beer-going public; not as serious as Cicerone, but a great test for your continuing brew education.

LOCAL HOMEBREW CLUB OR ASSOCIATION: Be sure to seek out your local homebrew clubs. This is the best way to get your feet wet in brewing. They will often offer lessons in brewing and a great space to give it a try. Local homebrew associations may also have beer-centric events like style contests, for which you can enter your homebrew and get some good feedback while tasting the fruits of other homebrew laborers.

Okay, hit the books. Perhaps you are ready to go back to school, study for the Cicerone, or take a class through the American Brewer's Guild. Or maybe you prefer to be homeschooled, where you can find every last brewing book or history on beer and study in the comfort of your own living room with a beer by your side.

Lay out the tablecloth and chill your beer. Or just get the BBQ going—whatever you like, as long as craft beer is a part of your gatherings. People are eager to have new dining experiences, and if you give them a beer tasting or dinner, they will be grateful. Even if you know your group is made up of wine lovers, be bold; give them quality beer backed with your love and knowledge of it, and watch them follow your lead. Those you least expected to love beer will be hosting a beer tasting next week. We hope, by now, you are a master of beer and understand it on a philosophical level. Hell, you even described the last beer you had as "a bit too diacetyl" for your liking and mused that the addition of some Fuggles hops might make for a better balance. It looks like it's time for us to let you go, to leave you to your own decisions. Oh, we'll always be right here for you, even if you don't need us anymore. Go...be free. See the world. Continue on your never-ending Beer Journey. We'll run into you along the way.

Parting Is Such Sweet Sorrow

When we first learned about the finer points of beer, we promised that we would take what we learned and pass it along. We feel that we've done that with this book. You are one of the converted, and now *you* can spread the word of great craft beer all over the world.

As you travel along on your Beer Journey, your path will cross with other beer explorers. You'll laugh at the Neophyte mistakes newbie beer drinkers are making. (They're so cute, aren't they?) You'll have deep conversations over a session beer with your Sophomore beer-drinking friends. You'll give knowing glances over a rich, complex vintage Trappist Ale with your Devout brethren. You'll take it all the way and dare to drink a shockingly hoppy 12% Quad IPA. Yeah! High five! Right here!

You'll bring beer home, stocking your fridge so that you'll always have what you need. Hell, you might even start a collection (we're so proud). Your friends will remember your beer pairings at the last dinner party and begin a Beer Journey of their own. You'll even make your own beer and, with a sense of accomplishment, proudly label the bottles with your name. You'll philosophize about beer, and you'll never stop searching, reaching, tasting, and learning, until you take that final Beer Journey in the sky. If you take nothing else from this book, we hope you will embrace the fleeting pleasure of a craft beer passing your lips. The impermanence of life is celebrated in great beer, to be consumed as a thing of beauty—not held onto for too long.

So, that's it. The only thing we can do now is to let go and hope that we raised you right. Cheers to you. Enjoy your new enlightened life.

Make us proud and always remember...beer is good.

Glossary

Here are your beer terms. Now that you are a bona fide part of the beer world, you gotta speak the lingo.

ABV (alcohol by volume) Standard measurement of the amount of alcohol present in a beverage.

Adjunct Unmalted grain (such as oats, rye, or wheat) and other sugar sources added as a supplement to malted barley for brewing.

Ale Beer made with top-fermenting yeast at warm temperatures.

All grain/full mash A brew made with all grains—like raw malted barley—instead of malt extracts. This requires space and time, and is quite advanced in the brewing world. This is often the practice of professional brewers.

Alt (Old German) Refers to German-style beer, similar to Pale Ale.

AOC (Appellation d'Origine Contrôlée) Meaning "controlled term of origin," this is a certification designated to agricultural products produced in certain regions of France.

Aroma hops Added last to the boil, meant to lend hop aromas without bitterness or flavor.

Attenuation Amount of fermentation that has occurred and how much the original gravity has decreased. Refers to the final ABV.

Bacteria Single-celled organisms responsible for a vast diversity of human experience, from disease to digestion, medicine, cheese making, pickling, and fermentation.

Barrel Traditionally made of wood, a cylindrical vessel with a 31-gallon capacity (this capacity is particular to barrels intended for beer). Can also be filled with monkeys.

Base malt Malt used as the main source of sugar for fermentation.

Bavarian Reference to the German state of Bavaria, an area thickly populated with breweries.

Beer-can chicken A recipe that uses a beer can shoved up a chicken's butt.

Beer-geek Us. And possibly you.

Beer snob One who uses his or her knowledge of beer to exclude, alienate, and judge rather than share, guide, and spread the love.

Bianco (Italian) White.

Bittering hops Used early in the boil to bitter the beer, not to add aroma.

Blanche (French) White.

Blanco (Spanish) White.

Bohemian Reference to the region of Bohemia (now in the Czech Republic) that boasts the cities of Budweis and Plzen.

Bottle conditioned Carbonated by living yeast in the bottle.

Brettanomyces Genus of yeast often employed in brewing.

CAMRA (Campaign for Real Ale) Group devoted to the protection of quality beer.

Cask Wooden barrel used to ferment or mature beer, wine, and other potent potables.

Cask conditioned Carbonated by a second fermentation in the barrel.

CO_2 Carbon dioxide.

Coupler Connecter that joins a tap to a keg.

Creamer faucet *See* Nitrogen tap.

Decoction Mashing technique by which a portion of the mash is removed and boiled, then returned to the whole to raise the temperature.

Dégorgement (French) *See* Disgorgement.

Devout Believer in beer.

Disgorgement Process for removal of sediments accumulated in the neck of a bottle during riddling.

Dry-hopped Beer in which hops are added after fermentation to lend supplementary hoppy character.

Dunkel (German) Dark.

Esters Compounds responsible for most fruity aromas in beer.

Extraction The process of transferring an ingredient's flavor, aroma, color, and essence into the final product. In beer, this usually refers to the process of extracting the flavor from the malt into the wort through boiling, much like one would with tea leaves.

Fermentation Metabolic process by which yeast convert sugars to alcohol and carbon dioxide.

Final gravity Measurement of the density of the wort after fermentation. By comparing the original gravity and final gravity, you can calculate the ABV.

Flavor hops Used later in the boil to add flavor and slight aroma.

Flavorings Extras added to some beers solely for flavor, such as fruits, some spices, and coffee.

Gluten Protein present in many grains, such as wheat and barley.

Grist Mixture of grains that are crushed in a mill and prepared for mashing.

Gruit Medieval herb blend used to flavor beer before the widespread use of hops.

Half barrel Vessel with the standard capacity of 15.5 gallons of beer.

Hefe (German) Yeast.

Helles/heller (German) Pale.

Hop pellets Little things that look like gross vitamins, used by most homebrewers in lieu of dried or fresh hops.

Hop-head A person addicted to the bitterness characteristic of hoppy beers.

Hops Flower cones of the hop plant, used in brewing for their aroma and bitterness. Originally employed for their preservative powers.

Hydrometer Device that measures the density of a liquid against the density of water. Taking a measurement of the density of the beer before and after fermentation helps you figure out the ABV of the brew.

IBU (international bitterness unit) Scale for the measurement of bitterness in beer.

Kolner Stangen/Stange (German) Stick or, as we were told (by a leering drunken German ex-pat), pole or rod.

Lager Beer made with bottom-fermenting yeast at cold temperatures. The term *lagering* traditionally refers to a prolonged, cold-storage maturation.

Malt Grain (usually barley) that has germinated and been dried or roasted.

Malt extract Concentrated liquid formed from wort that contains the sugars needed for brewing. This is what most homebrewers use.

Mash Process in which the crushed grains are mixed into hot water, and enzymes change the starch into fermentable (sometimes unfermentable) sugars for the yeast to eat.

Mash tun Vessel that contains the mash during all-grain brewing.

Methodé champenoise (French) Traditional method of Champagne production, in which secondary fermentation occurs in the bottle.

Microbrew The product of a brewery that produces less than 15,000 barrels per year.

Mouthfeel Sensation in the mouth exclusive of flavor, as texture, body, and carbonation.

Neophyte Beer newbie.

Nitrogen tap Tap system that introduces nitrogen into beer during the pour, resulting in creamy texture and weighty mouthfeel.

Original gravity Measurement of the density of the liquid wort before fermentation; important for later ABV determination.

Partial mash A wort made partially from grain and partially from malt extract.

Pasteurization Process of terminating microbial growth by means of heat.

Pitch Term for adding the yeast to the cooled wort, as in "Time to pitch the yeast!"

Priming Addition of sugar (priming sugar) to beer that has already fermented. This occurs as the beer is being bottle or kegged to promote more flavor nuances, more alcohol and carbonation, or all three.

Prohibition The bad time.

Promiscuous Experimenting with beer.

Rack Process of moving beer at different stages of homebrewing.

Rauch (German) Smoke; usually refers to lager made with smoked malts.

Remuage (French) *See* Riddling.

Riddling Method of slowly tipping a bottle from horizontal to vertical, allowing sediment to settle in the neck for removal.

Saccharomyces cerevisiae Yeast employed in brewing. Also know as brewer's yeast.

Schwarz (German) Black; usually refers to a very dark lager.

Session/sessionable Beer with moderate to low alcohol content, suitable for drinking in quantity over a leisurely stretch of time.

Sophomore The newly initiated.

Sparging Comes after the mash, when grains are removed and the liquid is separated, becoming the wort.

Specialty malts Small amounts of malt used for flavoring and nuance. These can be steeped like tea instead of turned into a mash.

Steeping grains Used to add flavor, nuance, and color for brewers using a malt extract. These do not need to be converted to sugar and can be steeped like tea.

Terrior (French) Most often associated with wine, this is the flavor of the land, or the concept that the geographical origin of a food or drink lends flavor and character particular to the very soil of the region in which it grows.

Weisse (German) White; refers to a wheat beer. *See also* Weizen.

Weizen (German) Wheat; refers to a wheat beer. *See also* Weisse.

Wet-hopped Beer made with the addition of fresh, undried hops.

Wit (Flemish) White; usually refers to Belgian-style wheat beer.

Wort The gross name chosen for the liquid that is extracted from the mash. Pronounced WERT.

Yeast Single-celled fungi responsible for the fermentation process.

What, We're Not Enough for You? Building a Library

F erris Bueller said it best when he said, "The world moves pretty fast." That sentiment couldn't be truer than in the craft beer world. There's always a new beer or a new craft brewery springing up. There's always some kind of limited special release that's only available for sale one day of the year when the moon's full in June or something. To keep up with the beer times, we check our favorite beer-centric magazines, websites, and blogs. A few short years ago, people seeking beer information only had one or two resources. Of course we keep updated by writing and blogging on our own beer aficionado site and blog called the Naked

Pint (www.thenakedpint.com). But in addition to craft brewery sites, nowadays there are *lots* of websites dedicated to beer out there. How do you know who's giving the straight skinny? Here are a few of our favorites to get you started.

The Big Boys: Can't-Miss Websites

Here are four major beer-centric websites that we visit virtually every day. These sites are one-stop shops where you can find the most updated information on almost everything you need to know about beer.

- **BEER ADVOCATE:** www.beeradvocate.com
  Founded in 1996, this portal is one big daddy in the beer world, with over 10,000 active members participating in beer-centric forums and groups as well as hundreds of thousands of user-generated beer reviews. Also to be found are reviews of beer bars, events, and beer tutorials. Founded by brothers Jason and Todd Alström, who live by the credo "Respect Beer," this site is an invaluable resource for beer novices and experts alike.

- **RATEBEER.COM:** www.ratebeer.com
  Since 2000, this amazing site has become one of the most visited beer sites on the Internet. It boasts over a million beer reviews, listing tens of thousands of different beers. Maintained by volunteers, this site's mission is to "provide independent, unbiased, consumer-driven information about beer and breweries and to enhance the image and worldwide appreciation of beer."

- **BROOKSTON BEER BULLETIN:** www.brookstonbeerbulletin.com
  Jay Brooks, the former general manager of the renowned beer newspaper *Celebrator Beer News*, started this beer website to "support the craft beer industry and do whatever he can to help promote the culture of better beer." This massively comprehensive site focuses on West Coast craft breweries and keeps an eye on the big breweries. In addition, there are some really great original articles because Jay's always got something interesting to say.

⟩ **THE BREWERS ASSOCIATION:** www.beertown.org

The Brewers Association's mission is to "promote and protect small and independent American brewers, their craft beers and the community of brewing enthusiasts." But you don't have to be a member of any association to use this website as a great resource. Features beer news, events, homebrewing, and beer-writing gems from the association's president, Charlie Papazian.

The Little People: Beer Bloggers

Want to find the best beer to get your girlfriend if jasmine is her favorite flower? Need to find out where in Indianapolis you can find Three Floyds Dark Lord? Want to find out what that newly opened gastropub is all about? These are all questions that can be answered by an often underrated contingency. These are the people on the streets, in the bars, and sometimes on the floor, who know their shit and who are giving their blood, sweat, and tears, mostly for free, to bring you the most current beer news. These are the beer bloggers! (*Insert sound of roaring crowd.*)

⟩ **BEER FOR CHICKS:** www.beerforchicks.com

This is where it all started for us. Seeing that there was a definite lack but want of beer knowledge among her fellow home girls, Christina started this website as a female-friendly place where women could come for some good beer news, knowledge, and reviews, and a little social networking. BTW, it's not just for chicks; her membership is 50/50 men and women.

⟩ **BEER AND NOSH:** www.beerandnosh.com

This San Francisco site is evidence that the foodie world is finally embracing the beauty of beer. A modern take, with beautiful pictures and recipes exploring "the endless possibilities of beer and food together."

⟩ **HAIL THE ALE:** www.hailtheale.com

For when you want some beer news but there's not a lot of time. This site has nice, punchy beer reviews, news, and humor.

○ **CONFESSIONS OF A BEER GEEK:** www.confessionsofabeergeek
.com

   "Spreading the gospel of craft beery goodness, converting one bitter beer face at a time," written by Eli "The Mad Beer Man" Shayotovich.

○ **HAIR OF THE DOG DAVE:** www.beerjobs.org and www.beergeek.la

   Want a beer job? Want to find out what's happening with beer in La La Land? Check out David Stickel's websites and get the latest on the California beer scene.

○ **HOT KNIVES:** www.urbanhonking.com/hotknives

   Alex Brown and Evan George are rad. Both are former line cooks. One is a cheesemonger and one is a writer. They bring the avant-garde to beer (including beer and music pairings). They believe in "cheap groceries, cooking with high alcohol content beer and free leisure." Oh, and they hate "weak sauces."

○ **HOOSIER BEER GEEK:** http://hoosierbeergeek.blogspot.com

   Touted as "Indiana's Favorite Website Ever," Hoosier Beer Geek is actually a collaborative group that calls themselves the "Knights of the Beer Roundtable" and is chock-full of interviews, reviews, news, and school. Go Hoosiers!

Anything Else You Wanna Know? Specialty Websites

In addition to the all-encompassing beer-centric websites are some specialty gems that can really help if you need to know how to pronounce *gueuze*, or you need the newest, craziest recipe for beer-braised duck, or you just want to sit back and watch a good show about beer.

○ **THE BEER MAPPING PROJECT:** www.beermapping.com

   Want to know exactly where you are and exactly how far away you are from your next good beer? Check out this site. Punch in your location and you'll know.

THE BEER COOK: www.beercook.com

Lucy Saunders, the prolific beer writer and author of *The Best of American Beer and Food: Pairing and Cooking with Craft Beer* writes this great site full of cooking-with-beer recipes, and beer and food reviews.

BEER TAP TV: www.beertaptv.com

Tired of all this reading? Beer Tap TV is a cable channel on the web that focuses solely on the best beverage on earth, with several entertaining and educational shows. "Taste Buds" is our favorite. Erik and Dusty rule.

THE BEER GEEK: www.thebeergeek.com

The couple that drinks beer together and travels together, and travels to drink beer together, stays together. Check out Chris and Meredith's adventures and live vicariously while they "see the world one pint at a time."

GUIDE TO BELGIAN BEER PRONUNCIATION GUIDE: http://belgianstyle.com/mmguide/pronounce/speak.html

Do you have absolutely no idea how to pronounce Westvleteren, St. Feuillien, or even worse Corsendonck? Go to this site, where you can hear an audible track of these tricky beer names. The site is a little bit rustic, but you won't sound like an ass when you order one of these tricky beers. Hooray.

Subscribe and Delight: Beer Magazines

Some say that the printed word is dead, but we have to say that there's nothing like opening your mailbox and finding the latest edition of your favorite beer magazine, ripe with new beer reviews, information about beer from around the country, and the hippest beer trends and styles. There are some great ones out there, and here are our favorite beeriodicals:

ALL ABOUT BEER: www.allaboutbeer.com

Now in its 30th year, this is the foremost magazine on contemporary beer culture. This magazine is for the serious beer drinker. It contains solid information on topics ranging from the culture, history, and variety of beers to marketing traditions, home brewing, storing, innovations, travel, entertaining, and beer politics that could affect your beer-drinking pleasure. It publishes six times a year, with two bonus issues each year.

BEER ADVOCATE: www.beeradvocate.com

Both the monthly magazine and the website are a staple for most craft beer lovers. With sections like "Style Profile," "Cuisine à la Bière," and "Ask the Beer Geek," it approaches beer in a fresh and modern way. Each issue of the magazine also offers reviews of new beers, perfect for building a wish list, and features the beer spots of a different city. With contributions by well-respected beer writers from all over the country, this magazine covers all aspects of beer and brewing, including features of specific breweries, with the history of the owners and brewers and the beers they offer.

CELEBRATOR BEER NEWS: www.celebrator.com

Touted as "America's Premier Brewspaper," this bimonthly is one of the most beloved craft beer papers among beer-geeks. This periodical has great national news, but it's also worth checking out for the great regional beer news that's sometimes hard to get. It has a great online version with upcoming beer events, blog links, columns, and a "CBN Evening Brews" Internet show!

DRAFT: www.draftmagazine.com

Based out of Arizona, this is a well-crafted magazine whose cover often features a celebrity beer lover. This bimonthly is very accessible and approaches beer in a way that even the novice can enjoy. Draft is also not confined to just the craft brews. This magazine is spreading the word to anyone who will listen. They also have a pretty sweet website presence.

This bimonthly magazine isn't all about beer. Imbibe includes all drinks, from coffee to spring water, from wine to tea. But when this magazine turns its focus to our beloved beverage, it does it right. Calling itself "the magazine of liquid culture," it gets deep when it comes to drinks. More than just merely scratching the surface, this magazine embraces the "history, ingredients, preparation, artistry and consumption" of all drinks. This glossy publication includes recipes, great pictures, travel, profiles, and reviews celebrating the world in a glass.

The Stacks: Books to Have at Home

In writing this book, we realized that we could write an entire book on almost every subject that we hit upon. Thankfully there are many books out there that cover a wide range of beer topics. Some are written specifically for the avid homebrewing technician, the beer traveler, the Belgian beer enthusiast, and yes, the "dummies." Whatever the focus, you can probably find it. We wrote *The Naked Pint* to be accessible to all beer fans and to provide a base of knowledge to get your feet wet and from which to jump into the big adult pool of beer. You could just read our book, start tasting different beer styles, keep updated on our website, and live a fantastic life with beer. Here are some books that we recommend. This is not a comprehensive library by any means, but if you want to delve a little deeper, these books helped us cultivate our beer love:

Calagione, Sam, and Marnie Old. *He Said Beer; She Said Wine.* New York: Dorling Kindersley, 2008. Have a friend who is a wine snob and refuses to listen to you about beer? This book is a fun look at the similarities and differences between the two drinks. Marnie Old, a knowledgeable and sophisticated wine sommelier, and Sam Calagione, the rock star of beer and owner of Dogfish Head Craft Brewed Ales, square off and go head-to-head on pairings for a variety of foods, flavors, and recipes for pairing dinners. A great read if you need to go toe-to-toe with a "non-beer drinker" and defend the best beverage in the world!

Deweer, Hilde. *All Belgian Beers.* Oostkamp, Belgium: Stichting Kunstboek, 2008. Fellow beer chick Deweer has painstakingly put together this 1,568-page volume with great care and precision, highlighting each beer on two pages with a picture, a flavor description, beer style, fermentation style, brewery, ingredients, ABV, color, appearance, serving tips, serving temperature, and other pertinent information.

Jackson, Michael. *Ultimate Beer.* New York: DK Publishing, 1998. Written by the late Jackson (moment of silence), the greatest beer writer of all time. The *New York Times* said, *"Ultimate Beer* is chock full of almost life size color photographs of beers from around the world, and text that is equally cosmopolitan.... His descriptions are so vivid...he seems to enjoy cooking as much as he does drinking. Instead of joining him at the pub, maybe you'd rather follow him home around supper time."

Ogle, Maureen. *Ambitious Brew.* Orlando: Harcourt, 2006. This is a fun romp and a very interesting read about the history of beer in America starting from the mid-1800s to the present. She talks about Prohibition, the industrialization of beer, the big breweries, and the craft beer revolution. This book was an eye-opener for us and helped us see where the misconceptions about beer started and how to move past them.

Oliver, Garret. *The Brewmasters Table.* New York: HarperCollins, 2003. This book is a must-read for any beer enthusiast. Not only does it cover every style in amazing detail but it talks about food pairing and the theories and history behind those pairings. It will open your eyes to the possibility of mixing fine dining with beer, which, as you know, is our mission.

Saunders, Lucy. *The Best of American Beer and Food.* Boulder, CO: Brewers Publications, 2007. Written by an English literature major, this book talks about food and beer pairing as well as specializing in cooking with craft and artisanal beers. The explanation of how beer can enhance your enjoyment of food, often much better than wine can, makes this book great. And can you really go wrong with recipes like shallot and stout-glazed steak with cumin-pepper onions? And we haven't even mentioned the Barleywine banana split. Forget about it.

Skilnik, Bob. *Does My Butt Look Big in This Beer?* Plainfield, IL: Gambrinus Media, 2008. We must admit, as women beer experts, we get asked about the nutritional and caloric content of beer on a daily basis. You can't find it on a beer label, but you can find it in this book, which lists the alcohol content, carbohydrates, calories, and Weight Watchers' points for more than 2,000 beers. This self-published book is a much-needed treasure. Thanks for keeping our butts in check, Bob.

BEER-TASTING NOTES

DATE:

NAME OF BEER:

STYLE OF BEER: ABV%:

BREWERY:

BREWERY LOCATION:

YOUR LOCATION:

DRAUGHT or BOTTLE: GLASSWARE:

APPEARANCE:

AROMATICS:

FLAVOR:

FINISH:

NOTES:

SCORE:

Base this on your own personal scale, like 1–4 stars or numbers 1–5 (1 being a below-average beer and 5 being an excellent one).

BEER-TASTING NOTES

DATE:

NAME OF BEER:

STYLE OF BEER: ABV%:

BREWERY:

BREWERY LOCATION:

YOUR LOCATION:

DRAUGHT or BOTTLE: GLASSWARE:

APPEARANCE:

AROMATICS:

FLAVOR:

FINISH:

NOTES:

SCORE:

Base this on your own personal scale, like 1–4 stars or numbers 1–5 (1 being a below-average beer and 5 being an excellent one).

BEER-TASTING NOTES

DATE: _____

NAME OF BEER: _____

STYLE OF BEER: _____ ABV%: _____

BREWERY: _____

BREWERY LOCATION: _____

YOUR LOCATION: _____

DRAUGHT or BOTTLE: _____ GLASSWARE: _____

APPEARANCE: _____

AROMATICS: _____

FLAVOR: _____

FINISH: _____

NOTES: _____

SCORE: _____

Base this on your own personal scale, like 1–4 stars or numbers 1–5 (1 being a below-average beer and 5 being an excellent one).

BEER-TASTING NOTES

DATE: _____

NAME OF BEER: _____

STYLE OF BEER: _____ ABV%: _____

BREWERY: _____

BREWERY LOCATION: _____

YOUR LOCATION: _____

DRAUGHT or BOTTLE: _____ GLASSWARE: _____

APPEARANCE: _____

AROMATICS: _____

FLAVOR: _____

FINISH: _____

NOTES: _____

SCORE: _____

Base this on your own personal scale, like 1–4 stars or numbers 1–5 (1 being a below-average beer and 5 being an excellent one).

BEER-TASTING NOTES

DATE: _____

NAME OF BEER: _____

STYLE OF BEER: _____ ABV%: _____

BREWERY: _____

BREWERY LOCATION: _____

YOUR LOCATION: _____

DRAUGHT or BOTTLE: _____ GLASSWARE: _____

APPEARANCE: _____

AROMATICS: _____

FLAVOR: _____

FINISH: _____

NOTES: _____

SCORE: _____

Base this on your own personal scale, like 1–4 stars or numbers 1–5 (1 being a below-average beer and 5 being an excellent one).

Index

alcohol by volume (ABV) (*cont.*)
  overview in, 27–28
  in Quadrupels, 23, 151
  in red ales, 92
  in Robust Porter, 110
  in Russian Imperial Stout, 147
  in Saison, 119
  in smoked beer, 144–45
  in steam beer, 86
  in stout, 111
  in Tripels, 130
  in Witbier, 74
ale. *See also specific styles*
  in Britain, 89–90
  lager vs., 14–15
Alesmith Speedway Stout, 147
Allagash Brewing Company, 242
Allagash Curieux, 132, 143, 172
  flourless chocolate cake with, 208–9
Allagash White, 74, 132
all-grain mash, 218, 227
all one style theme, for beer tasting parties,
    268
Altbier, 84–85
Amarillo hops, 230
amber ales, 91–93
  Sunset Boulevard Amber Ale, 240–41
American all-malt lager, 22
American Brewer's Guild (ABG), CBA of, 278
American IPAs, 158–62
American Pilsner, 65–66
American Stouts, 112–13
American Strong Ales, 158–62, 175
American Wheat Beer, 75–76
American Wild Ale (AWA), 156–58
Anchor Porter, 110
Anchor Steam, 51, 85–86, 132
"angel's share," 141–42
Angel's Share, The, 132
Anheuser-Busch, 66–67
Anvil Ale ESB, 47, 99
Arctic Devil, 150
Armstrong, Govind, Two-Can Chili: Heirloom
    Bean and Beer Short Rib Chili recipe
    by, 203–6
aroma hops, 220
aromatics
  of ale, 14
  in American Wheat Beer, 75

beer style and, 21
  carbonation and, 14
  in Hefeweizen, 71
  from hops, 16–17
  in Kölsch, 82–83
  yeast and, 18
Arrogant Bastard Ale, 161, 171
artisanal beer. *See* craft beer
astringent
  hops and, 16
  mouthfeel and, 55
attenuation, 220
Augustijn Grand Cru, 129
Australian Suzuki with Beer-Braised Mussels,
    Leeks, Trumpet Royale Mushrooms,
    and Chorizo, 194–95
AWA. *See* American Wild Ale
Ayinger Altbairisch Dunkel, 103
Ayinger Celebrator Doppelbock, 108, 132
Ayinger Jarhundert Bier, 69

bacterial contamination, off-flavors
    and, 25
balance
  carbonation and, 14
  of flavor components, 46–47
  in pairing beer with food, 180–81
Baltic Porter, 110
Barleywine, 149–50, 175
Barney Flats Oatmeal Stout, 114
barrel-aged beers, 139–43
base malt, 219
beans, Two-Can Chili: Heirloom Bean and
    Beer Short Rib Chili, 205–6
beer. *See also* cooking with beer;
    entertaining with beer; *specific styles*
  aging, 173–76
  calories and carbs in, 116–18
  description of, 8–9
  drinking of, 33–34
  fermentation of, 12, 14
  food in, 186
  grocery list for, 171–72
  history of, 39–42
  ingredients in, 9–12
  off-flavors in, 24–26
  ordering of, 28–32
  returning, 34–36
  styles of, 21–24

final gravity, 220
Firestone Twelve, 133
Firestone XII, 133, 143
Flanders Red Ale, 155–56
flavor
  adjuncts and flavorings and, 19
  of Altbier, 84
  balance of, 46–47
  of Baltic Porter, 110
  of Barleywine, 150
  in barrel-aging, 142–43
  beer style and, 21
  of Bière de Champagne, 138
  of Biére de Garde, 120
  bottle conditioning and, 60
  of Brown Porter, 110
  of Double IPAs, 159
  of Dubbels, 130
  of Dunkel, 101
  of Dunkelweizen, 104
  of fruity wheat beer, 78–79
  of Gueuze, 154–55
  hops and, 16–17
  of Kristallklar, 77
  malt and, 15–16
  of Munich Dunkel Lagers, 102
  of Oatmeal stouts, 111
  of porter, 110
  returning beer and, 36
  of Robust Porter, 110
  of Saison, 119
  of Schwarzbier, 103–4
  of smoked beer, 144
  of steam beer, 86
  of Sweet Stout, 111
  water and, 17–18
  wheat and, 70
  yeast and, 18
flavor hops, 220
flavorings
  examples of, 19
  flavor and, 19
  for homebrewing, 228–29
  mouthfeel and, 57–58
  Witbier and, 74
Flourless Chocolate Cake with Allagash
    Curieux, 208–9
flute, 165, 168
food
  in beer, 186

for beer tasting parties, 272–73
  matching beer with, 180–85
Foreign Extra Stout, 112
fruit beer, 24
  Pomegranate Tart, 255–57
fruity wheat beer, 78–79
Fuggle hops, 230
Fuller's ESB, 99
Fuller's London Porter, 110
full mash, 218
Funke, Evan, Kölsch-Braised Rabbit with
    Wild Ramps and Roasted Porcini recipe
    by, 196–98
Furious, 141

Garbee, Jenn, Rosemary-Thyme Beer Bread
    recipe by, 188–89
GBT. See Great Beer Test
geographic region theme, for beer tasting
    parties, 268
German beer purity law. See Reinheitsgebot
German Pilsner, 65–66
Girardin 1882 Black Label, 155
Girardin Faro, 133
Girardin Gueuze, 133
glass
  drinking from, 32
  returning beer and, 36
glassware, 164–69
  drinking from, 32
  glass quality, 166–67
  for home, 167–68
  returning beer and, 36
  shape of, 164–66
Glazen Toren Saison D'Erpe-Mere, food
    paired with, 183
goblet, 165, 168
Golding hops, 230
Gordon, 141
Gouden Carolus Tripel, 131
grain, history of, 40
Great Beer Test (GBT), 278
Great Depression, 43
Great Lakes Edmund Fitzgerald Porter, 110
Greeks, 41
Green Flash Hop Head Red, 93
Green Flash Nut Brown Ale, food paired
    with, 183
Grilled Fennel and Orange Salad, 191–92
Grimbergen Blonde, 69

About the Authors

Christina Perozzi, Beer Sommelier and "The Beer Chick"

Named Best Beer Sommelier in Los Angeles by *Los Angeles Magazine*, Christina Perozzi has gained a large following as the top female beer expert in the United States. She was born and raised in St. Louis, Missouri. Graduating with degrees in journalism and speech communication from Indiana University, Christina realized her affinity for the beer world while managing the famous Father's Office in Santa Monica, California. Seeing the need for beer education everywhere, she founded the popular website Beer for Chicks (www.beerforchicks.com) and started working as a consultant, a beer educator, a writer, and a beer sommelier in 2006.

Christina has been featured on Evan Kleiman's popular radio show on KCRW, *Good Food*, and was also featured as guest host for a segment of KNBC's TV show *Your LA* and as a guest expert on Los Angeles's KTLA *Morning Show* and KCBS's *Evening News*. She has been featured in *Gourmet* magazine, *Los Angeles* magazine, Patterson's *Tasting Panel*, Daily Candy, Urban Daddy, YumSugar.com, Metromix.com, and the Thrillist, as well as Forbes.com, *Delta Sky* magazine, Yahoo! Food, Metromix, *Angeleno* magazine, *Los Angeles Times*, *Imbibe* magazine, *Eating Well* magazine, and *Market Watch*.

Christina hosts beer tastings, gives seminars, and teaches classes, and also teams with chefs from around Los Angeles hosting beer-pairing dinners. Christina's consulting clients include celebrity chef Govind Armstrong's 8 oz. Burger Bar, Rustic Canyon Wine Bar and Seasonal

Kitchen, Violet Restaurant, Library Bar, Laurel Tavern, Charlie's Malibu, and the Essex in Hollywood. She also lends her beer talents for charitable organizations, such as Heal the Bay, Break the Cycle, and the Geffen Theater.

Christina's mission is to dispel the myths that women have about beer and to bring beer to the forefront of modern dining. She is currently drinking a deliciously spicy Saison Foret Belgian Ale with hints of lemon rind and pepper.

Hallie Beaune, Beer Expert

Hallie Beaune grew up in the lovely desert of Scottsdale, Arizona, where her first beer was from a can (and it wasn't good). College took her to the Northwest, where she earned a BA in theater at the University of Puget Sound. In this mecca of craft beer, Hallie discovered the enlightened world of microbrews.

Her Beer Journey brought her to the famed beer bar Father's Office in Santa Monica, California, where she met fellow beer chick Christina Perozzi. Her knowledge of hops and malt quickly elevated her to manager. At Father's Office, she taught the illustrious F.O. Beer School to eager, thirsty students. She was also featured on the hit cable foodie show *After Hours with Daniel Boulud* as F.O.'s resident expert and beer sommelier. She has been featured as a beer expert on KNBC *Evening News* and KTLA *Morning News*.

Hallie writes about beer for the web magazine *Rundown* (www .rundown.com), as its resident beer expert, and for Beer for Chicks (www.beerforchicks.com), spreading the good word of beer all over Los Angeles. Hallie has worked with Christina on sold-out beer dinners at critically acclaimed L.A. restaurants Rustic Canyon Wine Bar and Seasonal Kitchen, which was featured in the *Celebrator*; Three on Fourth;

and Violet. Hallie has also co-hosted charitable beer tastings for Heal the Bay and the Geffen Theater.

Hallie is on a spiritual quest to find the finest beers around the globe and then drink them. She is currently enjoying a nice, dry, earthy, and complex glass of Orval Trappist Ale.